Digital War

Digital War

A View from the Front Lines

Robert L. Bateman, editor

★
PRESIDIO

Published by Presidio Press
505 B San Marin Drive, Suite 300
Novato, CA 94945-1340

Library of Congress Cataloging-in-Publication Data

Bateman, Robert L.
Digital war : a view from the front lines / Robert L. Bateman, editor.
p. cm.
ISBN: 0-89141-685-4
1. Military art and science—Automation. 2. Military art and science—Data processing. 3. United States. Army. I. Title.
UG478 .B38 1999
355.4—dc21
99-31-044
CIP

Printed in the United States of America

Contents

Preface

This is a book with a purpose, a method, and a desired end state. "Purpose," "method," and "end state" are components of the concept of a "commander's intent" put forth in the 1996 version of the U.S. Army's capstone doctrinal document, *Field Manual 100-5*. Intent is part of the standard field order format used in the U.S. Army. The idea is that when commanders state their intent for a military mission in their orders, all other instructions included therein become supplementary information. The intent is, in effect, their guidance. That this book should adopt the same framework is unsurprising when one considers the biographies of the authors; with one exception, we are all soldiers. In all cases we are people intimately familiar at the practical level with the military profession.

Our purpose is to stimulate discussion about the course and direction of the military in light of the effects of digitization, among practitioners of the profession of arms, those interested in the profession of arms, and those who might have an influence upon the same.

Our method is to present to the reader a collection of essays with a logical organization suitable for intellectual dissection. The book is subdivided according to the various levels of warfare. Unlike any other book currently available, this set of prognostications on the future of warfare is not written by academics or members of a think tank. While several of the authors do have advanced degrees, this is not their primary qualification. Their primary qualification is their personal experience within the armed forces; the various Ph.D.s and master's degrees that several of them have collected are only secondary.

These are the ideas of those who are serving in the forces today. With one exception, each author has more than a decade in uniform. These are the ideas of soldiers and leaders familiar with the sound of a 120mm main gun and the smell of JP fuel. There is a legitimacy to these ideas that may only be earned through long years of service.

Our desired end state is a book that is dog-eared and covered with notes. If this book does its job, it will start more arguments than it settles, it will raise more questions than it answers, and it will serve as the basis for a host of articles as a new generation comes of age and begins to wrestle with the realities of digital warfare. To accomplish all of this, the book must start at the most basic place, with a common definition. For our purpose, the most important term that must be defined is "digital revolution." Just what is a digital revolution, anyway?

Unfortunately, answering this question is almost an impossible task at this time. Today, a digital revolution is just about anything; its meaning is entirely dependent upon the profession, agenda, and intention of the person using the term. One will not find the term in a dictionary or phrase book, nor is there a well-defended common doctrinal definition in any United States military manual; that is to say that the definition has not remained constant for any significant period. Therefore, we must create one. Before proceeding to a full definition of a digital revolution, however, it is prudent to explore what we mean by a "revolution."

In 1955, noted historian Michael Roberts delivered an important lecture titled "The Military Revolution: 1560–1660." In this lecture, and in a subsequent book, he asserted that changes in tactics, strategy, and the size of armies during the Thirty Years' War had increased the impact of warfare upon society by an order of magnitude. Swedish King Gustavus Adolphus became, with the stroke of a historian's pen, the "father of the military revolution." The transition from mass to linear tactics that Adolphus demonstrated against Tilly at Brietenfield; the national mobilization of Swedish assets designed to field a well-trained professional force; and the appearance of a relatively large army (given Sweden's size) were considered the turning points in a new way of warfare.

This model of how Western warfare changed European history stood virtually undisputed until 1976, when historian Geoffrey Parker challenged Roberts's thesis. Parker expanded both the scope of the model and the period to include all of Europe and events over a three-hundred-year span, from 1500 to 1800. By adding the idea that technology had a major effect upon the course of history through warfare and the economic impact of warfare (or the preparation for warfare), Parker redefined the accepted definition. Parker's thesis, that technology was a major causative factor behind the military revolution, became even more widely accepted with the 1988 publication of his book *The Military Revolution, Military Innovation and the Rise of the West 1500-1800.*

Historians, however, are nothing if not a contentious lot. Parker's thesis became a target for military historians. Capitalizing upon this tendency, then-graduate student Clifford Rogers (now a professor of military history at the U.S. Military Academy) collected essays from a host of prominent military historians and published an anthology titled *The Military Revolution Debate.*

Tucked between the covers was Rogers's own chapter and thesis. In it, Rogers suggested a new model for understanding the idea of a "military evolution." Borrowing loosely from the field of evolutionary biology, he put forth the concept of "punctuated equilibrium" and applied it to military history. This theory suggested that there were in military history relatively long periods of nearly static behavior in military affairs, interspersed with short periods of massive change. Rogers's thesis stands essentially unchanged today.

In 1994 Andrew Krepinovich added the final refinement to the idea of a military revolution when he defined it as a short period when the application of new technologies in a significant number of military systems combines with innovative operational concepts and organizational adaptations in a way that fundamentally alters the characteristics of warfare. Although the general exclusion of societal, economic, and political elements weakens his definition, his contribution serves as a decent starting point for us today. Krepinovich suggested that no fewer than ten revolutions have already occurred; in this book, we are seeking to define and refine our understanding of what may be the eleventh.

We have now covered the evolution of the revolution, generating a common definition of a revolution in military affairs: a fundamental change in the nature of war occurring in a relatively short period, stemming from changes in organization; military doctrine; economic, social, or political factors; or technology.

As an example, consider the "infantry revolution" of the fourteenth and fifteenth centuries. Prior to that era, the dominant branch in Western warfare was the mounted cavalry, exemplified by the medieval knight. When the infantry revolution started depends upon which scholar you prefer to read, but the phenomenon they all describe is the same. In that time, the dominant force upon European battlefields changed from mounted knights to masses of well-disciplined and organized infantry operating in unison. The battlefields of Agincourt, where the longbowmen of Henry V laid out the cream of French knighthood, and Laupen, where Swiss pikemen did much the same, attest to the same process. The rise of the common man, operating in concert, changed the nature of warfare at that time.

Similar changes occurred with the introduction of gunpowder (a technological factor), the transition to linear tactics (an organizational/doctrinal change), and the *leveé en masse* of the French Revolution (a social/political and economic factor).

The next step is to attempt to come to some common understanding of the implications of this newest "revolution." Unfortunately, this leads us to yet another roadblock. Most agree that the effects of digital communications and computer technology have the potential to fundamentally change the nature of warfare. The rub arises from disagreements about how this change will play out.

Is the true significance of digital communications and computer technology the fact that they make precision munitions a practicality, and therefore true stand-off tactics centered around indirect fire instead of maneuvering become possible?

Or is the most important aspect of these changes the idea that through the manipulation—the collection, analysis, and dissemination—of data, even conventional forces may be made more efficient by an order of magnitude? This might be so if digital forces know exactly where they are (the friendly situation), where the enemy is, and all aspects of the environment between the two. Obviously, access to knowledge of that sort might enable a unit to move more precisely, thereby massing combat power only when and where it is needed.

Or perhaps the real significance of digitization lies in the hands of the soldiers up front. Perhaps the leaders on the front, armed with accurate information, will begin to network themselves, obviating the need for some levels of the traditional command-and-control structure used by most conventional military forces around the world.

Which is the correct answer? We leave that up to you. As stated earlier, the desired end state of this book is to initiate discussion and dialogue. Ideas about the future of warfare and all that it encompasses flourish in an atmosphere of free and open discussion, and that is what this book is all about. Only through the exchange of ideas can we hope to arrive at the best answer for the future.

Ironically, the book you are now holding is itself a prime example of how this exchange process may be changing. Traditionally, the correspondence, writing, editing, and final compilation of an anthology such as this were the result of years of work. First, unless the collection was based upon the publication of a series of conference papers, the editor would need to collect a group of people to become authors. Letters and phone calls would cross and recross the miles as the editor sought contributors. Next, a tentative timeline would be established, a process that required something akin to a committee agreement conducted through the U.S. mail. Finally, manuscripts were submitted and the tedious process of editing began. All of this would occur before a publisher was even approached.

In the spring of 1998 I realized that I was maintaining correspondence with several of the greatest minds currently on active duty. For one reason or another I had come in contact with all of these men, primarily through mutual acquaintances. We shared ideas and tested concepts against each other through letters and articles. This contact was, appropriately enough, entirely via the Internet. To this day I have only met one of the authors face to face. Some of these men knew a few of the others, but it appeared that no one knew all of the others with whom I was exchanging ideas. Yet they all had important things to say. I realized that if I could harness the intellectual energy that we were spending on each other, there might be some greater benefit for the military as a whole.

This book, therefore, started with a single mass e-mail soliciting contributions. All authors responded within twenty-four hours. A timeline of four months was established and agreed upon within the next twenty-four hours. A proposal went to the publisher five months later, again partially via e-mail. The concept was accepted, and the manuscript went to the publisher one month after that. It was six months from concept to manuscript, thanks in large part to the Internet. The book has become a reality less than a year after conception. That is the power of the digital age.

For simplicity's sake this book adheres to a simple, albeit loose structure. The chapters are arranged into three broad subsections according to the level of warfare to which they most directly apply. There are, according to some authorities, four levels of warfare: the political, strategic, operational, and tactical levels. For our purposes we will only address three: the tactical, operational, and strategic levels.

A simple definition, although not an ironclad one, of the tactical level of warfare might read: The tactical level of warfare is that level at which soldiers meet and fight from the individual level through the division. It is the realm of skirmishes, engagements, and battles. Planning at the tactical level encompasses a time span roughly forty-eight hours into the future. The tactical level of warfare is where one sees the true face of battle.

Most weapon systems used in ground warfare operate at this level, as do some information systems. Speed at this echelon is sometimes measured in yards per day. This is the popular conception of war. This is war at the level of *Saving Private Ryan.* The battles on the beaches of Normandy in 1944 were purely tactical.

The operational level is somewhat more difficult to define and understand. Operational-level planning occurs with the intent of setting missions and objectives that will bend the enemy to your will in an entire theater of operations. It consists of a series of battles and engagements designed to win some strategic objective. The operational level of warfare is the realm of generals. Plans begin at forty-eight hours and may stretch out to cover months. They deal with the movements of entire corps, armies, and army groups. Again referring back to June 1944, the overall plan for the invasion of the beaches and beyond, known as Overlord, was an operational-level plan.

Finally, there is the strategic level of warfare. Over time there have been various definitions and subsets of this overarching term. There have been "grand strategy" and "national strategy" and "military strategy," all of which address slightly different aspects of the same general concept. This level concerns the planning and conduct of the war at the highest levels. Strategic plans aim for objectives leading directly to peace. In other words, these plans seek to answer the question, "How will we win this war?"

It is easier to understand strategic concepts not by assigning a force level as a definition, but by understanding the level at which decisions occur. Within the U.S. Army, strategic-level decisions occur at the highest-level headquarters in the field, most often in conjunction with and with the approval of the National Command Authority. This is the echelon that approves changes in force structure.

Strategic decisions also determine the allocation of some portions of a country's national resources. Decisions about production of materials and allocations of raw material and personnel occur at this level. Strategy involves planning campaign objectives, allocating forces, and choosing the theaters in which campaigns occur. The decision that the primary invasion of France in 1944 would take place at Normandy (as opposed to southern France) was a strategic-level decision. The decision to defeat Germany first, and then Japan, might also be considered strategic in nature.

Decisions regarding the allocation of resources available to the nation ("Do we build ten thousand tanks and two thousand planes, or ten thousand planes and two thousand tanks?") are strategic in that they determine indirectly the course and direction of the lower levels of warfare.

Finally, although we will not directly address it, there is the political level of warfare. The civilian government retains control over decisions about whether to go to war, whom to fight, and with whom to ally. Decisions at this level involve the interrelationships between allies, decisions regarding the factors of production, the national will, and societal issues.

In this book none of the serving officers will address this aspect; we will instead leave that largely (but not entirely) to the reader. Our one nonmilitary contributor is a professional as well—a professional who influences civilians through the power of the press. He is a reporter for a major newspaper. In his own way, he too might be considered as serving on the "front lines," albeit lines of a very different sort. However, because the political level involves the vague concept of a "national will," perhaps the chapter on the interrelationship between the military and the media in the digital age might apply to this level.

Obviously, all four levels are interrelated. There is no way to avoid that in the late twentieth century, and probably less so in the twenty-first. A political decision may result directly in a tactical engagement and even have bearing upon the conduct of that engagement. An example might be the decision to pursue Mohammed Farah Aideed in Somalia, a political decision that resulted in numerous skirmishes in the streets of Mogadishu. A previous political decision not to send U.S. armored vehicles to Somalia also affected the nature of these fights. The reverse may also occur; for example, tactical events in South Vietnam pushed President Nixon toward a political decision to conduct bombing operations over Hanoi and Haiphong in North Vietnam.

Cross-level influence is even more common between adjoining levels, but in general these levels remain valid as distinct mental constructs into which we may subdivide war for the purpose of discussion and theory. That the lines between these divisions may blur is to be expected. The separation between tactical and strategic warfare might become confused because these lines depend upon numerous factors such as the forces in a theater and the geographic scale of the theater. Yet for our purposes these divisions serve as an adequate starting point.

The purpose is outlined. The method is established. All that remains is for you to read on, complete the method, and arrive at the end state. Good luck.

Robert L. Bateman
West Point, New York

Acknowledgments

As an anthology, this is by necessity a child of many parents. All of the contributors have their own intellectual and material debts to acknowledge, and many of these are made in the following text. As the editor, however, I have the opportunity to be explicit about those that helped in the creation of this work.

As an institution I would like to extend my thanks and acknowledge the influence of the United States Military Academy at West Point. An assignment to the faculty here ensured that I would receive the training and come into contact with the many people which made this work possible. Within the academy I would thank the chain to which I directly respond, that of the Department of History, for creating an environment where intellectual contribution to the profession is acknowledged as a worthy goal. Most especially I would thank the men that make this vision into reality, Colonel Robert Doughty and Colonel James Johnson.

One common thanks should be passed to the editors of the several professional journals to which I and many of the other authors regularly contribute. These are, for the majority of the time, the forum for professional discussion, and often serve as the proving grounds for many of the ideas that are incorporated here. These editors, men and women like Lieutentant Colonel Terry Blakely at *Armor*, Mary Blake French at *Army*, Russ Eno at *Infantry*, and Colonel Lee Hockman at *Military Review*, have the courage to publish ideas that are not always in line with the current mainstream. They are the true heroes of any intellectual movement afoot within the U.S. Army.

Similarly there is the immeasurable assistance that many of the authors received from the various repositories of the Army's institutional memory. In my own case, for myself and for several of the others, I would like to thank Dr. David Keogh of the United States Army Military History Institute. His assistance and great patience with neophyte and developed intellectuals alike is one of the foundations upon which our institutional development rests.

For the challenges and intellectual support, as well as training in historical methods and guidance rather than direction, I would thank my advisor and guide through the swamps of academia, Dr. Allan Millett of the Department of History and the Mershon Center for International and Strategic Studies at the Ohio State University. I would also like to thank three other members of the Department of History at OSU, for their instruction, mentoring and friendship, Dr. John Guilmartin, Dr. Mark Grimsley, and Dr. Alan Beyerchen. Without the basis that these four men provided, my own chapter would be a poor creature indeed.

For their assistance in reviewing portions of this work I also extend a word of thanks to my peers here in the Department of History at the United States Military Academy, especially Dr. Clifford Rogers, Major James Haynsworth, and Captain David Toczek. Without the expertise of Mr. Frank Martini we would not have the charts and graphs that accompany this text. My greatest thanks go to my friend Captain James Fischer, for his patient reading and sympathetic ear when I would start off on an intellectual trip to nowhere in particular.

One other man deserves mention in this process, albeit anonymously. As a boss, he was known far and wide for his absolute insistence that we all wear our helmets. It was nearly a decade before I appreciated the real reasons for that inviolate order. He knows who he is, but may not realize that he is responsible for starting me on this journey in the first place, nearly ten years ago. It was from observing this man that I first realized that it was acceptable for infantry officers to write and pursue intellectual interests. He demonstrated that a grunt may "hump the Kahukus" one day and delve into the mysteries of Clausewitz the next without being struck down by lightning. Without the positive example that this officer set before a young lieutenant, I might never have committed a single idea to paper, and this book may well have never seen print.

For their steady and unwavering patience with a historian attempting to translate concepts lifted from physics into analogies applicable to history and military theory I thank my father, Dr. Robert L. Bateman, Jr. and my editors, Col. Robert Kane (Ret.) and E. J. McCarthy. My father started me down the track of synthesis, and Colonel Kane brought ill-defined but well intentioned concepts through to an understandable conclusion.

Finally, I would thank the people that really made this book a reality, my wife Debbie and my three daughters, Morgan, Ryann, and Connor. Their patience was the key to the creation of this book.

Introduction

Without overstating the matter, I am being credited or blamed for the "digitization" of the U.S. Army. I need to be very careful how I react to this praise or criticism because, in fact, the Army has been moving into the digital age for over 20 years and if anything, I could be correctly criticized for taking on a mantle not warranted. I am seeking no credit. For instance, Air Defense Artillery Systems were digital in 1992–1993, Field Artillery Fire Control Systems in 1980, Army aviation in 1989 and tanks in 1986 with the inclusion of the 1553 data buss. The keen observer of the scene could correctly note that we woke up in the early 90's to a powerful, ongoing trend and in turn made a virtue out of this inexorable movement.

An interlocutor once asked me to reflect on ". . . the decision to digitize . . ." as if to imply it was a decision of note. My answer surprised him I expect. As I told him, it was easy to make because it had already been made and frankly, I could have been quiet on the issue and it would have happened in the course of time.

If there was anything noteworthy which took place, it was the effort to explain to ourselves the implications of the term and, in turn, to ascertain how to harness the inherent power of this technology. It is obvious to all interested observers, as well as those who participated, that the experiments, battle labs, and Louisiana Maneuver T.F. were all pieces in a larger movement which is transforming the Army and all services and indeed having profound implications in our lives. This technological movement was, to be sure, hastened somewhat by our focus, but as in previous shifts, it is as if its time had come.

Frequency modulation, amplitude modulation, wireless technology like telegraph expanded the reach of commanders, reducing the soldiers per square mile while conversely expanding the scope of battlefields. Digital technology is having the same effect. It is not a transformation without growing pains, but this is not a new phenomenon. We tried to speed things up, experiment, learn, and integrate the force.

Who knows what kit the infantry soldier will carry? I doubt that any of us know, nor will we, until we experiment. The goal should be to protect this precious resource while making each infantryman more lethal and capable. I think we should be willing to push the envelope in this context while, at the same time, we must have the courage and wisdom to accept the fact that what at first seems like a good idea may not be good a idea.

I am encouraged by what I have read in this anthology; this book is overdue. We needed it in 1991. For valid reasons, I guess, it was not to be. Now, we are beginning to read ideas from "The Front" which are more than reflexive critiques. What we need are ideas, concepts, reflective of a world which is tough to predict—the future. Such ideas need not necessarily come from any place in the hierarchy, but they must come from interested and competent people—soldiers, citizens and defense-oriented civilians.

Thankfully, leaders in a healthy Army will always be debating the future. Soldiers can disagree about the future that faces them, the relative importance of the various arms and services in the fights that may await them, and the appropriate path from today's state of readiness to tomorrow's formula for victory. Without constructive debate on such issues, no Army would ever transform itself to meet new challenges.

This book is an important part of that dialogue and it might even start an informed debate on important issues: modernization force design, equipment training, C3. Most of its contributors are familiar to officers who try to stay informed on ideas about the Army's future, and all have written original, thoughtful essays that combine into a comprehensive, detailed, and convincing appraisal of important aspects of the future our Army might face. It is aptly sub-titled "A view from the front lines," because each of the contributors is most familiar with the challenges of the soldier at the tactical level and they are young enough to maintain the front-line leader's perspective on the imperatives for change.

When higher headquarters receive reports from the front lines, they expect each observer to give a full account of "what's in his lane." What is his or her assessment of the friendly forces within the command? What threats or opportunities can he see to his front? How does he assess his prospects? If we envision a view through time rather than space, each author has done a fine job of answering those and other pertinent questions. While the main emphasis is on the future, readers who are uncertain about details of current capabilities will find adequate discussions of current organizations, doctrines, or training requirements to read the futuristic passages critically. This is an important strength of the book, because current forces are complex and the forces at work to modify them are far from uniform and there are profound discontinuities in design as well as equipment in the force. The details available here give us solid footing for the integration/interpretation effort that every reader of any good anthology must perform.

That integration/interpretation effort is the real pay-off of this book. It helps us get beyond what we think we know into areas where theoretical and practical insights often depend on fresh ideas. We know that Army/Marine Corps partnership will be even more important in the future than in the past. These authors help us think about the challenge from both the light infantry and the joint task force perspective. While we are at the joint task force level, we can read another essay that gives us new thoughts on command, control, communications, and intelligence at that level. We can then assess those thoughts through essays that give us full-blown images of specific futures. The results are stimulating to all of us who worry about the Army's path to its future.

The soldiers in the front lines hope that headquarters will fill today's needs while facilitating tomorrow's operations. In our democracy, that can be tough to do at every level when war is raging. It may be even more difficult at the strategic level when today's force employment patterns do not fit historic patterns and tomorrow's requirements lie on the other side of a technological chasm in an ill-defined threat environment. If the front line views we encounter here are occasionally somewhat skeptical about higher headquarters' ability to get it right, we shouldn't be surprised. I don't believe anyone in "headquarters" is complacent on that point, and I expect this anthology will be debated just as carefully in the Pentagon as it will be in the Army's schools and units.

When I was about the age of these contributors we were reading General Sir John Hackett's *The Third World War.* (1978) We were engaged in equipment modernization, a training revolution, and a transformation to a doctrine-based Army. The "worst case scenario" sketched by Hackett, gave us a future we could agree upon so that we could easily gain internal consensus on lots of tough issues. Enough political leaders shared that view of the future so that we could resource those improvements that were most essential. For the ensuing decade, that single Cold War image of a future war between the two great coalitions provided an adequate framework for our defense debate. It helped to have a single view, an accepted view, of the future.

There is excellent food for thought about the future in these pages. Professionals of all services, as well as national defense oriented civilian leaders, can find much to think about. Most of these authors will be influencing the dialogue and our institutional direction for years to come. Their ideas are worthwhile.

Some readers, I expect, will correctly lament the paucity of fiscal resources to actualize some of these ideas. This has always been true yet, as most who read this know, money has not really ever limited imaginative thought, experimentation and growth—Naval air, amphibious operations and parachute assault, are good examples.

Now we need an entire shelf full of anthologies such as this if we are even to begin to capture the range of legitimate views associated with who we might fight, where, when, and with what. These authors have made an important contribution to that bookshelf. Now all of us who think about these issues need to do our part to add to the bookshelf and to raise our voices in support of a strong defense establishment that can rise to tomorrow's challenges. Captain Bateman and his team certainly have done their part.

General Gordon R. Sullivan, U.S. Army (Retired)

Robert L. Bateman III

Our definition of a revolution in military affairs states that it is a fundamental change in the nature of warfare based on changes in the areas of technology; organization; tactics; or social, political, and economic factors that make up how a force is developed, is fielded, and fights.[1] Many of the current prognostications about the U.S. Army's "Force XXI" and the "Army After Next" focus on the technology and methods that digital forces at all echelons should use on and around the battlefield. The focus here is on the tactical level. It appears that tactical doctrine and organizational structures are also changing as a byproduct of advances in technology.

What have not been examined are the potential effects of these changes on the men and women who will populate those future battlefields. In the past the army failed to appreciate the potential side effects of some technologies, especially the effects of two technologies operating together.

This chapter addresses some simple aspects of the human side of change. By looking at how the U.S. Army has failed in adaptation in the past, we may infer some lessons about pitfalls for the future. Technology has a tricky way of combining with other elements to create unintended consequences. When we mix technology with the human animal, the results are not always those originally predicted in the laboratory. For examples of this we need only look back a short time in military history.

This is obviously not the first revolution, if such a thing even exists, in military affairs. Historians and military theorists count between three and ten separate shifts in military dominance tied to technology, organizational change, societal change, or a combination of all three that have changed the way wars are won. From the infantry revolution of the fourteenth and fifteenth centuries through the advent of nuclear weapons, change is apparent at every turn. Yet we have within our own century an example that provides some ominous parallels.

Between the first and second world wars there was rapid development not only in the field of automotive technology (leading to better tanks) but in communications equipment as well. For the first time in human history instantaneous communication across long distances between units that could not see each other became practical at all echelons of military organizations. When some nations tied these advances in radio technology to the development of the tank, a synergistic system developed to pursue war in a new way.

The United States was not one of the nations that broke ground on this track. As late as 1940 the U.S. Army still included budget lines for the purchase, care, and feeding of pigeons. Our doctrine was suited for France, but a France of 1918, not 1940. How and where did our system break down? We need to identify this point so that we can accurately examine ourselves and guard against the same problem occurring in the future.

Specifically, we might ask ourselves, "What have we not accounted for in our predictions?" So many people are claiming that the face of war will dramatically change as a result of digitization; what constants then remain? There are at least two: fear and leadership. What are the effects of digitization upon these constants?

We must analyze today what the effects of these changes may be on our leaders and on how they lead, before the unanticipated effects of our decisions upend our desired end state. The army is looking at battle command and at creating templates to project the characteristics that successful future commanders might need, but is that enough? We must address the issue of information processing and the possible results of the explosion in available information upon leaders and leader development in Force XXI and beyond—now, before it is too late to adjust.

Leadership is needed to counteract a phenomenon common to war: fear. All soldiers, or at least most soldiers, feel fear. It is the one unifying element throughout the ages, recognizable in history texts and in science fiction set in the future. Reactions to fear may change in accordance with the social and cultural mores of an era, but the impetus remains a human constant. When confronted with a threat to their lives, humans have a biological reaction.

Military forces focus on training to reduce and leadership to alleviate fear, but they cannot eliminate it without altering the human body in some way. Because this is generally impractical, over time we have developed the idea of discipline. Discipline is the subordination of the real wishes of the individual to organizational goals.

At the current time our methods and levels of discipline are designed to deal with a battlefield that is essentially empty. The discipline of the past, even as recently as 150 years ago, is considered extreme and outdated, just as the tactics of that day have passed for similar reasons. Yet the discipline of that era, the era of linear warfare, was designed to hold men on the battlefield in the face of massive psychological assaults upon their bravery. The visual cues that a soldier's life was in danger were constantly present in the past.

In the twentieth century we have become accustomed to the phenomenon of the empty battlefield. Through most of this century soldiers have fought in open order. Once the shooting starts, the individual combatant's world is reduced to a small area—in essence, usually the space in the soldier's immediate vicinity that he or she can see while prone upon the earth. A few comrades and perhaps a few of the enemy are visible while in combat, but for the most part the battlefield is empty of everything but ordnance. What might happen when the battlefield, real or synthetic, is no longer empty? Might the age-old (but now not even defined) idea of shock return to the battlefield?

With these considerations in mind we should also acknowledge one other constant: change. How do we maintain a cutting-edge force even as we wrestle with the implications of each new technological progression? Admittedly the current system is supposed to adapt to and incorporate change, but it was designed for a tempo of change that was much slower than that in effect now. Today the U.S. Army's system of doctrinal review and institutional adaptation is glacial in comparison to the tempo of changes in technology.

If we accept that for the time being technology is a causative element in the changes in warfare, then we may need to reorganize ourselves to ensure that we stay ahead. Yet there is no way that we can afford to modernize the whole army every three years. This implies, when balanced against fiscal restraints, that perhaps we should adopt some form of deliberate and organizationally structured system designed to keep at least part of the force modern at all times. You may be the judge.

Pandora's Box

In my own mind, we are at the beginning of a revolution in the way we will command soldiers and tactical units in battle.

—Lt. Gen. Frederick Franks

It all comes back to doctrine in the end. Doctrine is a set of agreed-upon statements or beliefs about warfare. It is the synthesis of history, technology, and the culture of the nation whose military creates the doctrine. As the product of these elements, a doctrine is also a filter through which these elements are viewed. A military doctrine, once embraced, may cause a cultural shift within the military establishment. Doctrine may also have a profound effect upon the selection, development, and procurement of material and technology. Finally, doctrine may affect how a military institution views military history.

Despite initial appearances, this is not a closed-loop system. New technology developed for use by the supporting civilian society may appear. This technology may have battlefield implications that force the military to take it into account. Similarly, the military experiences of other nations at war become a source for new military history as time passes. Finally, the military or its supporting society may produce philosophical or cultural shifts that can cause changes in doctrine.

Today we are once again learning that it is far easier to create a doctrine against a specified threat than it is to do the same in a vacuum. As the twentieth century fades we find ourselves in a familiar position. Faced with shrinking budgets, no threats that are discernible to civilians, and an explosion of technology that we cannot afford to purchase as it advances by orders of magnitude within mere years, the U.S. Army struggles to define itself.

Toward that end, an analysis of where we have already been may assist military leaders of the present and future in avoiding the pitfalls that bothered their predecessors. Between World War I and World War II, the U.S. Army was faced with a set of conditions similar to those that we see today across the military. Following U.S. tradition, Congress cut the army to the bone following World War I and then did not provide the funds to reach even those troop levels that had been authorized. Simultaneously, communications and automotive technology expanded within the civilian sector at a terrific rate.

Finally, until the last years of the 1930s the army could not point toward a credible threat to the security of the nation. Modernization was the goal, but "do more with less" was the watchword. There was not enough money to fund the troop levels required to meet the security needs of the nation and to modernize as well, so choices had to be made. Some of those choices had unintended effects, some were the result of institutional inertia, and some were just wrong.

More ominously, in at least a few instances the institutional values that should have served the army by highlighting the shortcomings of the doctrine or the technology were undermined by the actions of officers imbued with a "win at all costs" mentality. Winning was defined in a personal rather than an institutional sense.

All of these factors combined to ensure that the U.S. Army entered the World War II era with outdated technology, an obsolescent doctrine, and a cultural habit of taking shortcuts. In essence, there were a lot of Courtney Massengales and not many Sam Damons.[2]

Doctrine is created by a professional military based on its understanding of history. Within the service schools of the military, military history is used to extract lessons learned from previous wars. These lessons learned are used to create or justify doctrine for the armed forces.[3] Since the Napoleonic era this has been a constant among Western armies. During World War I the German system of doctrinal change was a thorough and deliberate organizational phenomenon that resulted in well-conceived and well-integrated tactical changes.[4] The Allies' system of review resulted in technological solutions as well as doctrinal changes, but the impetus for both was the same: the stalemate and slaughter of the western front.

Following a war, this process is supposed to continue. The history of the combat that the military force experienced is recorded and dissected in a search for lessons. The military then applies these lessons to its existing set of assumptions about combat. The lessons derived from combat either validate or invalidate the existing doctrine.[5] Once the doctrine exists, it is used to train the force and serves as a guiding principle for the technological needs of the force. Subsequently training and testing (as well as observation of foreign military developments) provide new data for input into the cycle. When it works, this system should ensure constant refinement and change in light of contemporary developments. Sometimes it does not work correctly.

The untold story of the U.S. Army's radio development is an example of the technology-doctrine link. War Department General Order No. 29 dated 18 May 1920 declared, "Infantry troops will install, maintain and operate all lines of information within the infantry brigade."[6] Today that order does not seem in the least bit unusual or outrageous. But this is the end of the twentieth century, and that was far closer to the beginning.

Consider just the issue of the average infantry soldier's education, let alone his education in technology. A contemporary equivalent might be an order that proclaimed that infantry soldiers would build from raw components and install all software; resolve conflicts between all software applications; establish an Ethernet-based network; and operate without supervision their own Pentium II (MMX) 500-megahertz networked computers. This would be accomplished without diverting any resources to external training.

Unsurprisingly, problems developed almost immediately when the specially and uniformly trained signalmen were replaced by locally trained infantrymen. Part of the problem stemmed from the fact that as late as 1920 very few radios were actually in the infantry brigades. There were no radios at the platoon, company, or battalion levels and only a few sets at the regimental and brigade levels when the National Defense Act of 1920 went into effect.[7]

By 1922 new radios (originally designed for World War I but only then reaching the field units) were in operation at the battalion level, and technical (as opposed to human or pigeon) means of communication existed all the way down to the platoon level.[8]

By 1924 new equipment was being tested and personnel were being trained in its use. In a healthy and innovative system the influence of technology upon the existing doctrine is recognized during the course of training. Unfortunately, the U.S. Army was not this type of system at the time.

The newly developed and issued radio sets of 1922 were the SCR-77s.[9] Two factors conspired against the successful use of radios during interwar training. The first was the attitude of the users. A few brave officers writing in the *Infantry Journal* openly stated that the importance of communications was not recognized by their infantry brethren, nor was the importance of maintaining the radio equipment.[10]

Infantry officers on maneuvers regularly circumvented the communications system, thereby hiding the problems of the radios. In the opinion of infantry leaders, maneuvers were for maneuvering and training in the physical aspects of combat. All else was subordinate to this most important aspect of training. If communications could not be established and the maneuvers did not occur because of that, then "real" training could not occur and careers would be jeopardized. This avoidance, of course, limited the effectiveness of the training exercises because maneuvers lost that aspect of realism.

To overcome the effects of their lack of attention toward the radios, headquarters regularly leaked the details of upcoming maneuvers and in other ways allowed units to operate under conditions that they could not expect to enjoy during war. This situation was exacerbated by the attitudes of line infantry officers who not only bypassed the use of radios, but resented "wasting" soldiers on signals duty when they believed there was more important infantry training to be done.[11]

An article in the *Infantry Journal* of September 1927 demonstrates this attitude. The author was an observer during the summer maneuvers of the 2d Division.

> Radio within the infantry brigade was, as usual, of no value. Its equipment is delicate, and a disproportionate time is required for its personnel to attain proficiency. Then the neces-

> sity for coding and decoding all messages renders the radio unfit for practical use because there is always a faster and better means of communications at hand. At present the radio is no better than a very expensive toy. The Infantry and Signal Schools should continue to experiment with it because, quite possibly, some years from now, it may have lost its present vital defects. Meantime the troops should not have the burden of its care, and the personnel required for its service should be available for other duty.[12]

The radio set referred to in this quote was the now technologically antiquated but still serviceable SCR-77. With the pervasiveness of the negative attitude demonstrated in the *Infantry Journal,* it is possible to understand why a grand total of two tactical radio systems were fielded between 1917 and 1941.

The simple technological solution to the delicacy of the SCR-77 cited in the aforementioned account turned out to be the replacement of a single weak spring with a stronger one on the screwdriver condenser. The weaker spring had allowed the radio to be jarred out of calibration. (This was in the days before crystal-based control of frequency, or frequency modulation.[13]) The fact that this simple solution was not identified or the problem corrected for the better part of a decade helps demonstrate that the doctrinal control by the infantry over tactical communications resulted in relegating communications to a secondary role.

One other portion of the aforementioned quote crystallizes common army perceptions of the day: "There is always a faster and better means of communications at hand." The means referred to are the landline, the runner, and the pigeon—the communications systems of World War I. Given the scale of operations during a normal maneuver, the writer was correct. Then again, he observed training maneuvers in which nobody was being killed by enemy artillery or machine-gun fire.

If the infantry had been truly interested in radios or had allowed radios to play as important a part in maneuvers as they would in combat, it would have identified and pressed for a solution to the technical difficulties in radios earlier, as other nations did. As it was, the infantry's doctrine of a slow-moving, infantry-speed battlefield reinforced old prejudices. If the infantry controlled the training field, discounting the real environment of combat, it would never discover the need for reliable mobile radios.

Thus the cycle of history to doctrine to technology to new history (training lessons learned) came full circle. World War I provided the input of combat experience, while the National Defense Act of 1920 and the Field Service Regulation of 1923 dictated an infantry-based organization and doctrine. This doctrine trained the army using existing equipment.

Because the infantry could avoid the problems of the radio, it applied little to no pressure for the radio to be improved. Without lighter and more reliable radios there was little reason to attempt to develop new forms of maneuver or to consider that maneuvers could occur at a faster tempo. Thus the then-current training validated only the old system.

Other branches of the military saw the utility of mobile communication but lacked the political power or demonstrable need to force the signal corps to develop radios.[14] The result was stagnation.

The result of twenty years under this setup is best demonstrated by a 1940 article written by James Wilmeth a brave infantry lieutenant who was leading a tank platoon.

> No shielding of the engine, no bonding of the tracks, has yet made possible practicable radio transmission and reception between moving vehicles or tanks. (I discount the few times that after weeks of checking every connection with micrometer, slide rule, and Friss gauge, two tanks have engaged in moving communications for a few minutes until one of them ran over a chewing gum wrapper.) Except in theory, the tank is deaf.[15]

Wilmeth further noted that at the time of his writing the United States was the only major military power in the world still attempting to use pigeons with tanks. Had the U.S. Army adopted a mobile form of warfare not entirely tied to the infantry, at some point between the wars things might have worked out differently. The

United States had radios in all its tanks, but as Wilmeth pointed out, they did not work.

According to the chief of infantry when he rendered his final report in 1941, as late as 1937, "signal communications were behind developments in civil practice."[16] This was a gross understatement. In the end, it was only the adoption of FM radios used by civilian state police that saved the infantry and the army overall from its own interwar system. In 1941 the army adopted and fielded the SCR-293, a direct copy of the radios then in use by the Connecticut state police. These radios, unmodified, were installed in combat vehicles and saw immediate use in North Africa in 1942.[17] This is an example that army leaders might do well to remember.

In this case it was institutional values that undercut the modernization process. This was a military organization that intentionally or unintentionally promoted a system wracked by parochialism within the various combat arms. Branch fiefdoms appeared and were jealously guarded lest the funding for a given branch suffer in the least. It was not a healthy place to be labeled a dissenter.

Furthermore, there was an undeniable belief in the American myth of the Great War—that U.S. infantrymen would always be able to break through. The myth arose for political reasons, was sustained by the AEF for reasons of prestige, and was accepted into doctrine despite the evidence of the battlefield.[18]

Because of this myth the systems of the previous war were seen as sufficient. Doctrine did not have to change to accommodate new technology, especially since the tempo of war was not demonstrably different. The infantry establishment sustained itself with the myth and the doctrine of infantry supremacy. Those officers and men who suggested that the face of battle in the future might be radically different were gently chided and dismissed as extremists.

Wisdom Through History

This is where the U.S. Army stood firm between the wars. Tanks were primarily for the support of the infantry and would operate with and at the speed of the infantry. Some light tanks, also known for political reasons as "combat cars," were assigned to the cavalry.

There they were used on a limited scale, and the potential of command and control by radio was better appreciated. However in both cases, while the combination of tanks and radios was seen as useful, significant pressure to improve or field either was not applied.

Despite the presence of the occasional foresighted article in the professional journals of the period, there was no true debate. Some professionals of the time saw the synergistic potential, but they could not make their message heard. Those who suggested the need for a change in the army's system of fighting were brushed aside as messiahs to a single idea. Their ideas could therefore be readily dismissed.

The result was that between 1923 and 1940 the U.S. Army maintained a single doctrine, that of the Field Service Regulation of 1923. Despite the fact that massive changes in technology created the potential for great changes in the tempo and methods of warfare, the U.S. Army stuck to its position. Technology was viewed in discrete packets as it applied to narrowly defined areas. As a result the United States did not fully develop the possible combinations of technology with tactics between the wars.

Today, however, it appears that the shoe is on the other foot. Nearly everyone seems to agree that there are major changes in store and that these changes will be prompted by technology and its application to the battlefield. Various combinations of technology and tactical doctrines are tested on a daily basis. So perhaps we have beaten that bugaboo. We appear to be well on the way toward systematic discovery of the potential of various combinations of new technologies as they apply to the battlefield. What then remains?

What remains to be fully explored is the question of how humans will interact, individually and organizationally, with the new technology and with each other through the new technology.

Digitization of the battlefield may give maneuver commanders at the tactical, operational, and strategic levels an unprecedented ability to see themselves. Concurrent with this development is the continuation of an ongoing effort to break open the information stovepipes that allow us to see the enemy. These changes may allow friendly information and data about the enemy situation to be seen and known by everyone with the correct hardware configurations and communications assets. It is now a question of what they might do with this information that may prove to have unintended consequences in the future.

As postulated by the Tofflers in their books *The Third Wave* and *War Anti-War,* we are at the edge of a new type of society and by extension a new type of warfare. This information-based society and method of war will depend largely on the complete saturation of communications technology within the target element.

However, unless great care is taken to avoid it, this information explosion may result in the devaluation of at least one level of command and the eventual weakening of the fabric of our leadership development. The end state at which we find ourselves may not be the anticipated dynamic, decisive, and lethal leader-information combination. Instead, we may be a crippled force with indecisive leaders overwhelmed by information that they have not been trained to assimilate.

Digital Leadership

> In the term "Maneuver Warfare," maneuver refers to an entire style of warfare, one characterized not only by moving in relation to the enemy to gain positional advantage, but also—AND EVEN MORE—to moving faster than the enemy, to defeating him through superior tempo.[19]

> The Tenets of Battle Command: A commander's success on and off the battlefield depends on his ability to operate in accordance with nine basic tenets: initiative, agility, depth, integration, versatility, flexibility, judgment, intuition, and empathy.[20]

> *Auftragstaktik* is composed of four essential elements—obedience, proficiency, independence of action, and self-esteem. In order for *auftragstaktik* to exist, all four elements must be present.[21]

The battlefield is a tricky place filled with deception, fear, confusion, and even on the best of days no small amount of chaos. Much of military theory involves dissecting that environment to understand how we might reduce one or all of these elements. Military theories in turn often lead to military doctrine, which in a perfect world would result in common terminology.

This is not a perfect world.

The terminology used to define and understand the complex interaction of military battlefield leadership, the various strategies available to a nation, and the processes used to apply one to the other are confusing and at times contradictory. Therefore, this section contains more than the usual number of definitions to ensure that the reader understands the terms used in the same way that the author does.

Three strategies are available to nations and military forces. These are attrition, annihilation, and exhaustion. The first two have as their objective the destruction of the combat power of the enemy's military; the difference between them is largely one of time. The third strategy, exhaustion, seeks the erosion of the enemy's will or resources. All three strategies are effective. However, given the U.S. predilection for rapid and decisive action, the United States appears to prefer a general strategy of annihilation.

To accomplish this it must use one of two methods at the operational or tactical level: it may pursue annihilation through maneuver or annihilation through the physical destruction of the enemy (sometimes confusingly called annihilation through attrition). In general, the U.S. military ground forces claim to prefer maneuver over attrition at the operational and tactical levels. This leads to a stated preference for a particular style and method of command and control at the tactical level.[22]

Various military theorists expound upon these methods. We will use the British terms for concepts that probably originated with the Prussians in the nineteenth century. The competing concepts are called orders tactics and mission orders.[23]

Orders tactics require a rigid command structure and total adherence to a centralized plan and system of control. These tactics are suitable for top-down control and centralized control of a force.

Mission orders emphasize subordinate initiative and adherence to only a generalized intent published by a higher commander.[24] These tactics are suited to changing situations in which the reality of the front line is not necessarily well reflected on situation maps in the rear. Executing mission orders (also known as *auftragstaktik*) requires a mindset and an imbedded system of values that support the independent thinker, decisive commander, and risk taker. Many claim that mission orders are the key to successful maneuver-based warfare.

This linkage between a system of warfare (maneuver versus attritional) and the command process required to successfully execute it (mission orders versus orders tactics) is well established and decently supported by historical evidence.[25] At the root of all this is the assumption that the subordinate commander knows better than the senior commander what the local tactical situation may be at any given moment.

In the Industrial Age of warfare there has never been a technological solution that allowed commanders to see better when they operated farther from the front lines. Their field of vision might increase, but at the same time the accuracy of what they perceived would decrease in direct proportion to the number of filters (read "analysts") and amount of time that had passed since the data (read "reports") were initially recorded and sent up the chain.

Thus, even in the era of mechanization the decisive point for the maneuver commander has always been forward, preferably in a position from which the commander can personally observe the battle and thereby issue commands that may influence its course.

Communications advances of this century have freed the commanders of higher echelons from static locations and placed them on the battlefields with the means to issue orders to geographically separated units. This in turn has strengthened those leaders who have led from the front. Commanders operating at or near the front have gained flexibility because radios have allowed them to bring additional units or the effects of additional units (for instance, the effects of munitions from dispersed elements such as field artillery batteries) to the decisive points on the battlefields.

The ultimate example of this style of warfare and leadership is probably the Desert Fox himself, Erwin Rommel (although the author personally prefers the American example, P. Woods, commander of the U.S. 4th Armored Division during the race across

France).[26] In either case, the idea if not the terminology remains the same. Mission orders were a needed doctrinal leadership development to execute maneuver warfare for one great reason. It has been assumed, and has generally been true, that the commander forward knows more about the current situation than any higher commander not on the scene.

This implies that orders are written with the full understanding of all participants that should the situation not meet expectations, the commander on the ground has the ultimate authority to modify the plan as he or she sees fit in order to accomplish the intent of the higher commander. Mission and commander's intent are the overriding considerations; everything else is but a means to an end.

The empowerment of the junior leader and the reliance upon that leader's judgment are paramount because it is assumed that only at the lowest levels can a leader see through the "fog of war," if only for a short distance.[27] The lower the commander, the better he or she can visualize the strength and location of the various subunits and know the immediate threat; therefore the lower commander is better equipped to make decisions.

If a higher commander wants to influence a battle, that commander too must move forward to where he or she can personally observe the operations and their results. What happens when that higher commander is provided the means to see his or her units and those of the enemy over the proverbial hill better than the commander who is on the ground in the most forward position?

Digitization and the Emasculation of the Subordinate Commander

Force XXI and the theory of informational warfare rely heavily on the concept of "breaking down the stovepipe information structures."[28] Translated, this means that information that traditionally flowed vertically from one echelon to the next because of system hardware or organizational processes may now be accessed by a greater number of users spread horizontally across an organization without the requirement for formal distribution at each level. Anyone who needs information can access it from any other echelon, provided that the data is somewhere in the system.

Conceptually, this may greatly increase the effectiveness of our corps, division, brigade, and battalion staffs both in garrison and in the field. No longer will the Battalion S3 wait impatiently for information about an upcoming operation. As soon as the divisional graphics are created they will become available to all clients within the net. Parallel planning may begin immediately at both the brigade and battalion levels even as the division staff works to complete the plan.

Brigade planners may also have instant information regarding the status of their subordinate units as they work to create a tentative plan and select what element is best suited to being the main effort. Reporting of location, strength, and equipment status is available at the touch of a button for staffs and commanders to evaluate their situations.

Planning cells operating from digitally linked battle command vehicles (BCVs or C2Vs) may consult thirty-inch monitors to view accurate maps with the superimposed locations of all vehicles within their command. Intelligence officers may "look up" to access strategic and national reconnaissance assets to "see the enemy," greatly enhancing the speed and accuracy of their situation templates. Then with another toggle they may "look down" and receive digital photos from scouts and units on the front lines, which may refine their situation templates even more.

Finally, the battalion and brigade commanders of this digital force may enter their command vehicles, personally process the visual and perhaps auditory information available from the screens and their staffs, and make decisions. This is, after all, what commanders are trained to do.

But what about the most forward commander—the one in a turret; the one on the front line who does not have multiple large-screen monitors and a staff to help analyze the reams of potentially available information? What about that lowly company commander?

Standing in the cramped turret of his combat vehicle, he looks out over the battlefield. To his eyes the battlefield looks the same as it might have during World War II: largely deserted, potentially dangerous, and definitely lonely. He may have access to most of the information available to the staff and commanders above him, but to see it he's going to have to squint. His little twelve-inch screen tucked in under the deck of his tank turret can only access one piece of information at a time, provided that it works and is not splattered with mud or washed out by sunlight.

Given a minute he can easily access the digital information that shows the actual location of his team's vehicles on a map with the latest graphics. But because of the size of his monitor, expanding the view beyond the scale of his company or team is not practical. The map covers too much and the pieces are too small without that large screen to spread across. Of course he may scroll the screen wherever he likes, but he then loses the big picture. His is not the problem of information overload but of not being able to access enough information simultaneously. For the first time in history, the frontline commander actually knows less about what is going on in his immediate area than does the higher commander.

Of course, this may not be all bad. After all, it is only at the battalion level that any synchronization begins to occur anyway. The frontline commanders receive their missions, move out, and draw fire. Theirs is the mission of closing with and destroying, and they may operate using mission tactics as their guiding principles. After all, when the operation kicks off, their plan becomes a guide. The frontline commander who will see the situation in real time is expected to react as he or she sees fit to accomplish his or her commander's overall intent.

But wait. What about that higher commander at the battalion, brigade, or division level? In our Industrial Age army that commander's place has always been up front so that he or she can see what the company commanders see, become mentally oriented regarding the enemy, decide on a course of action, and act.

But in the information-based Force XXI, the best place to see the battlefield may be from within the command post vehicle. The battalion or brigade commander who wants access to all information is tied to a command-and-control vehicle—that is, if that commander wants to stay ahead in the "observe, orient, decide, act" cycle. Not only that, but because this commander has better information faster than his or her subordinate commanders, he or she may end up telling them how to maneuver their subordinate units.

This is not without nondigital precedents. For example, during the crossings of the Meuse River by the German army in May 1940, the personal presence of officers up to and including division commanders often became the critical factor in the crossing. This was not because of any inherent leadership abilities of these generals. Rather, it was because the personal observation of the tactical situation plus the rank needed in a hierarchical system to issue orders to a large number of troops were combined in one general laying prone, under direct fire, on the banks of the river.[29]

Leadership examples from the U.S. attack in the other direction four years later also indicate these characteristics. So the precedent is there—partially. Commanders from higher echelons sometimes come down and directly influence the action on the ground. The qualifying element here is that these commanders have heretofore needed to be physically present to effect efficient command influence.[30]

Imagine this scenario: a battalion-equivalent task force moves forward from its tactical assembly area into a meeting engagement. The battalion commander in his battle command vehicle simultaneously surveys three large screens displaying the entire area of operations with graphics and actual vehicle locations, confirmed enemy locations, and critical logistical information in a user-friendly format.

His company commanders bouncing across the terrain have little time to look at their own displays unless one of their lieutenants wanders off into the mist again. Instead they rely on their senses and voice commands. Of course their senses are degraded, not physically but because of the increased area that the new digital force covers. Companies that once could only spread out over a mile now cover several miles. They will not get lost or separated because they are digitally aware of each other.

Suddenly, in the battle command vehicle, the battalion commander observes a new icon on the screen. Enemy tanks have just started their engines and have been detected through thermal emissions by a friendly unmanned aerial vehicle. The enemy tanks are on the immediate flank of one of his company's platoons. He immediately broadcasts the warning directly to that platoon leader (who is himself separated by miles from his company commander during the approach movement), describing the threat and the immediate actions he must take.

The lieutenant does not question his battalion commander, nor is there time to confirm this with his company commander; he *acts*. It is only after the threat is avoided and the action well under way that the company commander has time to look at his display, rewind to see what happened, and mentally confirm that the battalion commander gave the correct orders to one of his platoons.

Still the task force moves forward. Again in the battle command vehicle the battalion commander sees what his commanders on the front line cannot. As the breach is initiated and supporting fires lay a smokescreen for the engineers, the commander notices another downlink, this time from a Joint Surveillance Target Acquisition Radar System (JSTARS) aircraft. The enemy reserve has not been pinned or delayed by the field artillery scatterable minefield (FASCAM) fired on its location, and is in fact moving forward from its concealed position along an unexpected route.

Again the commander has beaten the enemy in the decision cycle, so he orders his own reserve to move forward and occupy a position below a ridge that is over the next hill from its current location. The reserve company commander protests. "What ridge?" he asks. On his monitor the resolution cannot pick out the gap in the contour intervals, and he is leery of placing his command in an exposed forward slope position against what to him is an unknown force.

The battalion commander knows better and repeats his orders. He has seen this ground through the unmanned aerial vehicle and has confirmed that it is an ideal location to meet the attempted flanking counterattack. From his swivel chair he turns and directs the fire support officer to place fires in the grid where he has placed his cursor. The cursor becomes a fire mission even as the enemy counterattack arrives. The breach created in the enemy defenses is a success and the task force rolls on. The battalion commander has learned that information is power, and he has certainly acted upon that information with lethal effects.

Back to those other commanders—the dirty ones in the turrets. They have learned a lesson as well: obey orders from on high because higher does know better. The information stovepipe may have been broken open, but they do not have large enough buckets to catch all the information flowing out to them. They have seen their platoons issued direct orders by a higher level and they have themselves been forced to execute missions that, based upon their personal observations, appeared irrational—but that were in fact the best in a given situation.

Their commander knew as much about each of them as they themselves knew, and knew it at the same time or even before they did. While moving they had little time to look down, manipulate their computer interfaces, and access the same information sequentially that their commander could see simultaneously. Most importantly, they rarely got the chance to make independent decisions regarding the employment of their own units.

In this scenario I painted a picture at the company level. It could just as easily occur at the battalion-brigade level or the brigade-division level. Moreover, although this example uses what appear to be direct-fire ground-maneuver units (either mechanized infantry or armor), this does not limit the applicability of the concept and warning to only those units. The idea that the dominant maneuver of the future is defined as the maneuver of effects spreads the implications of this scenario evenly across all combat arms, from field artillery to aviation.

Implications for the Future of Force XXI

In the scenario previously described, the decisive force on the battlefield was the battalion commander. A U.S. Army publication, *Battle Command,* states that technology has the potential to revolutionize the way we command in battle by becoming "the tool that will allow the commander to move freely about the battlefield to where he can best influence the action without separating himself from his staff and other sources of information, communications and control."[31]

To that might be added the realization that on the digital or information battlefield, "moving freely about the battlefield" may not mean the physical movement of the commander. Instead the commander may move only his or her "eyes" (the unmanned aerial vehicle and various downlinks and uplinks from other assets) to where they can best see for the commander. The commander may have become tied to the information node from which he or she will command.

Another example to illustrate the point is an experiment of sorts. Place a battalion, brigade, or division commander in the training analysis facility at the National Training Center. Allow this commander full communications with his or her subordinate units and observe how the command becomes centralized around the commander.

At the division level something similar has already occurred. Division-level exercises with the 4th Infantry Division during the past several years appear to demonstrate that in an information-rich environment, a commander with the assets must be aware of the potential for (and deliberately avoid) overcontrolling.

Ironically, given the American distaste for anything that smacks of overcontrolling, this may not be all bad. It almost certainly is an effective method to increase our own decision-cycle speed past any potential enemy and may therefore save lives. The army currently has enough leaders with the proper qualifications to assimilate a vast amount of information rapidly and thus make timely decisions. This is what we have been trying to inculcate into our leaders for years. But what kind of commanders will those officers who grow up under this system become?

They have learned not to question orders and operate according to their own assessment of the situation to accomplish their commanders' intent. Instead they have developed under a system in which control is central and higher knows better. Their company commands were really glorified platoon-leader positions, while the battalion or brigade micromanaged their actions in an effort to increase speed by bypassing the company as an independent element.

Mission tactics will have died with the last nondigital company command. In the original definition of the term, the German idea of *auftragstaktik* had four components: obedience, proficiency, independence of action, and self-esteem. The U.S. Army has generally attempted to adopt these. However, if any one of these components was considered paramount, it was the tradition of independent action. It now appears likely that this cannot and perhaps should not survive on the digital battlefield of the future.

There are, however, several implications of this conclusion that military leaders of the future will wrestle with for some time to come. The idea that leadership and command and control may change is not particularly surprising or alarming if we recognize the potential for this change. If we decide that we would like to counter the potential shift toward centralized control at the forward edge of the battlefield, training and doctrine may overcome the byproduct effects of the new information technology.

But what about the effects of the new digital information technology at the absolute lowest level, that of the soldier on the future battlefield? How might information technology affect the way that this soldier perceives and reacts to the battle? More to the point, are we opening a new Pandora's box by allowing information that has not been available to the common soldier for more than one hundred years out of the realm of command and control and back onto the battlefield? How will Joe Sixpack react to digital information that tells him that he and his tank stand squarely in the path of the Sixth Guards Army?

> SHOCK (shôk) n. -intr. Archaic. To come into contact violently, as in battle; collide. [Old French choc, from choquer, to strike (with fear)][32]

Shock is a common term in the military lexicon of Western armed forces. It is typically considered an asset—something one wishes would happen to the enemy. It is often stated as a goal in a tactical operation. Yet how many people have considered exactly what they mean by "shock action"?

Shock has the potential to be a terrible and effective weapon in its own right. An understanding of the phenomenon of shock is critical for the commander hoping to employ it effectively as a component of a plan, or as the objective result of planned actions. Does the potential for shock exist on the modern battlefield? This portion of the essay examines shock not only so that we can use it more effectively, but also so that we can better understand how it might be used against us.

Reviewing Shock

For as long as people have attempted to better one another in physical matches there has been shock. Within the modern era the first military theorist to truly examine and develop a coherent theory on the behavior of men in combat was French Col. Ardant du Picq. He found that the one constant in human behavior in battle was abject fear. This fear was cumulative in its effect on masses of men. Du Picq was, for all intents and purposes, describing what we might now define as the phenomenon of shock.[33] His theories deal with methods that can be used to delay or prevent shock.

In more recent times military historians and sociologists have begun to take up this forgotten area of study and attempt to analyze the behavior of large groups of humans in the environment of combat. Many of them are interested in the effects of shock on human organizations. One of the scholars who has been most successful at this, Bruce Allan Watson, describes in sociological terms the possible effects of military disintegration using several events from military history as case studies.[34]

Despite the value of these and related studies, it appears that they are not being applied to the modern U.S. military. Du Picq was a combat leader writing just prior to the Franco-Prussian War of 1870, a period as full of technological changes as today. Watson, writing in the present but using historic examples ranging from the Peninsula War of the Napoleonic era through the Vietnam War, uses modern analytical tools to create a coherent picture.

Putting the lessons of both together should be the mission of doctrine today. We should understand human behavior in combat and from that develop doctrine to help us decide what tools we will use in the future. We must understand shock so that we may inflict it rather than having it inflicted upon us. Current U.S. Army doctrine, however, is silent on the topic.

One finds neither a definition nor a broad use of the term within Field Manual 100-5 (*Operations*) or the subordinate tactical manuals. Failing a definition from these sources one turns to the dictionary. For general military purposes we will define shock as having two components: physical force (expressed in terms of mass and velocity) and psychological force. Physical force is the enabling component; fear is the active and primary component. This definition will be the basis for our dissection. Yet this definition did not appear from whole cloth; shock is a recognized aspect of combat that has been widely documented if less often defined.

The mounted knights of the Middle Ages rode upon warhorses, which made them a potent combination of mass and acceleration and produced a fearsome visual impetus for shock. In the fifteenth century the European destrier, or warhorse, was a genetically refined and well-trained complement to the mounted knight's basic style of fighting. Just as size and endurance might be bred into a mount, so might psychological characteristics such as aggression.

Reinforced with training to accentuate its natural tendencies, the warhorse of the Middle Ages was a fearsome beast in its own right. Trained from the time it was a colt to obey the subtle commands given by leg pressures from its rider, it was also trained in more violent actions. Biting opposing horses or kicking dismounted warriors in the melee, this two thousand pounds of directed mass could impart a mighty impact by itself. When coupled with a knight and his intelligent mass at a velocity of nine meters per second, which could be converted into a rapid deceleration upon impact, the mounted warhorse was a weapon system made for producing shock.

There was one major problem, however: mounted knights were not inclined by training or culture to act in a truly concerted manner. Although their tactical disposition might loosely reflect some form of organization, they were in the final analysis still individual warriors. Knights or men-at-arms, grouped into battles under the standards of their respective noble commanders, were not trained for massed coordinated behavior beyond the simplest of tactical movements: attack, fall back, and so forth.

For a long time this was enough. The knights stood dominant against all but similarly equipped foes throughout the Middle Ages, until they ran into an even more efficient weapon: disciplined infantry operating in concert. Although much has been made of the

English longbowmen as the model for this, the example on which we will concentrate here is the Swiss phalanx of the fourteenth and fifteenth centuries.

Success for the Swiss relied on both aspects of the phenomenon of shock. At the time of the Swiss ascension, shock was the sole purview of the mounted heavy cavalryman and his steed. The infantry was relegated to a supporting, largely defensive role on the battlefield. The Swiss changed this equation with their attacks in massed columnar formation wielding eighteen-foot-long pikes.[35] In their attacks the Swiss were helped not only by the physical component of shock but also by the psychological component, upon which they capitalized. The Swiss took no prisoners and were known for bowling over their opponents in nearly fanatical attacks.[36] This was the basis for the reputation of the Swiss *Eidgenossen.*

Key battles fought by the Swiss demonstrate both elements of shock in operation. At the battle of Sempach in 1386 they attacked in a deep column formation, sometimes described as a wedge because of its unusual depth-to-front ratio.[37] This formation permitted the *Eidgenossen* to literally bowl their opponents over. As they closed for the attack the entire formation would increase its velocity until the men were nearly running just prior to impact. This was the physical component in action.

Later, in what may have been their ultimate example of the power of fear as a weapon, the Swiss attacked a numerically superior combined arms force raised by the Duke of Burgundy at Grandson in 1476. The Burgundians and their allies, faced with the sudden onslaught of opponents who had never retreated, never accepted a surrender, and never lost while there was still a man among them alive, dissolved before the Swiss ever had the chance to make contact with the opposing infantry. From that point on it was no longer a battle but a pursuit leading to a massacre.

Moving forward into the age of gunpowder, Napoleon's attacks with *L'Ordre Mixte* again demonstrate the power of shock when a mass of combatants attacked in a columnar formation.[38] Even that far into the gunpowder era, the threat of cold steel could and did break many formations facing the charge of French troops in column. The visible physical mass and combined will of the French formations were often enough to cause others to break, despite their inherent lack of firepower (which resulted from the reduced frontage of the column relative to a defender "in line").

Later, in the American Civil War, similar tactics were again attempted. Recent studies using the medical records of the Union army reveal that in those fights that contained successful bayonet charges, surprisingly few wounds were inflicted by the bayonets. Units apparently broke before the attacking ranks collided with the defenders. How did this happen?[39]

A mass process appeared to occur in which the defenders continually evaluated the attackers' chances for success. If the attackers began an assault that the defenders did not feel they could stop with firepower, they might break. The break appears to have been a function of their discipline and training.

Similarly, in the attack a "culminating moment" could occur when the attackers individually and collectively conducted a similar analysis.[40] If in their minds they had passed the point at which they believed they could succeed, the attackers too might quickly dissolve. Classic examples are the "high water mark of the Confederacy" at Gettysburg and the failed attack of Napoleon's *Grognards* (the Imperial Old Guard) at Waterloo.[41] In the case of Waterloo, the cry of *"Le Guard recule"* set in motion the dissolution of the entire *Grande Armeé.*[42]

The First Component of Shock: Force

Force is defined in terms of mass and velocity. A simple equation results—one which is repeatedly demonstrated every fall weekend in stadiums across the United States. While the mechanical method that delivers the force may differ from the *Eidgenossen* to the Big Ten linebacker or a battalion task force at the National Training Center, the same principle applies. That force has a large role in warfare is obvious; what is not so evident is the role of force as a component of shock.

Shock, as we hope to inflict it, is not an individual phenomenon. It affects the reactions of large bodies of soldiers, causing the retreat or surrender not of scattered individuals but of entire units. The shock we would like to inflict upon our opponents (and avoid having inflicted upon us) affects whole companies and battalions, perhaps even brigades. The disintegration of Napoleon's *Grande Armeé* is what we are aiming for as a goal. How then does force apply within this context?

First, force must be demonstrable. The cause of the effect must be present and visible for force to develop any psychological impetus. Further, the effects of force, whether from a single weapon or the massed effects of many weapons, must be visible to numerous members of the opposition. Both elements must be present when force is applied for shock to develop.

This partially explains why few units have ever surrendered as a result of the pummeling received from airpower alone.[43] Similarly, artillery, while it may contribute to effects on morale, remains by itself less than decisive. Attack aviation, while meeting the criteria of visibility and presence, also fails. It may attack and infuse shock, but any opponent facing an attack helicopter knows that it cannot drive home its attack.

Mass

Although weight and size are not exactly equivalent to mass, they are close enough for our purposes, since mass and velocity are the primary components of force.

To fully understand this we must turn again to the historical record. How did physical force affect the recipients of the *Eidgenossen* attack? The Swiss pikemen faced armored knights fighting both on horseback and on foot. How did they develop the force required to defeat the armor of the knights, and was this physical force sufficient to explain their long series of one-sided victories?

It is doubtful that most *Eidgenossen* pike tips actually penetrated the armor of knights standing ready to accept the rushing charge of the Swiss phalanx.[44] What they did was bowl over their opponents, killing some in the initial rush and stabbing others as they lay on the ground while the *Eidgenossen* walked over them, continuing their attack.

The result was a wake of dead bodies trailing in a path behind the *Eidgenossen* phalanx. Their deep formations permitted them to accumulate sufficient kinetic energy through additional mass to make up for what they lacked in acceleration. The results were visible, gruesome, and apparently (to their opponents) inevitable for any that stood up to the charge of the Swiss.

For a similar reason some of the attacks of the British tanks at Amiens in 1917 met with unprecedented success for a time. The physical presence of an impenetrable object rolling over German trenches and destroying those machine gunners who stayed by their guns at ranges of as little as four to eight feet, combined with the visible presence of mass (represented by the tank itself) and the undeniable power of its numerous machine guns or cannons, produced shock.[45]

Mass, therefore, is visible and demonstrable power. This may be in the form of human organization or mechanical harnessing of energy. In either case, it is modified by a second element.

Velocity

Velocity is speed with a direction. In modern military terms it should be subdivided according to the echelon of warfare to which it applies. Tactical speed relates to the movement of units or individuals upon the battlefield. Operational speed is the movement of units between engagements or campaigns. Strategic speed is the movement of forces into the theater of operations. Today the U.S. Army seeks to increase all three. In this the army is struggling through a series of tradeoffs.

Generally speaking, providing a ground force with the ability to achieve high strategic speed (today through the use of strategic airlift aircraft) virtually ensures that it will have limited tactical speed once on the battlefield because of the limitation on the amount of material that can be airlifted. An example of this is the 82d Airborne Infantry Division. On the other end of the spectrum are mechanized infantry and armored formations that have the lowest strategic mobility because of the material that they include, but the highest tactical speed once on the battlefield.

All of this relates only to the ability of any given type of unit to traverse the ground. As some recognize, there is more to battlefield mobility than mere speed. The fog and friction of war often combine to ensure that at least some portion of the distance an average unit will traverse is wasted, either because of misdirection or variations in the terrain. There is, however, another aspect to velocity that may be exploited today.

With the newest generation of command and control technology, the army claims that it will increase the speed of units. More accurately, it should be stated that the army hopes to increase the velocity of units.

Velocity is a vectored component combining both speed and direction. By decreasing the average wasted distance traveled by a normal unit, the army should be able to reduce the average time it takes to move from point A to point B. Specifically, if digitization ensures that all battlefield leaders know where they are and have accurate representations of the terrain and the disposition of friendly and enemy forces, they should be able to plot and follow the most efficient route to any given point. This, at least, is the theory.

What has not been explicitly stated is the effect that speed may have at any given echelon upon the enemy.[46] Generally, the army hopes to use a relative advantage in speed at all echelons to achieve surprise or gain positional advantages. Surprise is a worthy goal, but this does not take the potential of velocity far enough. Surprise, like shock, is a term that currently is too loosely defined. Here, however, we can at least provide some sense of how velocity contributes to shock as a battlefield phenomenon.

At the tactical level, one classic example occurred on 3 July 1863, during the Battle of Gettysburg. Many readers are familiar with the famous charge conducted by the men of Confederate Major Generals Pickett and Pettigrew. Some thirteen thousand men attacked across rolling but open terrain against the center of the Union line. Most Union troops involved were situated behind a low stone wall at the point of the attack. One unit, however, was at a forward outpost beyond direct supporting distance of the rest of the army. This unit, the 8th Ohio Volunteer Infantry, had about 180 men at the time of the Confederate infantry assault.

The unit's position initially appeared to be astride the route of march of roughly one-half of the entire Confederate attack force. Since the soldiers were not permitted to retreat and would be destroyed if they stayed where they were, their commander made a decision that appears rational only in hindsight. He attacked.

He formed his men in a single line on the reverse side of the low spur they occupied and ordered a charge at the double-quick directly at the nearest Confederate brigade to their front. This brigade, damaged badly in the first day's fighting and by all accounts poorly led, saw the line of Ohioans charging over the crest at a full run with their regimental colors flying. The Confederate brigade immediately folded, running from the field without firing a shot. The shock of the sudden appearance of the Union regiment was too much for the six hundred Confederates who had already suffered so much.

In this case speed and direction were the determining factors. Had the Ohioans moved slowly it is doubtful that the Confederates would have dissolved as they did. They would have had the time to see that it was merely a single regiment, and an understrength one at that, attacking them. Similarly, had the angle of attack been anything but head-on, it would have been less likely that 600 soldiers would cede the field to 180 without firing so much as a shot. High speed and direction compensated for decreased mass to impart a moral force, shock, on the Confederate troops.[47]

In any examination of speed at the operational level of war one is inevitably drawn to the examples left to history by Napoleon Bonaparte. Although there are a multitude of examples of Napoleonic speed from which to choose, one case will illustrate how his speed forced his enemies into a reactive role, thereby giving the advantage to Napoleon.

In 1805 Napoleon fought a series of battles across Bavaria and Austria, known collectively as the Ulm and Austerlitz campaigns, which set his mark upon the wall for all time. At Ulm he surrounded an enemy force of Austrians, forcing their surrender on 20 October 1805. This in itself was a massive accomplishment, but what followed was even more impressive.

Almost immediately after forcing the Austrian surrender, Napoleon reconsolidated his forces in the vicinity of Munich and started out after the remaining forces of the alliance, who were then retreating eastward. On 26 October, Napoleon and his *Grande Armeé* were in and around Munich. Less than a month later, on 23 November, this force was deployed in the area of the small town of Austerlitz three hundred miles away.

As incredible as Napoleon's speed was, it was the result of this speed that made a difference. More than any other factor, his speed threw his opponents off balance. When he stopped and withdrew slightly it only compounded their confusion.

This gave Napoleon the luxury of selecting the place of battle and conducting a thorough reconnaissance of forces to lure the enemy into an attack by convincing them that his forces were weaker than they actually were and too dispersed to fight together in any case. This dispersion of his subordinate elements lured Napoleon's Austrian and Russian opponents into an ill-advised counterattack, one met by a united *Grande Armeé* that had some corps marching eighty miles in less than two days to reach the battle. The result was a massive defeat for the Austrians and Russians.

Although the Austrians and Russians may have enjoyed near parity on some areas of the battlefield, they were undone by their perceptions of Napoleon's forces at any given location because of the speed with which the French operated. Operational and tactical speed contributed to the force being out of proportion to the mass at any given location.

As examples of the power of force in ground combat, these episodes speak for themselves. Force is the physical component. It may be relayed by manpower or explosives or a combination of both, and it consists of mass and velocity. Yet as stated, shock has a second element, one which is prompted by force.

The Second Component of Shock: Fear

We need to dissect fear to understand how we use it as a weapon. Fear produced by shock cannot be replicated in training and is one of the great imponderables of warfare. By what physical process may fear be conveyed? How is fear transmitted?

Fear may be imparted by several methods. On a strictly physical level the senses that receive messages that might induce fear are obvious, with the auditory and visual senses being primary. Fear is not directly transmitted, of course, but here we will consider a series of sensory inputs that, when combined with knowledge inside a human, create fear. It is that combination that the *Eidgenossen* and other successful forces since their time have managed to use to great effect. Placing visual and auditory sensory signals, which combine with the opponents' knowledge of their enemy's reputation, upon the battlefield can create fear and is a worthy goal for our forces.

Of these signals, auditory inputs are easiest to demonstrate. Anyone who has ever been near a large body of marching or jogging troops, let alone the roar of a large diesel engine or the reverberations of a tank main gun discharge, understands the feeling of power conveyed by sound alone. Massed rifle fire in volley is especially impressive.

The French of the Napoleonic era used drums, helping the French soldiers to maintain their step in the close-order formations of the day, but there may have been a second effect as well. The drums almost certainly heartened the French and struck fear into their opponents. As early as the Battle of Valmy in 1792, when French revolutionary forces confronted the Prussians, the French chanted "Vive la France" in time with the drumbeats as they marched into the attack. Certainly the sound of thousands of voices operating in concert conveys a feeling of power and force.

In our own century we can see that mere sound still retains a place on the battlefield. The physical force of the Luftwaffe's JU-87 Stuka dive-bomber was not increased by the addition of the famous screaming dive sirens that were added to the aircraft. Many of the men who suffered through Stuka attacks, however, would attest that the siren was a weapon—a psychological weapon designed to increase fear.

Conveying a threat through the sense of vision is another way to express force without physical contact. Organized masses are considered dangerous, sometimes out of proportion to their size. Consider recent examples such as those occurring during the U.S. involvement in Somalia in 1993. Soldiers of the 10th Infantry Division learned such lessons by experience. Somalian rioters, when faced with small contingents of U.S. troops, barely paused in their activities. The U.S. troops acted in dispersed elements in order not to appear confrontational to the "peaceful" Somalians.

In squad (nine men) and fire team (four men) -sized groupings, these U.S. troops were initially dispersed throughout a troublesome area; their effect was negligible. However, when the same number of troops combined into a platoon or company-sized riot formation, their effect was sudden and visible upon the Somalians.

The simple act of forming ranks by the U.S. troops was enough to convince the rioters to cease their activities and cause some to disperse—until they learned that U.S. forces would not resort to physical force unless attacked or fired upon. This lessened the effectiveness of U.S. troops considerably. The visual stimulus of a massed and coherent force has more effect than the same number of troops in a loose formation.

Audible and visual inputs combined would be useless without some knowledge of what these stimuli might mean. It is the interpretation of the stimuli and the human imagination acting upon that interpretation that create fear.

One does not become afraid until one has something to be afraid of: a bogeyman or the *Eidgenossen*. Further, being confronted with an object is not enough; one needs an imagination. Fear affects reality when an input stimulus and mental object combine and the mind imagines what the effect of the object of its fear might be.

From their beginning as a unified and cohesive force at Morgarten in 1315, the Swiss created for themselves a reputation of invincibility and utter contempt for the human lives of those who opposed them. Later they would add to this an apparent disregard for their own lives. Their actions at the Battle of St. Jacob-en-Birs are a prime example that reinforced their reputation.[48]

Fear requires a stimulus, most often visual or auditory. The stimulus acts upon a preconceived notion regarding the force that the enemy will impart upon the subject. In other words, a person asks, "What will happen to me when that tank that I hear or see decides to attack me?" If the threat is sufficient and the message clear, that individual is likely to break, becoming ineffective in combat; but that is only one individual. Shock affects entire units.

How does this occur? Surely different people have differing tolerances affecting their behavior. Societal norms, personal upbringing, and institutional forces combine within a person to create a unique point at which he or she will decide, "Enough is enough," and try to escape the arena of combat as an individual. This leads soldiers in the first soldier's vicinity also to break, eventually incapacitating an entire unit. This is the essence of the military definition of shock.

Fear and Dissolution

In his classic work *Battle Studies,* Ardant du Picq examined the ancient battles of the Romans and Greeks. Attempting to merge what he personally knew of human behavior in combat with the various accounts of several battles, he arrived at some simple conclusions. An individual is prone to fear, but people in large groups may reinforce each other's courage under certain conditions.

Du Picq's studies also determined that not all accounts of these battles made sense. Yet he was able to reconcile the accounts through insightful analysis. He developed truisms that he sought to apply to the French military experience of his own generation. At their core was the idea that the most critical element in combat effectiveness is morale. Faced with the effects of increasing battlefield dispersion, du Picq sought unit cohesion to counteract the human emotion of fear.

Today we are once again facing increasing physical dispersion, although ironically this may be due to increased communications means and apparent visibility. What is true today is that human nature and emotions have not changed. We must therefore attempt to forecast how our technological innovations may interact with the least common denominator of the battlefield: the soldier. To do this we should look, as du Picq did, to history. He studied the ancient battles and found lessons for his day. One hundred thirty years later, this essay looks toward medieval battles for a lesson in human nature applicable to the twenty-first century.

Returning to the Swiss, one cannot help but wonder how they were as efficient at killing as the historic record indicates they were in the fourteenth and fifteenth centuries. The Swiss eighteen-inch pike was a horrible individual weapon. In fact, the only time that it was efficient was in the initial onslaught and upon a foe that was giving way before the attackers. For the Swiss to experience the success that they enjoyed so often in the early years of their primacy, 1338 to approximately 1450, they must, therefore, have faced irresolute opponents.

When the forward motion of the phalanx was stopped, the invariable Swiss response was to bring forward their true killing weapons, the halberds. But when an enemy was not so inflexible and gave way, the pike could be very effective. Its force would carry men off their feet to be trampled by the onrushing Swiss formation and often crushed or stabbed to death while on the ground by the swords or halberds of those in the sixth, seventh, or following ranks of the *Eidgenossen* formation. This was how their opponents died. The process was accelerated by the presence of fear in the enemy ranks.

Facing the initial onrush of the Swiss attack, many men in the front ranks arrayed against the Swiss would pull back from the hedge of pikes. Some would die in the initial thrust, while others might be wounded and fall to the ground. Still more would trip as they backed away, and their falling could create a shock wave of its own.

Imagine a tightly packed crowd. Knock down a man in the leading edge of this crowd and literally dozens will be carried to the ground with him. None within the crowd have the room to catch their balance, which causes them to fall into others in the same predicament. Prone opponents are easier to kill than standing ones. If you are *Eidgenossen* and have no qualms about this minor breach of medieval protocol, you can take advantage of this event.

But this scenario is not complete. Even given the self-perpetuating nature of what is described above and adding in the continuing force of the *Eidgenossen* themselves, not enough damage is inflicted to explain the crushing defeats handed out by the *Eidgenossen* in their early years of dominance.

Du Picq pointed out that more men are killed in the retreat than are killed while facing the enemy.[49] It is also true that when a unit broke, the break started from the rear of the formation.[50] This would appear to be counterintuitive, but the observations recorded by contemporaries are clear.

These observations led to the "file closer" role of the early noncommissioned officer. Stationed at the rear of the formation with his sword or pike extended lengthwise, he closed the files and added strength to the most vulnerable location in the formation. Breaks in the rear of the formation were most often the result of a pyramid effect which densely packed formations have upon the men within these formations, but with a message bearing psychological force rather than a physical force being the impetus.

A message of impending assault passed from the front ranks (who could see the reality) to the rear ranks may move like a sentence in a game of "I've got a secret," becoming amplified at each successive rank until the rear ranks receive a message of doom. If fear is the current, then massed formations serve as excellent conduits.

This brings us forward in time to the twentieth century. This is the danger that forces experimenting with digitization should consider: the idea that we may now be inadvertently creating an entirely new conduit for those messages to pass. It may be, in fact, a resurrection of a phenomenon that disappeared with the last of the linear battle formations one hundred years ago.

The Fading of Shock

If there has been one constant on the twentieth-century battlefield since World War I, it has been the phenomenon of the empty battlefield. Today we rarely consider during our tactical decision-making processes that there might have been another way; every soldier and leader currently in service has served with this as a given. Yet the shock described up to this point relies upon a massed formation to transmit its message of terror efficiently and quickly. The implications of the modern battle characteristics are similarly evident in the historical record. Shock, at least the mass version of shock, has faded.

Without a large body of soldiers passing a defeatist message to each other rapidly, the classic effects of shock, although pursued, have seldom been attained. Rarely in the twentieth century have entire battalions, divisions, or corps literally quit the battlefield when their reserves of courage were expended. This is obviously not because of a lack of applied violence or a greater level of courage possessed by the soldiers of this era compared to all the rest of human history. What has been missing is the ability for one soldier suffering from shock as an individual to pass his or her message of despair to a large number of other soldiers simultaneously.

With modern soldiers dispersed and fighting in increasingly smaller and more autonomous elements, their actions have not had personal relevance to the same number of personnel as in the past. In those cases in which troops have been shocked and broken by an event, they have most often been rear echelon units attacked and surprised by an enemy conducting a breakthrough or deep penetration. They have not been frontline combat elements, as was the case earlier.

This partially explains the greater significance of the breakthrough or penetration in modern tactical and operational thought. The common denominator for most apocryphal stories in this century is that they refer to combat units that held out against improbable odds in separated pockets of resistance. Histories of the attack of the German Wehrmacht in the Ardennes in winter 1944 are rife with such accounts.

Anomalies occur, however, when the weapon itself is sufficient to convey a message to all who see the weapon, let alone encounter its effects. During the twentieth century this has been the almost exclusive purview of the heavy tank in an offensive role. A single tank, unlike an entire company of infantry, is extremely visible. While the infantry relies upon the earth to serve as both protection and concealment, the tank with its massive bulk finds this much more difficult.

As a result, the tank has had the potential to convey shock to ground units as has no other force. Its visible presence replicates the effects that an implacable formation of *Eidgenossen* might have had upon a defender. From this effect, no less than the ability to impart force upon the enemy, has armor earned the sobriquet of the "combat arm of decision." Yet now, given our new understanding of the effects of discipline and morale upon a unit and of how shock affects an enemy both physically and psychologically, what can we say about the future?

The Future of Shock

Does shock have a role to play on the battlefield of the present and the future? For the present I would suggest that the Iraqi army has provided us a definitive answer of yes. However, as most professionals will readily concede, the Gulf War was custom-made for the employment of U.S. heavy weapons and doctrine. What of those future less-than-perfect wars? How might we convey shock there?

Shock will play a role in war as long as human animals continue to feel fear. Perhaps more important, and until now unconsidered is the question: How might we prevent our forces from being shocked? This last leads to one critical question toward which the U.S. Army should devote some attention. Are we, with our new reliance and emphasis upon the digital warrior and total information dominance, opening ourselves to a new era of shock?

Let us review what it takes to be affected adversely by shock. First and foremost there must be a threat. Some physical entity must be able to convey real force. This can be firepower. Artillery, close air support, attack helicopters, the main guns of M1A2s, or the fires from M60 machine guns all meet the requirements. Choosing the appropriate weapon and placing that weapon in a position where it can inflict real damage is the traditional definition of the art of war at the tactical level. These weapons are often most effective when used in combination. "Combined arms," therefore, has been the byword of professional organizers of mass violence for several centuries.

Following the impact of physical force there must be a mental image of the attacker, some reputation which the force of the weapons being employed serves to reinforce in the mind's eye of the attacked.

This aspect has an obvious counterforce acting upon the subject: the combined elements of discipline and morale. There is an inverse relationship between the effectiveness of a threat upon a subject and that subject's morale or discipline. The higher the morale or discipline, the more firepower will be required to impart sufficient mental violence upon the subject to cause that person to break. Conversely, a defender with low morale or discipline requires less firepower before deciding to quit the field of battle.

What do these obvious statements about warfare have to do with our future? Here the third factor applies. In the situations that have been discussed, the actions and forces acting upon a single individual were considered. On the empty battlefield of the twentieth century it was typically only a single element that might be affected. Thus, more and more firepower was required to affect enough individuals in a single area so that a breakthrough might occur.

In effect, we have come to rely upon the physical destruction of the enemy and disregard almost entirely the potential for psychological destruction. We are using only half the shock available to us. The cumulative effect of the two components disappeared with the massed formations of the nineteenth century. Now, however, we are planning to place the ability to see the whole battlefield in the hands of every soldier in a way that has not been possible since the nineteenth century. This may open the door once more to shock.

Even in the least visionary of these proposed technological schemes, every soldier has at least a limited ability to see most of the battlefield on which his or her unit is operating. Graphical map displays embedded within a clear visor worn by the infantry private show the location and relative position of all of his or her fellow soldiers. The Intervehicle Information System display, which a sergeant may call upon within his M1A2 today, will show how many friendly units remain—and how many have died. A lieutenant may examine the positions and strengths of the entire battalion task force. This alone opens an ominous chink in our armor.

The Signal Corps is understandably concerned about protecting the integrity of our signal transmissions. This may become doubly important, because the information conveyed by these transmissions may soon show our soldiers that they are under attack by a force ten times the size of what actually faces them. What do you suppose the young men and women raised on Nintendo 64 will believe? The message conveyed by their eyes—"No enemy in sight yet" or "There is only one company attacking this platoon"—or that of their information warfare machines—"There is an entire regiment headed toward this exact location"?

These men and women of the future, many of them in diapers today, are growing up believing in the reality displayed upon a screen by pixels of varied color. Icons may well define reality to these soldiers of the future, who will operate the equipment that we field in this decade. What if those icons lie? What happens when a number of icons go dim? Have we opened ourselves to a new era in which true and massive shock might again become a tactical reality?

There is a lesson and a warning within this essay that is beyond my ability to fathom. It may be that we have inadvertently reopened a door once closed that will cause the most technologically gifted army in the world to react as though they were nineteenth-century troops of the line.

Shock is imparted by physical force, which acts not only upon the flesh but upon the minds of those on the receiving end. When other armies of the world follow our lead, as they inevitably will, the field might again level out. But until that day, some thought should be devoted to blunting the effects that our own weapons of information may have upon our soldiers, leaders, and units.

Conclusion

We have all experienced it recently. The massive burst in information technology has changed the way we live our lives and run our units. Paperwork once done on a typewriter now appears on a computer screen in a word-processing program. Slides and graphics, once simple and rare below the division level, now appear as major works of art at the company level and are used for every occasion. Faxes, modems, e-mail, and the Internet are integrated into our daily existence.

It is said that the sum of human knowledge took one thousand years to double in the Middle Ages; by the nineteenth century it took only one hundred years. It is estimated that human knowledge now doubles every three years, and that time span is dropping. Even at the lowest level in the army this change can be felt, and devil take the hindmost on the latest computer upgrade.

A mere eight years ago the standard for microprocessor chips was a clock speed of eight to ten megahertz. Since then there have been major leaps in this measure of computer speed. Moore's Law runs rampant across the field of battle. Today's top-of-the-line chips operate at five hundred megahertz or better, and we have yet to see the horizon, if indeed there is one. It's not that the old 286s no longer work; they just aren't as good in a relative sense. Officers who graduated from West Point in 1989 may now return to their alma mater to find an example of the computers that they were issued as cadets residing in the museum.

At a larger level this is the same problem faced by our army today. We cannot afford to buy thousands of major items only to see them outdated before they are fully fielded. Technology is moving too fast, and morally we cannot accept sending our soldiers to the field of battle with third-rate equipment. Moreover, as this chapter illustrates, significant pitfalls must be examined and dealt with in response to this latest revolution.

Even if we could afford to, should we adopt a fielding plan that sends the same technology out across the entire army, in light of the potential and unintended effects it might have upon our own troops? What other potential pitfalls lurk in the shadows of the future? If we do adopt such a plan, how do we then escape the vicious cycle of procuring equipment that needs to be upgraded before the field force has fully received its new gear? How do we experiment with and create an applicable doctrine for the new technology? The answer is the deliberate and planned creation of a modular army.

What is a modular army? This is an army that as a whole operates synergistically, consisting of nonstandardized parts that are interoperable at some base level. This concept is designed to be applied to the major weapons systems and tables of organization and equipment of the future. Instead of the current practice—to research; design; test; develop tables of organization and equipment; develop tactics, techniques, and procedures; field; and use the technology across the entire army—we must adopt a more streamlined process.

We must field at least two forces within the active army. Call them first and second echelon, first string and second string, or what you like. The fact is that there always will be a force that is ready to go and others that are not because of budget and resource constraints. We must accept this and let it become a strength. Set a priority and follow it through. If this means fielding only one corps that has the latest and greatest equipment, so be it. In ten years their positions will flip. Those using outdated equipment today (five years old based on current estimates) will become the new first echelon when they in turn field the latest equipment.

How do we field this concept? Start today with Force XXI, now one brigade of the redesignated 4th Infantry Division, the 1st Cavalry Division, and III Corps Headquarters, as already planned. Plan to buy only enough to equip that force. Do not modify the rest of the force structure to accommodate the new equipment, because it is apparent that they will never get this particular generation.

Then look to the future with a goal of having a new MBT, IFV, artillery system, rotary wing aircraft, and command, control, communications, and intelligence system ready for fielding in 2005. Say at that time that the reflagged 24th Infantry Division and 1st Infantry Division become the first echelon. They are fielded Tank-X, IFV-Y, Artillery System-Z, and the latest tribe of helicopters. We do not dump the old M1A2s from the system; they continue until the time between failures becomes too great, by which time the cycle should be complete and we should be ready to field a third (or fifth) generation of combat systems.

Advantages: We do not have a period in which all of our systems are outclassed for years by anyone on the planet; nor are we faced with constant upgrades to keep the equipment that we have competitive. Disadvantages: We do not have an army that is nominally capable of interchangeability at all levels. Division X cannot do what Division Y might be capable of. But we do not have that now.

We are also faced with the prospect of changing how we train and develop doctrine. The "schoolhouses" cannot effectively follow the developments occurring among troop units as new equipment is fielded. We cannot segment the schools and effectively train everyone on three sets of equipment depending on where each soldier might be assigned. There must be a concurrent revolution in personnel management (as described in another essay) and logistics. This concept is not the safe way to do business; it is referred to as "accepting risk," and we must now practice what we preach in the procurement and doctrinal arenas.

Logistics support remains the same. No matter how the systems are configured they must be fueled by the same equipment. The new concept applies to major weapon systems; combat service support elements at the ground level may not be affected. Food, fuels, and lubricants are areas that must be designed into future systems with an eye toward interoperability.

Future vehicles and systems must be designed so that they can be serviced and recovered by the equipment in the inventory of the combat support and combat service support units. Moreover, their new weapons must be designed with combat service support in mind. Creating a weapon that requires new equipment in combat service support units in order to reload after contact is a recipe for disaster. An example would be artillery shells that are twice as effective but so large that only one-third of the normal basic load can be carried by the same combat service support unit that can currently transport a double basic load. Common sense must prevail.

Communications, while a fast-moving area, must be standardized across the force. We cannot afford incompatible systems, which we have now in some reserve units. The future communications suites must be designed for integration across the force in all systems.

This imposes a second restriction on combat forces. Their communications equipment must be uniform whatever the system and must be designed to accommodate the least common (or capable) denominator. This will allow upgrades across the force without major modifications from a base design. The goal is to achieve something like what the computer industry has in place: a Plug and Play system. We must design communications equipment so that no matter what peripheral is placed in the system or "plugged in," it can be recognized and used immediately with no modifications by the user.

As noted earlier, this concept requires major changes to our current centralized schoolhouse system of education and doctrinal creation. It will require sustained innovation at the tactical level to create and record new methods to adapt new equipment to existing tactical doctrine. Alternately, it may require the complete decentralization of the creation of tactical doctrine. If we field a force with different generations of equipment, we ought to allow those who use the equipment (or those who will use it) to experiment with and create the appropriate tactical doctrine for its use.

At the same time, leaders equipped with the latest and greatest will be able to afford to train in the use of their gear, reducing through the traditional standbys of training and repetition the potential effects of shock. As we accept risk in the degree that we modernize at any given instant, we must mitigate the risk through the devotion of additional training funds.

In this it appears that once again the historical record provides us with the key. In the past several decades we have been slipping toward an increasingly synthetic training environment, training with computer simulators for a phenomenon called fear that can only be represented, not felt. The auditory and physical sensations are not there, and perhaps if we wish to consider the potential effects of shock they should be.

All of these manifestations are already apparent in the civilian sector. Yet the U.S. Army, because of the unique environment in which it plans to operate, holds back from major structural changes in its organization.

We started down the correct trail with the creation of the Force XXI concept. This was, in effect if not in intent, the basis for a modular army. Somewhere between here and there, things changed, and it appears that we are once again moving along the same old intellectual trails at all levels of war. My fear is that these trails will lead the U.S. Army to the same destination that it has traditionally reached just in time for the next war.[51]

Notes

1. Scott Maryott, *History of the Military Art, Course Notebook* (West Point, N.Y.: United States Military Academy, 1998), 98. This definition is a derivation of Captain Maryott's collaborative definition.

2. Anton Myrer, *Once an Eagle* (New York: Holt, Rinehart, and Winston, 1968; reprint, Carlisle, Pa.: Army War College Foundation Press, 1996). The protagonist of this work of historical fiction is Sam Damon, a hard-working and selfless career officer. His antithesis is the dilettante martinet Courtney Massengale, a self-serving and ruthless "ticket-punching" officer. Although a work of fiction, this book is considered by many professional officers as a military classic. The ultimate evidence of the high regard that officers in the U.S. Army have for this work is the fact that the book was reprinted by the Army War College itself.

3. Allan R. Millett, "American Military History: Clio and Mars as 'Pards,'" in *Military History and the Military Profession,* ed. David A. Charters, Marc Milner, and J. Brent Wilson (Westport, Conn.: Praeger Publishers, 1992), 5–9. In this essay Millett states that there are at least five kinds of military history. One of these is military-utilitarian, that is, the deliberate use of history by the military establishment for specific purposes. One purpose that Millett identifies is the role that this type of history has played in the creation of military doctrine. In describing the role of military history at the U.S. School of the Line and Staff College at Fort Leavenworth, Millet states, "Military history developed operational doctrine and strategic vision within the officer corps."

4. Timothy T. Lupfer, *The Dynamics of Doctrine: The Changes in German Tactical Doctrine During the First World War, Leavenworth Papers, No. 4* (Leavenworth, Kan.: Combat Studies Institute, 1981), viii. Lupfer demonstrates that the German army of World War II deliberately and systematically developed, refined, and implemented a series of doctrinal changes in response to its experiences on the eastern and western fronts of World War II.

5. Robert A. Doughty, *The Evolution of U.S. Army Tactical Doctrine, 1946–1976, Leavenworth Papers, No. 1* (Leavenworth, Kan.: Combat Studies Institute, 1979), 2.

6. C. N. Sawyer, "Infantry Signal Communications," *Infantry Journal* 17, no. 5 (November 1920): 474–475.

7. Ibid., 477.

8. L. D. Davis, "Communications," *Infantry Journal* 21, no. 1 (July 1922): 51.

9. Dulany Terrett, *The Signal Corps: The Emergency, History of the Signal Corps,* vol. 1 of *The Technical Services,* subseries of *U.S. Army in World War II,* gen. ed. Kent Roberts Greenfield (Washington, D.C.: Government Printing Office, 1956), 28. SCR at this time meant "set, complete, radio."

10. Davis, "Communications," 52.

11. Ibid., 53. See also evidence of the peacetime strength of assigned personnel in F. M. Harris, "A Communications Platoon in China," *Infantry Journal* 31, no. 1 (July 1927): 197. Harris was a signal platoon leader at the regimental level. Normal authorized strength for his platoon section was fifty-four men; Harris had seventeen on hand.

12. "2nd Division Maneuvers," *Infantry Journal* 31, no. 3 (September 1927): 537.

13. W. J. Tack, "Radio in the Infantry," *Infantry Journal* 31, no. 5 (November 1927): 470.

14. Robert L. Bateman, "Shifting Gears: Tanks, Radios and the Changing Tempo of Warfare, 1919–1940" (M.A. thesis, Ohio State University, 1998).

15. James D. Wilmeth, "Hear No. See No. Speak No.," *Infantry Journal,* Vol XLVI, No. 2, (March-April 1940): 232–234.

16. Final Report of the Chief of Infantry, 1941, Lynch papers, U.S. Army Military History Institute, Carlisle Barracks, Pa.

17. Terrett, *The Signal Corps,* 183.

18. Millett, "Cantigny, 28–31 May 1918," in *America's First Battles,* ed. Charles E. Heller and William A. Stofft (Lawrence, Kan.: University Press of Kansas, 1986), 149–185. See also Timothy K. Nenninger, "American Military Effectiveness in the First World War," in *Military Effectiveness,* ed. Allan R. Millett and Williamson Murray, (Boston: Allen and Unwin, 1988), 117–156.

19. George Lind, "The Theory and Practice of Maneuver Warfare," in *Maneuver Warfare: An Anthology* (New York: Doubleday), 1994.

20. Department of the Army, *Battle Command, Draft 2.1* (Ft. Leavenworth, Kan.: Battle Command Battle Lab, April 1994).

21. Ronald Bashista, "*Auftragstaktik:* It's More than Just a Word," *Armor* (November-December 1994), 17–18.

22. This stated preference may be overcome by doctrinal evolution in response to the apparent success of precision-guided munitions. In *Army Vision 2010,* the chief of staff of the army claims that "dominant maneuver" is a vital goal for army development. However, this document defines "dominant maneuver" as "a massing of effects . . . not forces." This reignites the continuing debate about the supremacy of fires versus ground maneuver forces. However, because this chapter deals with command and control as a separate issue, the definition of what is being commanded and controlled is somewhat academic.

23. The German terms for these concepts are *befehlestaktiks* and *auftragstaktik* (the literal translation would be "task tactics"). These concepts derive directly from the writings and influence of the Prussian Gen. Helmuth von Moltke and the earlier Prussian military theorist Karl von Clausewitz.

24. Helmuth von Moltke, "The Battle, Leadership in Battle," in *Moltke on the Art of War,* ed. Daniel J. Hughes (Novato, Calif.: Presidio Press, 1993), 123–133. One quote is telling: "Given the current extended battlefield, a unified command of an army on the day of a battle is possible only in a very general way. Commanders of army corps and even divisions must judge the situation for themselves and must know how to act independently in consonance with the general intention."

25. John Arquila and David Ronfeldt, "Cyberwar Is Coming," *Comparative Strategy,* Vol.12, No. 2, Spring 1993.

26. F. W. von Mellenthin, *Panzer Battles* (New York: Ballantine, 1976). See also Hanson Baldwin, *Tiger Jack* (Ft. Collins, Colo.: Old Army Press, 1979) for the best example of American maneuver warfare in action, the 4th Armored Division in the race across France in 1944.

27. The concept of a "fog of war" is a constant in military history. The term is credited to Prussian military theorist Karl von Clausewitz in his book *On War (Vom Krieg).* "War is the realm of uncertainty; three quarters of the factors on which action in war are based are

wrapped in a fog of greater or lesser uncertainty." Karl von Clausewitz, *On War,* indexed edition, ed. and trans. Michael Howard and Peter Paret (Princeton, N.J.: Princeton University Press, 1976), 101.

28. Gen. Gordon Sullivan, "Force XXI: Digitizing the Battlefield," Army RD&A Bulletin, November-December 1994.

29. Paul W. Thompson, "A Panzer Division Crosses the Meuse [The Little Picture]," *Infantry Journal* 48, No. 5 (May 1941), 45–47. This source describes the German crossing at the Belgian village of Houx on the morning of 13 May 1940. The author describes how the German assault crossing had stalled when "there appeared on the river none other than the commanding general of the division. He had come forward the hard and dangerous way, crawling and freezing and bounding the hard and dangerous way, and taking his chances just like any other soldier." The general subsequently assessed the situation and ordered up supporting units, artillery, and armor to force the crossing at that particular location, which he apparently had determined through personal reconnaissance was the best site.

30. The counterexample pointed out by several people to the author is that the infantry experienced a similar phenomenon in Vietnam when commanders operated in stacked helicopters. These commanders, physically and emotionally separated from the small units on the ground, were wont to issue orders to the units on the ground that they could not accomplish.

31. Department of the Army, *Battle Command,* 2–1.

32. *American Heritage Dictionary,* New College Edition, Ed. William Morris (Boston: Houghton Mifflin Company, 1982)s.v. "shock."

33. Ardant du Picq, *Battle Studies, Ancient and Modern Battle,* trans. from eighth French edition by John N. Greely and Robert C. Cotton (New York: Macmillan, 1921), 88–89. In analyzing ancient accounts of close combat, du Picq suggests that units that broke did so not from the front but from the rear. "Then by that natural instinct of the soldier to worry, to assure himself of supports, the contagion of flight spreads from the last ranks to the first." He suggests that there is a "sphere of moral tension" wherein men not in physical contact with the enemy were nonetheless subject to developing fear. These men, deprived of the opportunity to act and thereby re-

lieve some of the tension, were the ones most susceptible to what we would now refer to as shock.

34. Bruce Allan Watson, *When Soldiers Quit, Studies in Military Disintegration* (Westport, Conn.: Praeger, 1997), 196. Watson's book walks the thin line between two academic fields between which little love is lost, and he does so successfully.

35. Initially, the Swiss formations relied primarily on another long weapon, the halberd. The eight-foot-long halberd was capable of slashing and holding off cavalry and was a decent individual weapon. However, over time there was a transition from a majority of halberds to a majority of pikes in the Swiss phalanxes. It was in trying to understand why the Swiss adopted the pike (an inefficient weapon in almost any situation other than massed formations) that I developed my theories regarding the phenomenon of shock. Special thanks to Dr. John F. Guilmartin for his role in helping me refine these thoughts.

36. C. W. C. Oman, *The Art of War in the Middle Ages* (1885; reprint, Ithaca: Cornell University Press, 1993), 79. "Oath Brothers." This title for the Swiss derives from the fact that they did not swear fealty to any feudal rulers but rather to each other. Some see this as a primary motivational source for their high level of cohesion in combat.

37. J. F. Verbruggen, *Art of Warfare in Western Europe in the Middle Ages*, vol. 1 of *Europe in the Middle Ages Selected Studies*, ed. Richard Vaughn, trans. Sumner Willard and S. C. M. Southern (Amsterdam: North-Holland Publishing Company, 1977), 60.

38. Gunther Rothenburg, *The Art of Warfare in the Age of Napoleon* (Bloomington, Ind.: Indiana University Press, 1978), 117. It should be noted that although these formations can be described as columns, they do not fit the modern description. They were still wider than they were deep, massing men across a front of up to forty while only maintaining a depth of twelve ranks. However, twelve deep was still four times the norm of three deep in line formation.

39. Dave Grossman, *On Killing, The Psychological Cost of Learning to Kill in War and Society* (New York: Little Brown and Company, 1995), 367. Grossman, a trained psychologist as well as a professional army officer, has developed a theory that there is a natural human reluc-

tance to kill other humans in the modern era. This reluctance may be partially overcome through physical (and therefore psychological) separation from the object of the violence. This separation can come from actual distancing (for example, stand-off weaponry) or from the use of tools that reduce the apparent humanity of the object of violence (such as mechanically aided optical sights).

According to Grossman, as distance decreases, so generally does an individual's ability to bring himself or herself to kill. At the closest distance, that of the bayonet for example, one side or the other will almost always break contact prior to the moment of impact.

Although Grossman's theories have been somewhat tempered through academic criticism of some of his sources and conclusions, his underlying statements retain considerable credibility within the profession of arms.

40. In U.S. military doctrine the culminating point in an attack is that point at which the commander determines that he or she no longer has sufficient combat power to continue the attack successfully (the attackers' relative combat power no longer exceeds that of the defenders) and must therefore make a transition to defense. I suggest that in most of human history this is an individual decision. It is, furthermore, a decision with cumulative effects in that the decision of ten soldiers that they cannot succeed will cause them to stop where they are. Thereafter, all other soldiers' personal calculations of the relative combat power of the attacking force are affected by those ten soldiers, which may cause an eleventh to stop, and so on.

41. George R. Stewart, *Pickett's Charge* (Boston: Houghton-Mifflin, 1959), 245–246. The "high water mark" was a closer thing than many realize. Opposing the charge of the Confederates at the clump of trees was but a single line of infantry. These Union regiments, although undamaged by the preceding cannonade, were nonetheless severely understrength. The Confederates actually attained their objective for a brief period as fierce fighting occurred within "the angle"; then something—nobody can say for sure what it was—motivated the 72d Pennsylvania to countercharge.

This desperate rush broke the will of the Confederates. Brutal hand-to-hand fighting occurred and men literally attempted to choke each other to death, but it lasted only for seconds. Then the Confederates broke. One Sergeant Kimble stated, "For about a hundred yards I broke the land speed record."

42. Keegan, *The Face of Battle,* 178.

43. Robert Wallace, ed., *The Italian Campaign* (Alexandria, Va.: Time-Life Books, 1978), 23. In May 1943 the Italian garrison of the island fortress on Pantelleria surrendered after five weeks of continuous bombardment. This island stands between northern Africa and Sicily, so its capture was critical for the following invasion of Sicily. On 10 May 1943 British forces landed; the sole casualty was a Tommy bitten by an ass. The ass's name, rank, and unit were not recorded.

44. The force of a pike on armor is equal to the force of armor on the pike. Therefore, the force applied by the tip of a pike is equal to the force needed to bring pike-bearing *Eidgenossen* to a stop.

45. Col. S. D. Rockenback, "Tanks in Battle of Amiens," *Infantry Journal* 21, No. 2 (August 1922), pp.141–149.

46. The most outstanding exception to this general rule is Robert Leonhard's *Fighting by Minutes* (Westport, Conn.: Praeger, 1993). Leonhard's theoretical analysis suggests that the most efficient way to conceptualize the battlefield is not in terms of distances but in terms of time.

47. Bateman, "The Eighth Ohioan at the High Water Mark," currently awaiting publication in *Timeline,* the journal of the Ohio Historical Society in Columbus, Ohio.

48. Oman, *The Art of War in the Middle Ages,* 96. At St.-Jacob-en-Birs a Swiss force of between 1,000 and 1,500 men deliberately crossed the Birs River and assaulted a force of French troops numbering roughly forty thousand. All of the Swiss were killed, but not before the French lost more than two thousand of their own. This deliberate disregard for their own lives, coupled with the ferocity of their attack, convinced the French commander that further progress in his planned invasion would be suicidal. The Swiss attacking him had been merely the advance guard, not the main body he could later expect. The French returned to Alsace following this engagement, and the Swiss reputation was sealed.

49. Du Picq, *Battle Studies,* 88–89.

50. Keegan, *The Face of Battle,* 174–175. Keegan follows through on du Picq's ideas and provides a short analysis of the effects of mental shock upon those soldiers in following ranks while describing the action between infantry units of the British and French at Waterloo in 1815.

51. See Charles E. Heller and William A. Stofft, eds., *America's First Battles* (Lawrence, Kan.: University Press of Kansas, 1986).

John A. Antal

Lieutenant Colonel John Antal (M.A.) is an armor officer. A career soldier, Antal fits the mold of the classic soldier-scholar. He is already the author of four books: *Armor Attacks, The Tank Platoon* (1991), *Infantry Combat, The Rifle Platoon* (1995), *Combat Command* (1997), and *Proud Legions* (1999). He also penned three of the chapters in *The Maneuver Warfare Anthology*, the now classic work on the subject published by Presidio Press in 1993. Since 1985 he has published more than twenty-two articles in professional journals. In addition to writing, he is a frequent speaker on the Arts and Entertainment Network's series "Brute Force." He recently completed the U.S. Army's prestigious War College and is currently stationed in the Pentagon.

Colonel Antal brings us into a dark and certainly disturbing future with this hypothetical scenario set in the mid- to late twenty-first century. Extrapolating from military theories and nascent doctrinal concepts now beginning to gain credence, Antal takes us forward to an era when military forces are expected to operate in total accordance with a plan because the plan is always correct. It is an era that appears limited in that the objectives and national assets are constrained, but is this a new era of limited war? Infantry soldiers trained to operate as spotters for the United States' impressive arsenal of stand-off precision weapons relearn a hard lesson that many of their forefathers may recognize: stand-off is OK, but you need to stand-on before you own a piece of ground.

Elite soldiers trained to expect what might appear to be a twenty-first-century version of the seventeenth-century phenomenon of limited war are shocked when faced with an enemy that operates in accordance with an older set of rules. They are forcibly reminded of the lesson that Marlborough learned at the Battle of Malpalquet in 1709: that "limited" in warfare only applies to the strategic level. Down on the ground at the tactical level, things can still get nasty. As the saying goes, "When you are the guy they are shooting at, your war is total." The lesson they learn is a hard one and suggests a second lesson to the reader. This is that technology, especially information-based technology, is most definitely a double-edged sword.

Battleshock XXI

Sergeant? I guess this knife throwing is fun . . . but why do we have to learn it? What possible use is it?"

"Well," answered Zim, "suppose all you have is a knife? Or maybe not even a knife? What do you do? Just say your prayers and die? Or wade in and make him buy it anyhow? Son, this is real—it's not a checker game you can concede if you find yourself too far behind."

—Robert Heinlein[1]

"All three companies have landed and occupied their sectors. Robot scouts are initialized and in place to designate targets for the second precision strike," a tall, leathery-faced sergeant announced without the slightest trace of emotion. The man sounded as if he were an extension of the machine he carried on his back. "But sir, we're having some problems with the data flow rate."

The colonel turned his head, a shocked look on his hard face. "Say that again, Sergeant Harper."

"The flow rate is intermittent. I've checked it twice," the gruff veteran sergeant answered. "The sensor link is good but the info stream is noncontiguous. It's unusual, but probably nothing more than a software glitch. I'm running parallel diagnostics."

"Just fix it," the colonel answered sharply. "We're already off simulation."

Sergeant Harper nodded, clearly comprehending the seriousness of being off simulation. "It's not on our end. It's as if someone is interrupting the stream at the opposite end of the data link. I'll run another decision variant based on what I've seen so far."

The colonel shook his head at the man in front of him. Harper was the picture-perfect image of a twenty-first-century high-tech soldier.

The six-foot-two-inch sergeant wore a camouflaged flexible-armor fighting ensemble.[2] On his back he carried a command communications pack—a sophisticated package of Hypernet communications equipment for the brigade commander. In his left hand he held a smart rifle.[3] Harper was all muscle and appeared to be in his early thirties, but his looks were deceiving. His biogenetic engineering masked the fact that he and most of the soldiers in the brigade were in their fifties. Harper was one of the young ones. He was only fifty-one.[4]

"Maybe when this mission is over, we'll study war no more." Harper grinned. "I'm getting too old for this kind of work."

"Don't count on it," Pierce replied, as a smile flashed across his face. "Your enlistment isn't up for another twelve years. You've found a home in the mobile strike force."

Harper returned the grin, his large white teeth a peculiar glow in Pierce's thermal viewer. The colonel turned and stared out the window of the third floor of the abandoned warehouse. It was pitch-dark outside, but through the thermal optics of his helmet Pierce viewed the city as if it were day. As he scanned the city with his thermal viewer, the sight automatically changed from one to three and then sixteen power as his eye focused on various structures.

The battlefield was quiet. With any luck he could still get back on simulation.

Pierce contemplated Harper's hope—"to study war no more." In spite of the absence of superpower conflicts, global peace and stability in the twenty-first century had remained an elusive dream. The world was still dangerous, although world wars comparable to those of the twentieth century had been avoided. In the twenty-first century the monopoly held by the advanced powers over the info stream of the Hypernet—the super information system that had evolved from the twentieth-century Internet—had brought them cascading wealth and tremendous power. The growth rate in the underdeveloped world was not as impressive. From this difference grew the seeds of conflict.

The Hypernet was essential to life in the twenty-first century. To succeed, you had to be connected. Connection cost money—and the price was more than some could afford. Those who could not afford connection fell continually behind. In the 1990s wars had been fought over oil and free access to oil resources. In the new millennium, information had replaced oil and many other physical resources as the major commodity of trade, wealth, and power.

Countries, cities, and corporations that could not afford connection paid on credit. National and corporate debts grew, while at the same time, millions of people in the developing world were thrown out of work by the advanced world's precision industries. The result by 2017 was a world of many failed nation-states that had devolved into rule by local warlords and criminal oligarchies.

The Hypernet had created a powerful new tool for good and evil. Unlike the primitive Internet, the Hypernet was not just e-mail, news, games, and the latest stock quotes. The Hypernet was the medium of transfer for commerce and communications. It was the central means of political and social interaction. Old notions of wealth had blurred in a virtual marketplace in which the Hypernet was money, communications, and politics.

The Hypernet was seamless, innocuous, essential, and everywhere. The United States in particular had gained tremendous economic, political, and military power by regulating the Hypernet. By 2018 the Hypernet had become so closely linked with everyday human life that it was unconscionable for any person or group to contemplate attacking the system any more than someone would attack the air or the water.

The history of humankind, however, is fraught with examples of people or nations doing the unconscionable. It was inevitable that some of the less successful groups in the world would view the Hypernet as a form of global taxation. Enter the Neo-Absolutist Coalition on the world stage.[5]

The Neo-Absolutist Coalition could best be termed a cybertribe. Unlike the participants in wars of the twentieth century, when power had been concentrated in nation-states, the Neo-Absolutists were not a state but an alliance that coalesced only on the Hypernet. The coalition obeyed no laws and, flaunting its anonymity, had launched a synchronized and highly sophisticated attack on the Hypernet.

The colonel checked the BSD screen—his battle-sensing display. The BSD was a small monocular data screen suspended in front of his left eye. Although the BSD was only a few inches in diameter, it presented the illusion of a full data-fusion screen for the war-tech user. Attached to his MK77 battle helmet, the BSD screen served as his data-link viewer to the Hypernet. In addition, the BSD combined the capabilities of a range finder, night vision equipment, a friend or foe designator, and a tactical battle-space display.

Colonel Pierce muttered an unintelligible curse. His mind raced as his eye scrolled down the latest pictogram on his BSD. A large three-dimensional holographic-video battle grid appeared before him. He scanned the latest report from Captain Sharnberg, the commander of C Company. The target of their raid was not where it was supposed to be. This was bad news.

I'm off simulation, Pierce thought, *and there's no enemy on my screen. What could be worse?*

"Sir, the transmission link is up. It's the president."

Pierce's BSD screen immediately glowed blue, red, and green as the holographic image of the president appeared in full view. Pierce seemed to be transported to the Oval Office. He was standing in front of the president—but of course this was just an illusion of depth, space, and distance created by the BSD monocular. The president, looking spruce in an expensive turquoise tunic, was flanked by two advisors—a man, the director of the Department of Information; and an older woman, the director of national security. The president, a concerned, youthful-looking woman of fifty-seven, was smiling.

"Mrs. President, the brigade has landed and secured the enemy headquarters building," Pierce reported.

"Good," the president replied, smiling to the woman to her left. "How much longer until the Neo-Absolutists' comp-trans is captured?"

Pierce's expression soured. "I'm afraid our intelligence reports are wrong, Mrs. President. It's not here—at least not where it was reported to be."

The pleasant, dignified expression on the president's face quickly vanished. "What do you mean? You're off simulation?"

Pierce winced. "Off simulation" meant being off the plan—out of synch with the computers. It was as bad a thing as could happen to a military commander in the twenty-first century.

"Affirmative, Mrs. President. Our precision strike flattened the enemy in the objective area and within ten kilometers of the enemy complex. The Neo-Absolutists have taken massive casualties . . . but there is no headquarters here, just an empty complex. We're searching the complex just in case they moved the computer transmitter to another floor or another building. My computers are running alternative decision variants to determine where it might be."

"Colonel Pierce, you must get back on simulation," an agitated, gray-haired, thin-faced man to the president's left announced. "The Information Department has Hypernet proof of the comp-trans location. This fact was figured into the simulation. It has to be there."

Pierce's anxiety increased. Virtual was not in synch with reality. He had never been off simulation before. Simulations reduced uncertainty to insignificance. Simulations controlled the planning process. Being "off sim" added chaos into the equation—and chaos was anathema to the twenty-first-century military doctrinal tenets of precision fire, target sensing, and certainty.

"Pierce, thirty hours after the EMP strike, the Neo-Absolutists Hypernetted their second set of demands to the White House," interrupted a large round-faced woman, the secretary of national security, referring to the electromagnetic pulse bomb strikes.[6] "These Neo-Absolutists threaten to strike Washington and San Francisco if worldwide free access to the Hypernet is not established in the next twenty-two hours. You must find the comp-trans that detonates these devices."

"Madame Secretary, I'm well aware of my mission," Pierce responded, resentment and concern visibly etched on his chiseled face.

A sudden silence filled the room.

"Pierce," the president interjected, reasserting command of the discussion, her voice noticeably disturbed. "We won't stand idly by while this coalition of cowards tries to blackmail us. You must find the comp-trans before the deadline."

"Mrs. President, is there any more information on the terrorists?" Pierce asked.

"Nothing more than you have already received in your hypnobrief concerning the Neo-Absolutist headquarters in Bactria," the president answered, with a nervous glance to the woman on her left. "The fact is that we don't know exactly who set off the EMP bombs in New York and Philadelphia—although we haven't ruled out the possibility that Marshal Weng Chung, the generalissimo of the northeast coprosperity region, is involved. What is clear is that you are not dealing with just a lone terrorist group. These guys have plenty of Hypernet credits, lots of low-tech forces, and some disconcerting high-tech help."

Tell me something I don't already know, Pierce thought as he observed the president's face.

"You must get back on sim," the director of national security ordered. "It is only a matter of time before economies collapse and governments fall."

Pierce flinched. No one had to tell him how high the stakes were—nothing less than world stability and peace. He knew the score and was painfully aware that the enemy had already thrown him off simulation.

A deafening blast resonated in the distance. The power of the explosion shook the concrete walls of the empty warehouse like an earthquake. Dust fell from the concrete roof of the dark factory building.

"What the hell was that?" the president asked.

"Mrs. President, we're under attack," Pierce replied tersely. "This is most unusual. I don't have the enemy on my sensors."

The president looked at her round-faced secretary of national security with a look that straddled the line between panic and despair. "How is that possible?"

"Mrs. President," Pierce continued, "I can search the headquarters building for the comp-trans or call in my V-22s and pull out. What do you want me to do?"

A bright flash erupted on Pierce's BSD screen. The holographic image of the president went blank.

"Damn! What the hell caused that?" Pierce screamed at Harper. "Use your backup system to retrieve the data stream."

"Sir, the stream is down," Harper replied, his words rolling quickly as he fiddled with his belt touch pad. "I don't know why. Give me a few minutes. Systems diagnostic check initiated."

Pierce felt terribly uncomfortable. His BSD was blank—no president, no Oval Office. With a quick movement of his eye he switched to tactical. No battle grid. He had never been in a situation in which the data stream was down. In the past he had always followed a carefully orchestrated and detailed plan as prescribed by the system of systems.

"Sir, I'm switching to the alternate UAV data stream," Harper announced. "You should have your battle grid back in a few seconds."

Colonel Pierce viewed his BSD. It glowed bright blue, but still nothing registered. The UAVs, or unmanned aerial vehicles, hovered high over the battle space, automatically tracking enemy targets and searching areas at Colonel Pierce's command. The UAVs doubled as a backup communications stream in emergencies. Normally the UAVs sent their data streams directly to satellites. Harper was reconfiguring their transmissions to send data directly to his command pack.

Pierce waited. Tense seconds flashed by as he heard the muffled sound of explosions in the city. It was unnerving to hear a battle going on and not see the enemy on his BSD screen. He knew that he had to find that comp-trans.

Information from the detailed hypno-briefing cascaded through his mind as he retraced the steps that had led to his current situation. A number of outlaw states and other agents had formed an alliance that was labeled the Neo-Absolutist Coalition. Forty-eight hours ago terrorists had attacked the Hypernet nodes in New York and Philadelphia. In spite of recent security advances to protect the Hypernet, the enemy attacks had totally shut down the northeastern portion of the country. Washington was operating on an emergency info stream that rerouted connections only to key government agencies. The resulting data-stream loss had thrown the United States into turmoil as billions of dollars were lost for every minute of the information blackout.[7]

For the first time in history war had been waged with EMP bombs.[8] The EMP weapons were nonlethal weapons that fried electronic systems and disrupted data-stream transfers. The Protocols of 2007 had been championed by Microsoft's ambassador to the United Nations. These banned the development of the anti-info-stream EMP devices, which were added to the list of prohibited weapons of mass destruction.

An outraged U.S. public was demanding vengeance, but these twenty-first-century terrorists were difficult to find. The leaders of the enemy coalition hid in cyberspace, united in a virtual community of interests. The Hypernet dramatically empowered distant partners with diverse backgrounds, goals, and aspirations to act with anonymity. At the same time, the military applications of Hypernet connectivity had become more significant than the raw military power of the remaining one hundred aging Midgetman intercontinental ballistic missiles, sitting silently in their underground silos across the American Northwest.

The search for these terrorists was the job of the U.S. Department of Information. This department merged the previous duties of the Central Intelligence Agency, the National Reconnaissance Agency, and Microsoft's Computer Intelligence Agency. Twenty-four hours after the initial attack, only a handful of the terrorists and their accomplices had been captured. Interrogation of the captured prisoners and their accomplices revealed little. The supergeeks at the Department of Information then did what the government had publicly pledged that it would never do: they surreptitiously broke the cipher of the secure Hypernet.

Since the Neo-Absolutists were a cybertribe, the Hypernet provided the only way to locate them. Within twenty-four hours of the terrorist deadline, the Department of Information had found the location of the command detonation device. It learned that the terrorists controlled the EMP bombs from a Hypernet cipher device located at their headquarters in Bactria. If the Hypernet cipher controls could be captured, all of the EMP bombs could be deactivated simultaneously. If not, the bombs would self-destruct according to a preplanned schedule.

The Hypernet clues led to Bactria, a failed state with a government that acted as a front for a powerful warlord. The Department of Information discovered that this warlord had received his Hypernet credits from a Neo-Absolutist Hypernet address. The Bactrians didn't have a navy or much of an air force, but they had several divisions of troops. These soldiers were armed with upgraded early twenty-first-century armored vehicles and artillery and a newly upgraded air defense system. The Bactrian government openly declared that it was not part of the Neo-Absolutist cause, but it would not accept incursions onto or over its sovereign territory.

The United States immediately sent a powerful precision-fire strike force to the region, and the U.S. Navy ordered one of its four remaining aircraft carriers and two arsenal ships into operational range. The U.S. Air Force scrambled its two manned bomber squadrons and eight robotic fighter wings.[9] The U.S. leaders knew, however, that bombing the enemy's headquarters into dust would not solve the problem.

The mobile strike force, or MSF, was therefore alerted. MSF planners immediately ran a series of computer simulations to determine several courses of action, and from them they developed a plan with an estimated 98.7 percent probability of success. The simulation proved that one brigade could accomplish the mission. This was fortunate because four of the six U.S. Army ground-force brigades were deployed in peace-and-stability operations in the worst hot spots of the underconnected world.

The MSF plan called for a "brilliant fire strike" to devastate enemy forces in the headquarters area. Pierce's mobile strike force, transported in V-22AE9 Super Ospreys, would then swoop in and capture the headquarters, search the area, and retrieve the comptrans detonator. After a careful study of the simulations, Pierce did not expect the raid to be much of a fight; it would just be a case of moving in and mopping up.

Pierce listened to the sound of distant explosions as he recalled the events of the last twenty-four hours. He remembered a quote from a great U.S. general who had said that the ideals with which an army fights are only slightly less important than the ideas for which it fights.[10] Pierce knew this to be true. The war-fighting doctrine of a nation is one of the most sensitive elements of national security policy. War-fighting doctrine by definition reflects the national character of the military force.

As early as 2005, the war-fighting doctrine of the United States had become one of distant punishment. The concept was simple: find the enemy electronically, plaster him with ultra-accurate fire from brilliant missiles and robot fighter-bombers, and force him to surrender or continue the punishment. This doctrine negated the possibility of friendly casualties.[11] By 2020 the doctrine had become etched in transparent titanium. It had become dogma.

Of course, the doctrine of distant punishment had not blossomed overnight. This development had grown from security-policy debates at the turn of the millennium. In the early years of the twenty-first century there had been several critics who warned against the false promises of a firepower-only solution. They argued for a balanced approach that would place maneuver and decisive action on a par with firepower. These arguments had ceased when the ascendancy of precision fires came to dominate doctrine.[12] The American way of war developed into a firepower solution fixed on superior technology. Distant punishment became the tool of choice for policymakers who feared the political fallout of the image of U.S. casualties splashed across the flat-view entertainment screens of the country.

Except for two brigades of MSF troopers, the U.S. Army was reorganized for maximum effectiveness in low-intensity conflicts. Force-projection problems were solved by opting for a light, high-technology force that could get there fast, designate targets for precision-guided weapons, and secure the ground after the fire strike. Close-combat operations were no longer necessary. Closing with the enemy was considered anachronistic. Besides, there was no support in the government for spending more money to develop systems to support maneuver dominance. Combined arms, the theory of warfare of the twentieth century, fell into the dustbin of history. The twenty-first-century motto of the U.S. military was: "Sensors find and blind; fire kills; infantry occupies."

Pierce commanded one of the ultramodernized U.S. Army MSF brigades. The brigade consisted of three companies, but each company had the firepower of a 1990s-style light infantry brigade. Each soldier had equipment that would have been the envy of a twentieth-century soldier. The ultramodern force soldier was genetically enhanced for strength, disease protection, and chemical and biological defense. Each soldier wore a smart uniform that sensed injuries and had the capacity to stabilize wounds automatically. The

MSF troopers wore ballistic armor developed through nanotechnology that could stop most small-arms fire like an umbrella holding off the rain.

Most importantly, each soldier was a battlefield transmission sensor node. Wired through a high-frequency Hypernet link, each soldier had perfect situation awareness of the friendly and enemy forces. The MK77 helmet was effective ballistic protection, and it also held the microelectronics for communications, all-weather thermal sensing, battlefield-grid visualization, and voice-message transmission. The BSD monocular attached to the helmet was the trooper's window to see in the dark, designate targets for destruction by brilliant munitions, and display and send tactical information.

This equipment was extremely expensive, which was the reason there had only been enough funding to maintain two MSF brigades. There were not enough funds to purchase armored vehicles or mobile platforms to balance the force, despite the revolutions in nanotechnology that had improved vehicle armor and power plant design. Instead, the V-22AE9 Super Osprey had become the company's maneuver vehicle.[13] The ultramodern force used the Super Ospreys as dragoons had used horses in the nineteenth century.

"Sir, I've got the UAVs functioning by switching to direct comm link. Six targeting satellites are back on line. I don't know what caused them to blink out . . . but we have another problem. The grid confirms enemy armored vehicles entering Sector Three. They're moving fast from multiple directions right down the highways . . . and Colonel, there's a lot of them."

Pierce viewed his battle grid. Harper was right; the UAV sensors were reporting what had been invisible from the satellite link. The enemy was counterattacking in force and had apparently found a way to fool the satellite sensors.

"We've got them now," Pierce crowed as he watched the pictogram that depicted the enemy advance. Enemy tanks and infantry fighting vehicles were moving from the east, south, and west at forty miles an hour across the scarred, devastated terrain. The enemy elements were only twenty kilometers away, racing toward the MSF perimeter along the Islawanda Highway exchange. "This will change the odds. They're closer than I'd like, but our missiles will grind them to dust."

Harper smiled back, displaying the grin of a hunter waiting for the hammer to fall on his unsuspecting prey. Both men knew what would happen next. Targeting satellites were plotting the enemy's movement. In a few seconds the precision-guided brilliant munitions would turn the enemy armored columns into so much jagged junk.

A holographic image of Captain Sharnberg appeared in front of Pierce, courtesy of his BSD imager. "Sir, my sensors have discovered the location of the comp-trans. It's only a kilometer from the headquarters building."

"Excellent," Pierce replied, giving a determined nod. "Get there and capture it. I'll take care of the enemy counterattack."

Sharnberg acknowledged the mission, and his holographic image dissolved. Pierce's BSD screen switched to the battle-space tactical map—the grid—projected in a three-dimensional holographic cube. Robotic fighter-bombers were moving in to launch stand-off munitions at the enemy columns. Pierce realized that he was off simulation, but as he eradicated the enemy's counterattack, Sharnberg would capture the comp-trans and his force could head for home. With luck, the MSF would accomplish its mission despite being slightly off simulation.

A brilliant arc of light shattered the night sky as several missiles were launched from somewhere southeast of the city. Pierce's BSD immediately shut off, the illusion of the three-dimensional battlecube grid fading before his eyes. For a second the room was very dark and quiet. His MK77 helmet screeched a cold, mechanical verbal warning: "Enemy missile launch—systems deactivated for 15.25 seconds."

In a flash of fire the sky brightened as a string of missiles detonated in the upper atmosphere. Pierce stared out the window, watching the night sky turn light and then darken again. Seconds later his MK77 helmet reactivated. He quickly checked his helmet diagnostics. The helmet checked out as fully functional and his BSD screen glowed green, red, and blue. It was not, however, receiving the tactical data stream.

The battle grid remained blank. He felt alone and disconnected.[14] Pierce shouted to Harper: "The data stream's down again!"

"Sir, their EMP bombs may have broken the Hypernet connection. The satellites don't even register. . . . Searching for UAVs," Harper replied as he stared into his BSD monocular. "There! Eight UAVs are still up. Switching now."

"Eight!" Pierce shook his head. Thirty-two had flown over the city in support of his operation just moments ago. With the data stream broken and only eight UAVs remaining, it was as if he were fighting with one eye closed.

A flashing icon in Pierce's BSD indicated an incoming voice transmission. He normally didn't use voice transmission, but with only eight UAVs up, there wasn't enough data stream to employ holographic video. With the movement of his left eye Pierce pulled down the voice-trans menu and initiated the audio data.

"Wizard Six, this is Wizard One. I can't reach you on video-holograph circuit so I've switched to audio. I've got trouble in the north, at Sector One. A mass of civilians are headed my way—maybe a thousand or more—intermingled with enemy soldiers. They've got women and children in the crowd."

The worried female voice that resonated in the earphones of Colonel Pierce's helmet was Captain Krepanovitch. Pierce's anxiety heightened as he heard the sound of explosions to the north.

"Activate your nonlethal generators," Pierce ordered, the tension rising in his voice.

"I've already done that and they're still coming," Krepanovitch screamed through Pierce's audio receiver. The sharp echo of her smart rifle sounded in the background of the transmission. "I've lost three troopers—I say again, three KIA. The bastards have tanks here too. I can't hold them!"

The colonel's eye darted to the top right of his BSD and activated a status report screen. Pierce's heart swelled with anger as he saw the names of the dead scroll across his screen. His force was taking casualties, something that hadn't happened to a U.S. force for a long time.

The enemy was using the population to infiltrate his perimeter—to get in close to fight him on more even terms. The NLGs—nonlethal generators that turned you ill and incapacitated you if you were within a kilometer of them—weren't stopping them. He had two choices: fall back or order Krepanovitch to fire on the crowd.

"Use all means to stop them from entering the northern sector of the perimeter, Krepanovitch! Empty your arsenal boxes if you have to," Pierce ordered, white-hot with anger.[15] Another status report flashed on his BSD screen. He saw that Krepanovitch's company, which normally had fifteen soldiers, was now down to nine troopers.

"I need help," Krepanovitch answered. "I've got more KIAs. The enemy is too close!"

Pierce ignored her plea and pulled down the next report. The BSD displayed Sharnberg's Bravo Company in the west in Sector Nine. Sharnberg's force was fighting enemy forces in the headquarters building, frantically trying to fight its way to the comp-trans device. Somehow the enemy had survived the brilliant fire strike, probably by hiding in bomb-proof basement shelters. Against stiff opposition, Sharnberg's company—down to thirteen soldiers—was moving too slowly.

Captain Martinez's Charlie Company had been hit hard by a large column of enemy tanks. It was all happening too fast.

"Sharnberg, fight your way to that comp-trans. You're the main effort. Capture that damn device!"

"Sir, we're fighting at close range, room to room!" Sharnberg replied hysterically. "Robot sentries aren't stopping them. They're too close and there's too much enemy fire. I can't move forward."

Pierce blinked, searching for options to support Sharnberg's force. "Martinez, gain me some time! Stop the lead elements of the enemy armored column. You've got six arsenal boxes at your disposal—use them! Robo fighter-bombers are inbound in two minutes."

A digital pictogram in Pierce's BSD confirmed that Martinez's soldiers were in close combat with the enemy armor. Martinez's FAF missiles—superfast fire-and-forget antitank missiles with a range of twelve kilometers, packed sixteen to an arsenal box—fired in rapid volleys at the enemy. Each FAF launch registered on Pierce's grid, but before the hits registered, the battlefield grid blinked off. A sinking feeling gripped Pierce's soul.

"Sir, the enemy is not appearing on the grid," Sergeant Harper announced. "They're jamming our signal. I've never seen this before!"

Pierce didn't answer. How could he fight without precise information about the enemy? The battlefield, a place that he had learned to deal with in real-time certainty in simulations, in which he saw the location of all friendly and all enemy forces all the time, was now a very confused place.[16]

"Sir, if we can't see the enemy on our battle grid, how can we fight him?" Harper questioned, his voice quivering. "Do you want me to call in the retrieval birds?"

"No, damn it!" Pierce screamed. He felt like a caged bear surrounded by hounds. "We're not quitting yet!"

A half-dozen hypersonic robotic fighter-bombers screamed through the dark, high above the city. Pierce looked up through the window to see their burning engines streaking across the night sky like laser-thin lines of light. He smiled. The rumble of smart hunter-killer munitions buffeted the ground, shaking the walls of the building. He had to find a way to get back on sim. Maybe he could still win.

Another series of superbright explosions detonated in the dark night air, high above the battlefield, but at a lower altitude than the previous explosions. Pierce covered his eyes with his right hand.

The rumble of the explosions echoed across the city as he dropped his hand and stared out the window in disbelief. The robotic fighter-bombers that should have decimated the enemy's armor were falling to the ground like rocks. As the robo craft crashed, they lit up the city in a series of bright explosions.

Understanding dawned on Pierce, and the situation abruptly became clear. The entire operation had been a setup. The comp-trans information was probably false. The enemy had trapped his brigade in a carefully orchestrated ambush. They had used EMP bombs and probably a sophisticated digital attack to blind and disrupt the United States' information and precision-fire systems. His striking power was gone.[17] Now the enemy was closing in for the kill.

A barrage of enemy artillery shells struck the empty parking lot outside, offering the promise of more to come.

"Incoming!" Sergeant Harper screamed as he fell to his knees.

Pierce didn't need any warning—he was already on the floor, hugging the cold concrete for dear life. His BSD went dead.

The room filled with light as the windows shattered, shooting solar glass in all directions. The explosion buffeted the building, lifted Pierce off the floor, and sent him two feet into the air. He landed with a thud and rolled over on his back.

Flattened and dazed, he pushed the button on the side of his helmet to reboot the sensor package. His BSD turned back on. His fighting ensemble sensors had registered the energy surge and shut down again just long enough to protect his nano-electronic systems.[18] For the time being, he was still functional.

He scanned his BSD for the latest report. Two UAVs had survived and were still relaying signals among the elements of his battered force. He sighed with relief at the knowledge that two were still operational. Apparently, the electronic-surge countermeasure defensive systems on the UAVs had held against the enemy's explosions—or maybe they had been shielded by the terrain. At this point it didn't matter. The two UAVs were his only means to stay connected.

Pierce looked over and saw Harper staggering to his feet. "That was a close one . . . too close. Sir, we've got to change plans or the grave registration teams won't have enough of us left to bury."

Pierce didn't answer. There were no grave registration teams in the twenty-first-century army, but he understood the drift of Harper's comment. He searched for a way out for his brigade. He felt as if he were in a huge vice and the walls were slowly crushing in on him.

Pierce smelled the acrid smoke of a dozen fires raging in the building. A large part of the city was on fire. His BSD flickered off for a moment, then recharged and displayed the layout of his forces. Two more soldier systems were down. He had only a handful of MSF troopers left.

He quickly pulled down the latest UAV report in his BSD. His sensors indicated that the enemy had exploded EMP bombs in the air above the city, knocking out the robo fighter-bombers. The EMP bombs had also degraded several of his soldiers. With their MK77 helmets fried, they were reduced to fighting within visual range, a task they rarely trained for.

Then he saw something he had never seen before. One of his companies—Charlie—had broken and was running back to Sector Twelve, the center of the defensive sector.

"Wizard Three, report!" Pierce shouted on his FM transmitter. "You have to hold Sector Three."

"Wizard Six, this is Wizard Three," Captain Martinez's panicked voice responded. "I stacked them up at the Afghanistan Memorial Bridge, but we can't hold without fire support. They're everywhere, and they keep closing the distance. I'm down to seven troopers. They're too damn close!"

The colonel stood in the dark room in silence. Pierce's airpower was gone; precision fires were ineffective; and he was running out of options. He scanned his ever-shrinking defensive perimeter. Time was running out.

"Wizard Six, this is Wizard Two," Sharnberg screamed over the radio. "I've located the comp-trans device in a truck inside a large open area, Afghanistan Square, just half a kilometer away. Their tanks are attacking. You've got to help me stop them."

Pierce checked his fire support options. Maybe he could still target the precision fires manually. The enemy's tanks were hidden on his grid, but the fixed bridges and choke points in the city were designated on the computer hard drive that generated his battle map. If he manually indexed the grids to these targets, maybe the precision fires could stop the enemy's advance.

"Wizard Three, leave a squad to hold the enemy in the east and pull back to support Sharnberg at the southern edge of Vietnam Street. I'm working a fire strike now. Stop the enemy armor from reaching Sharnberg."

Martinez acknowledged.

Rapidly, with quick movements of his left eye, Pierce pulled down the screens for fire support and ordered a precision strike. In seconds he watched the targets—a bridge near a burning industrial complex in the south near Afghanistan Square, two bridges and a tunnel just to the east, and a bridge and a narrow building-lined road to the west of the square—disappear under the strikes of the precision-guided weapons.

"That will hold them," Pierce said, nodding with satisfaction. "Sharnberg, make your move. Move quickly."

Pierce scanned his BSD and concluded that Sharnberg still had time to accomplish the mission. If he could hold the enemy back for a little while longer—keep them at a distance—maybe the precision weapon sensors would come back on-line and the balance would shift back to the MSF. He repeated the doctrine as if to reassure himself: "Sensors find and blind; fire kills; infantry occupies."

He watched the latest UAV real-time video reports as a widely dispersed column of enemy tanks and infantry fighting vehicles converged on Afghanistan Square. The lead vehicles in the column dispensed a thick white smokescreen. Pierce watched from his bird's-eye view as bridge-laying armored vehicles rushed forward to replace the destroyed bridges. He cross-checked his electronic targeting sensors. The battle grid did not register the enemy tanks at all.

Abruptly, the UAV screen went blank. His BSD registered the loss of both UAVs to enemy energy weapons. His battle grid now showed only the location of his MSF troopers.

"Damn it!" Pierce screamed, as he banged his Kevlar-armored fist against the wall. "I can't stop them!"

"Sir, Krepanovitch reports by audio that the enemy's attacking in strength. She destroyed the Dienbienphu Bridge, but they've found a way to bypass. They're breaking through."

Pierce listened to the audio backup system as Krepanovitch's forces engaged the enemy. Her soldiers were still fighting, but in the old-fashioned way, in direct close combat with direct fire.

The feeling of close combat was unnerving. As a veteran of countless simulations, Pierce had always killed his enemies at long range.[19] He never closed within direct-fire range to defeat an enemy.

"You can't see it on your BSD," Krepanovitch's voice shouted over Pierce's FM receiver. The sound of automatic smart-rifle fire and explosions resonated in the background of her transmission. "We've destroyed at least two dozen enemy tanks in Sector Twelve, but they keep coming. More of my troopers are down—don't know how many. I can't hold them!"

Pierce received similar reports from all sectors. The enemy was advancing regardless of losses—another situation he had never experienced before. It disheartened him to think that his opponents would sacrifice so many to accomplish their mission. Obviously the enemy's thinking was not very twenty-first-century.

Pierce's BSD registered then that Sharnberg had been killed. An electric shot of panic ran up Pierce's spine. The effect on Pierce was as if he had lost a son: traumatic and at the same time galvanizing. The rest of Sharnberg's company was quickly cut down as they were overwhelmed by the enemy.

The feeling of trauma was immediately replaced by rage. Nothing was working. The enemy—these puny, low-tech, industrial-age Neo-Absolutists—were out-generaling him. His force, the pride of the United States and armed with the latest technological wonders, could not stem the tide of battle.

The battle was lost; he knew that he would not get back on sim now. The enemy, smart and determined, had disrupted the system of systems. The battle had turned into a messy, chaotic, uncoordinated melee with each company fighting a desperate battle of its own, virtually in isolation. He was not prepared for this kind of battle.

He sent a digital report to all units to rally on Sector Twelve, the center of the perimeter. He saw the icons that represented his forces falling back to the center of the city. Now his plan was one of survival. He would defend this smaller perimeter and prepare for retrieval. He called for the retrieval ships. He prayed that the V-22s would arrive before his force was annihilated.

Pierce sweated out the final seconds as he waited for the retrieval birds. In a three-day campaign the Neo-Absolutists had crippled the U.S. economy and defeated a U.S. mobile strike force. The air force's multibillion-dollar robotic fighter-bombers had been knocked out of the sky, the navy's vast array of precision missiles had been rendered impotent, and the army was being butchered on the ground.

Pierce shook his head in disbelief at the events that had occurred in the past three hours. This wasn't the way it was supposed to be. Three weapons had revolutionized warfare in the twenty-first century: precision-guided fires, robotic air forces, and ultra-information-targeting systems. Warfare was now knowledge-based. What could be sensed could be killed by long-range missile fires. Direct fire and maneuver had ceased to be the primary forms of decision. Close combat was a thing of the past. Distant fires broke the back of the opponent, and the high-tech infantry flew in to mop up. This was how things were supposed to work.

But the Neo-Absolutists had set a cleverly laid trap—and had obviously gone to a lot of trouble and expense to turn this trap into a decisive battle.[20] Their use of EMP bombs and their willingness to take tremendous casualties had turned U.S. doctrine on its head. They were using chaos and shock—not the killing effect of precision firepower—to maneuver on the Americans and kill their opponents at close range. The destruction of the MSF would be a catastrophic blow to the United States and would probably determine the outcome of the war.

Enemy artillery blanketed the northern sector near Afghanistan Square. The ground shook with the blast of the explosions. The enemy was not holding back. Pierce listened in awe as the enemy devastated its own city to kill his brigade.

"Remarkable," he mumbled, as he suddenly realized the true nature of war. "These savages will stop at nothing."

"Sir, we'd better get on the ground if we expect to link up with the birds," Harper shouted over the sound of fighting that was raging outside.

Pierce nodded.

The two men quickly moved through the dark building, down the concrete stairs to an opening that emptied into a street leading to the pickup zone—a soccer stadium in the center of the city.

They arrived at the soccer stadium and joined what was left of their once-proud brigade. Captain Krepanovitch, wounded but still fighting, had formed the survivors into a tight perimeter along the walls of the stadium.

Pierce took a position near the pickup zone with Sergeant Harper. He now realized how badly the doctrine of distant punishment had failed. The system of systems had been overcome by a ruthless and determined enemy. The notion of high-technology, bloodless battles was a horrible lie.

He struggled to think of what he could have done differently. He realized that the first requirement of war was decisive action—not just killing. This meant you had to be prepared and willing to fight in close combat. You had to be trained and equipped to move across deadly ground under the enemies' fire and, if necessary, grind them into dust. If you were not willing to do this, the enemies would find ways to counter a firepower-only approach. They could merely dig in or develop an asymmetrical means to defeat your technology. In the twenty-first century, you still needed to dominate the enemy physically.

Pierce looked around at his brigade. His force was down to sixteen effectives; his high-tech brigade was decimated. A V-22 miraculously appeared, hovering over the stadium like an angel to the rescue. In a flurry of wind and dust, the bird landed. The pilot radioed Pierce that two more Ospreys were on the way. Pierce gave the order to withdraw. His soldiers ran to the V-22. Pierce, Harper, and a squad of soldiers from Alpha Company formed the rearguard. The swirling rotors of the V-22, the smoke, and the sound of gunfire gave the scene a surrealistic effect he had never experienced in the simulations.

The V-22 lifted off. As the Super Osprey switched pitch from vertical to forward acceleration, tears streamed down Pierce's dirty cheeks. He unbuckled his helmet and took off the heavy apparatus. His close-cropped hair was specked in sweat. He rubbed his head with his hands, then buried his face in them.

Pierce scanned the eastern sky, searching for the second flight of Super Ospreys. Explosions rocketed the city. His force was firing madly with their smart rifles. The squad with Pierce fired the last of the FAF missiles. The missiles roared into the sky over the walls of the stadium and swooped down to devastate an enemy tank platoon rushing west from Afghanistan Square. Now the arsenal boxes were empty.

As Pierce searched the sky, hoping to see the large whirling blades of another Osprey, he saw a large sign that designated the stadium's name. It read, "Mogadishu Field."

A bright orange-red explosion flickered in the northwest as an enemy antiaircraft missile struck the lead Osprey. A streak of orange-red flame registered the site where the Super Osprey had smashed into the ground. Bravely disregarding this disaster, the last

Super Osprey executed evasive maneuvers, fired a suite of antiaircraft decoys, and headed for Mogadishu Field.

The Osprey flew low over the stadium, hovered, and descended. In a strong blast of wind, the huge blades of the aircraft brought the forty-ton bird down into the center of Mogadishu Field. Pierce quickly put his helmet back on and flicked his eye, pulling down the screen in his BSD. He then gave the order he had never practiced: the order to retreat and save yourselves.

But it was too late. Enemy tanks had already closed the ground and broken through the gate of the stadium. A surge of enemy infantry entered Mogadishu Field, following the advancing tanks.

"Sir, let's go. The last bird has its ramp down!" Harper yelled.

In awe, Pierce watched as a group of enemy soldiers rushed the last V-22. He pointed his smart carbine at the group to his left and fired, dropping a dozen attackers. Then Pierce sensed a threat to his right. Spinning around, he caught a glimpse of a teenage boy carrying a rocket launcher over his shoulder, Cossack style. The boy had a knife in his right hand.

Pierce's mind registered the type of weapon—a knife, just a knife—just as the boy threw the blade. Six inches of steel sank into Pierce's chest, puncturing his body armor just below the right shoulder blade. He grabbed the knife with his left hand and staggered to the open ramp of the Super Osprey. A brilliant flash from an antitank missile shattered the gray early morning sky as the Osprey ignited in an orange-red explosion. The force of the explosion knocked Pierce unconscious before the flaming wreck of the blades of the Super Osprey cut him in half.

Notes

1. Robert Heinlein, *Starship Troopers* (New York: G. P. Putnam's Sons, 1959), 50–51.

2. Tanai Khiaonarong, "Soldiers May Soon Be Marching to New Tune," *The Nation* (November 7, 1997): 6.

"Smart suits would also help soldiers survive . . . to wear uniforms that could 'think' . . . [and] detect injuries. When a soldier is shot, for example, his clothes, which would have fiber-optic threads woven into the fabric, could determine the extent of the injury, its location and whether the damage is internal or external. All this information, once detected by the fiber-optic strands, would be transmitted to miniature processors, radio transmitters and satellite receivers located on the uniform. The information would then travel to a Global Positioning System to enable medics to locate the soldier's position. Doctors could then judge the nature of the injuries, prescribe medication, or determine if the soldier is dead. The amazing part may be the built-in antiseptic system. The uniforms would feature an antiseptic lining that would release pain killers if they are pierced by a bullet or a sharp object. This 'self-healing' property would help injured soldiers withstand the pain until proper medical attention arrives."

3. Charles Arthur, "Smart Bullets Set to Hit the Target," *Independent* (April 10, 1997): 2. "Ultimately miniaturization could make it possible to have hand weapons with smart bullets. A sniper equipped with a laser-sighted BLAM rifle would be able to hit targets several kilometers away."

4. Karen Jowers, "A 72-Year-Old Soldier a Possibility for Future Force," *Army Times* (January 5, 1998): 6. "Imagine the soldiers, sailors, airmen and marines of the year 2025. They have been 'genetically enhanced' to increase strength and flexibility. They are doing the job better than ever before. And they are 72 years old."

5. Charles J. Dunlap, Jr., "21st-Century Land Warfare: Four Dangerous Myths," *Parameters* 27, No. 3 (Autumn 1997): 29. Dunlap states that Neo-Absolutist war "would be a vicious form of conflict extending across the spectrum of warfare. It would differ from more traditional 'total war' by, among other things, the propensity

of the aggressor to focus not on destroying military forces, but rather on shattering the opponent's will."

6. *Webster's New World Dictionary*, s.v. "EMP": "EMP electromagnetic pulse: an immense surge of electromagnetic radiation caused by a nuclear explosion."

7. Gary H. Anthes, "Info Warfare Risk Growing," *Computerworld* (May 22, 1995): 1.

8. Stephen V. Cole, "Russians Exporting Microwave Bomb," in *For Your Eyes Only, An Open Intelligence Summary of Current Military Affairs* (Amarillo, Texas: Tiger Publications, 1998), 1.

9. Robert H. Williams, "Unmanned Aerial Combat Aircraft Age Is Rapidly Approaching," *National Defense* 82, No. 534 (January 1998): 22.

10. Tom Clancy with Gen. Fred Franks, Jr. (Ret.), *Into the Storm, A Study in Command* (New York: G. P. Putnam's Sons, 1997), 107.

11. Glenn K. Otis, "The Ascendancy of Fires, The Evolution of the Combined Arms Team," *Field Artillery Journal* (June 1995): 18–19. The article was an interview of General Otis (Ret.), former commander of NATO's Central Army Group and commander-in-chief of U.S. Army Europe. He said: "I believe we're at the threshold of a major change for the combined arms team—the ascendancy of fires. What that means is that we, as a nation, will fight conventional battles using firepower of all kinds from longer ranges, much of it indirect—not eyeball-to-eyeball using direct fire. We'll use long range fires as the spearhead of the attack to the extent that the ground maneuver forces may only need to mop up after the fires. That's a totally different concept of operations. This concept aims at achieving decisive results while minimizing the usual high casualties of the direct fire battle."

12. Gary Stix, "Fighting Future Wars," *Scientific American* 273, No. 6 (December 1995): 92. "In 1978, more than a decade before the end of the cold war, physicist Philip Morrison and political scientist Paul F. Walker wrote a book on military spending that suggested that a relatively inexpensive national defense could be built around precision munitions, thereby forgoing vulnerable weapons platforms such as the aircraft carrier. Budgets, they asserted, could be cut by 40 percent."

13. Anick Jesdanun, "We Have Liftoff: Tilt-Rotor Osprey, Aircraft Hybrid, Rises from Grave; The Combination Helicopter and Airplane, No Longer Grounded, Gets a Central Role in Pentagon Plans," *Los Angeles Times,* 29 August 1997, Orange County edition. "The Osprey can fly as far and as fast as the C-130 transport plane now used to fly military personnel and equipment to war zones. Once there, it can land in the battlefield like a CH-46. Helicopters now headed to another part of the world must be taken apart, loaded on a transport plane and reassembled at the destination; they fly too slowly to get there on their own. Using the self-deploying Osprey could shorten a mission by hours or days. Because of the Osprey's speed, the military can launch offshore attacks with greater surprise and distance from enemies' land-based missiles and underwater mines."

14. See Lt. Col. Robert R. Leonhard's excellent article, "Shedding Light on the 'Man in the Dark,'" *Army* (February 1997): 41–48, "It is this innate capacity to adapt that underlies the theory of combined arms and, incidentally, confounds theorists who envision a single arm or weapon system dominating a future battlefield. No single system will ever prevail in real war because no matter how effective it is the enemy will adapt itself to it."

15. The arsenal box is suggested by recent proposals by the Defense Advanced Research Program Agency to field the "rockets in a box" Advanced Fire Support System.

16. Richard H. Sinnreich, "To Stand and Fight," *Army* (February 1997): 15–19. "The objective of many of these technologies is to improve certainty, a goal as perilous as it is alluring. As with narcotics, dependence on certainty can become a habit. The history of war confirms that no habit more readily invites catastrophic failure in battle, especially among small isolated units."

17. See Heinz Guderian, *Achtung Panzer* (London: Arms and Armor Press, 1992), 204–205, for a discussion of striking power. "What after all is striking power? It is the power that enables combatants to get close enough to destroy the enemy with their weapons. Only forces that possess this capacity can be reckoned to have true striking power, in other words, have true offensive capacity. . . . A tank has this striking power to the highest degree."

18. Paul Rodgers, "Billion-Pound Atoms," *Independent on Sunday*, 14 January 1996.

19. George Seffers, "U.S. Army Plans Test for Early Entry Force Equipment," *Defense News* (December 15–21, 1997): 18. "The whole idea was to avoid close battle, to extend it as far as possible so that the force has a better chance of survival."

20. Chris Bellamy, *The Future of Land Warfare* (New York: St. Martin's Press, 1987), 19. "Surprise remains a decisive factor in attaining success, and with meticulous planning and execution can be attained even in spite of modern electronic and other surveillance."

Mike Pryor

Major Mike Pryor is a national guardsman in Louisiana. You might pass him on the street on any given day, none the wiser that he leads a dual life. Like many national guardsmen, Major Pryor qualifies as a professional in more ways than one. A fully qualified tanker, he is a graduate of the army's armor officer basic and advanced courses and has led citizen soldiers for more than fourteen years. In his civilian life he is a computer specialist. Qualified as a Microsoft professional, he knows intimately the state of the art as it exists at the cutting edge of civilian technology. Soon to be promoted to major, Pryor offers an unparalleled breadth to this book. His experience in one of the national guard's enhanced brigades tells us something about the future for the largest part of the army, the guard and reserves.

Perhaps because of experiences in his civilian job, Major Pryor takes for granted the coming of digitization and the information dominance that it promises. The hard questions that he wrestles with in this chapter deal primarily not with, "Will the technology work?" but with the larger issue for the total force of the army of, "How will we make it all work together?" Through careful analysis and concrete studies, he offers us a blueprint, down to the nuts and bolts, of one way that the army might continue the tradition of a total force operating with a unified doctrine.

Digitization, Simulations, and the Future of the Army National Guard

Captain John Simpson looked deeply into his screen. As he quickly scanned from left to right, he could make out the icons that represented all of his tank company team's vehicles. These icons were superimposed on a terrain-relief map of the area his unit was traveling across. Yep, he knew exactly where they were on the battlefield.

A glance forward to the extreme right of his screen showed the plumes that his soldiers had come to call rabbit tracks. They represented enemy positions compiled by a collection of surveillance assets available to the force. A characteristic of Simpson's generation of war fighters was that they had no problem trusting the icons displayed on their screens. This was partly because of the soldiers' upbringing as the "Nintendo generation." It was also because after years of use, these assets were proving themselves to be as good as advertised. In using them, Simpson always knew where the enemy was.

A part of the digital puzzle was missing, however. He was supposed to also see where all friendly units were. Looking at the top of his screen, he did not see the unit that was supposed to be on his northern flank. A moment's hesitation ensued, and then Simpson decided to surf. Grasping the joystick—his commander's control handle—with his right hand, he pressed his thumb on the mouse button to scroll toward the top of his screen. When his last unit icon was about to disappear from view at the bottom of the screen, he released the button.

"That's odd," he said aloud. He had thought the flank unit would be visible. He could not remember any reports of it stopping along the way. Another few seconds of hesitation followed before he decided to take action. He toggled his communication switch.

"Gunner, continue to scan."

"Roger, sir," came the metallic-sounding reply over his headphones.

"Loader, you got outside," he said, indicating that from his position, Simpson was going to look intently at his display. Like helicopter pilots, tankers had come to make a habit of passing off responsibilities for who scanned where. When the tank commander was "inside" looking at the computer display, the tank's loader was up in his hatch—"outside"—to monitor the local situation.

"Wilco," came the stilted reply.

Simpson grasped the control handle again and used the mouse to scroll backward. He hoped the flank unit had only lost contact and had remained at the last phase line. As he moved to the left of his screen, losing sight of his unit in the process, he came to the previous phase line. His heartbeat picked up when he found no unit there.

"Sir, dust clouds to our front," the loader reported.

"Roger, loader, continue to scan," Simpson replied absentmindedly as he began to scroll with renewed vigor even farther to the rear. There he found them. Or rather, what was left of them. A blinking black icon indicated the point on the battlefield where the northern flank unit had expired.

Simpson's mind and heart raced. "Geronimo Six, I show the Blackhawk element as a combat loss at grid."

"Missile fire, direct front!" from the loader interrupted Simpson's transmission. Captain Simpson froze for two seconds, allowing the incoming enemy missile to close enough of the one thousand meter distance to make his attempt to fire countermeasures in vain. A loud bang preceded quiet darkness.

After his computer went blank, the box on the right of the screen flickered and then lightened, revealing the face of his commander. "Simpson, Simpson, Simpson. . . . Where do you think you went wrong?"

The young captain hated doing things improperly and was embarrassed to be speaking face to face with his commander at this moment. "Um, sir, I think I was inside on the display too long?"

"Precisely, Comanche Six. You were so busy trying to find your flank unit that you weren't paying attention to the confirmed enemy positions to your front. You should have been surfing for them every now and then just like you glance at the side and rearview mirrors of your car as you drive. Then you might have seen Blackhawk getting ambushed on your northern flank before Phase Line Smash. Also, if you had engaged the battle-space indicator on your screen, you would have seen you were in enemy missile range when you started to scroll north the first time. When that is the case, you need to focus on your immediate threat and send digital traffic or quick requests over your FM radio to your flank units. The computerized report by your loader about the dust clouds to your front? That was queued in by me to attempt to bring you back to reality."

"Yes, sir," was all Simpson could manage as he took stock of his effort in this exercise. As part of Force XXI leaders' training initiatives for the total armor force, computer-based training had received a good measure of armor school funding. The national guard had enthusiastically volunteered to test new software designed to train leaders in tactics online. With computers, a modem, and an inexpensive digital camera attached to the monitor, tactical simulation was brought to an officer's desktop.

Simpson, assigned as the commander of Company C—"Comanche

Six"—a mere six months ago, had almost completed his first tier of training matrices. After successful completion of two more exercises, he would complete Tier I training and meet his pre-annual training requirements. Tier II training thereafter continued to meet armor-branch professional development criteria.

"What are the lessons learned here?" the battalion commander asked.

"Less time inside, and turn on my battle-space indicator."

"Roger, Comanche Six. Remember that the BI should be turned on no later than fifteen kilometers from your objective. That way the enemy's graphical red line shows you his ability to mass fires on your formation. OK, let's do a different iteration of Vignette 13B . . . on central European terrain this time. And Comanche?"

"Sir?"

"Let's get it done this time. If I don't take the kids to see that new Disney movie tonight, Household Six is gonna skin me alive."

"Roger that, Six."

"Good hunting," the battalion commander said as he leaned forward and flipped off his camera, blackening the audiovisual box on Simpson's screen. The young captain gazed into his monitor as the representation of his tank's display screen came into view.

The army national guard will continue to act as a strategic hedge against aggressive foreign enemies in the twenty-first century. Impending integration of national guard light infantry companies in active-duty brigades, the formation of two integrated divisions, and continuance of the separate enhanced brigade concept underscore the relevance of reserve component combat arms units.[1] A glance at how many active-duty troops are deployed at any given time also serves as an indicator that guardsmen must be prepared to mobilize, conduct postmobilization training, and deploy to deter aggression. When they deploy, national guard combat arms, combat support, and combat service support soldiers will be expected to accomplish their assigned missions with as much skill as their active-duty counterparts.

Because this is so, the national guard must be digitized concurrently with the active-duty army. If it is not, army commanders risk having to employ their subordinate units in dissimilar fashion. Primarily because of vast differences in command-and-control capabilities, digital and nondigital or partially digitized units cannot seamlessly integrate and perform like missions in a like manner.

That being said, the challenges of digitizing the national guard must be understood. To grasp the ramifications of such an effort, several questions require answers, because the decision to digitize requires fundamental changes in the way the guard trains.

Why is there a challenge to mixing digital and nondigital units? What are some of the characteristics of national guard training that weigh on the decision to modernize? What are the missions of the national guard, and how do they affect potential training of digital reservists? How can simulations aid the conversion effort? And how would a digital national guard unit train? These questions must be answered if we are to gain a proper perspective on the nature of the national guard as digital war fighters. An extensive use of simulations, such as in the previous example, and an ability to train with them using off-the-shelf computer equipment from a soldier's home will be key to this effort.

Digital or Nondigital: A Force Dichotomy

Comparing digital and nondigital forces is the proverbial apples and oranges discussion. The two simply cannot fight in the same manner. Digital units have command-and-control equipment that tells the entire force, down to each vehicle, the friendly and enemy situation in relation to the surrounding terrain. A nondigital unit must advance physically to acquire the same information. How does this affect the way the two fight?

Digital units, with an enhanced ability to "see" the battlefield, theoretically think and therefore act faster than nondigital units. For instance, in an attack, a digital unit knows the entire force's location based on radio signal updates broadcast by its vehicles. That unit also sees the enemy's positions because a number of reconnaissance assets download information to the unit's computer screens. This information is displayed in relation to the terrain based on grid coordinate locations. (In the not-too-distant future, maps will be added to the display along with three-dimensional terrain tools that will assist the commander in picking concealed routes of advance.)

A digital commander decides where and how to attack the enemy from a position of advantage before the unit is seen. The digital force can also choose to simply mass its weapons' effects from dispersed formations, attacking and demoralizing the enemy, again unobserved. Enhanced targeting capability and dispersion greatly increase the unit's survivability. It is almost as if the enemy's actions prior to contact are irrelevant.

Nondigital units must go forth and find the enemy physically. Most often when they do, the enemy becomes just as aware of their presence. This negates any advantage for either side, and a fair fight ensues. A technique that has been discussed is to place digitally equipped liaison officers in a nondigital unit's operations center.

The problem here is that the flow of information from which tactical decisions are made does not change from the way operations are currently executed. The digital liaison receives intelligence on his or her computer, then passes the information verbally to the commander at the tip of the spear. That commander does not move the element in dispersed formations. The situation is unclear, so the commander must have firepower available to mass on the enemy at any given moment. As the commander plots reports passed via the radio, the unit continues to move closer to the enemy, diminishing both its time and positional advantages. With enemy positions manually posted on the map, the commander must translate contour intervals and terrain markings to determine the best route of attack. In effect, the only advantage derived from the digital liaison is more accurate intelligence.

Since they fight differently, digital and nondigital units must be employed differently. A digital unit is most like Sun Tzu's unorthodox force—its enhancements make it ideal for attack by fire or economy of force (in an extended battle space), pursuit, and exploitation operations. A nondigital unit is the orthodox force—no real enhancements mean it is best suited for creating penetrations, deliberate attack, and deliberate defense missions that make up the close battle. While nondigital units can meet with success and make a transition to pursuit or exploitation operations, they are like a boxer with a short reach lining up opposite Mike Tyson. Ask anyone who might be forced to climb into the ring, and they would probably say they prefer to face a blindfolded Pee Wee Herman with one arm tied behind his back.

The decision to modernize the national guard is a delicate one. It requires a complete equipment makeover and an entirely new war-fighting thought process, with which the active-duty army is only now coming to grips. As with active-duty modernization, however, the introduction of digital systems should not make the national guard mission more difficult. There are already challenges to national guard training that do not need any added degree of difficulty.

Challenges in National Guard Training

If the national guard is to digitize, we must decide whether they are able to train for tasks to standard using the new equipment. Guardsmen, with a significant amount of college education throughout their ranks and a resulting exposure to computers, possess a high technical aptitude for digitization. However, limited time in uniform makes it difficult to train with the army's brand of digital equipment.

There are obvious, and in many cases substantial, differences in many of the software applications that the army uses. Ironically, in some situations it is a case of training backward. That is to say that because many army programs are written in proprietary software and used for extended periods of time (for the computer era, that is), some are archaic by civilian standards. National guardsmen used to the top-end computers of their day jobs find that they must learn new tasks to use army systems. In any event it is not merely a question of upgrading from Excel 5.0 to Excel 97.

With that in mind, several challenges driving the nature of national guard training must be understood. These factors conspire to produce an initial asynchronous effect at the beginning of each drill. To understand this observation, think of an eighteen-wheel truck trying to climb a hill from a standstill. The driver must grab the stick and shift through several gears, slowly getting the vehicle up to speed. Once up to speed and at the top of the hill, the driver can coast through a good part of the rest of the drive. The factors discussed following are the gears the guard shifts through to accomplish its mission each time its soldiers mass for drill. Guardsmen consistently deal with conditions that produce this asynchronous effect. If the national guard is to digitize successfully, it must plan to attack the asynchronous effect of these challenges directly.

Only Thirty-Nine Days a Year?

Do not let anyone fool you. Although the standard is supposedly "one weekend a month and two weeks in the summer," guardsmen over the rank of sergeant, E-5, often drill more than thirty-nine days per year.

As an example, a typical brigade combat team of the Louisiana army national guard is beginning its three-year train-up for a National Training Center rotation in July 2001. In training year 1998 the battalion task force S3 (operations officer) will attend his normal drills and annual training, an additional drill per month when the unit conducts gunnery (the battalion is split in half for gunnery because of resource limitations), a leaders' training program rotation at the National Training Center, and a command-post exercise at Fort Polk. Total days of service will be somewhere in the neighborhood of sixty days. During training year 1999, I estimate that this same officer will drill for ninety days.[2]

The part-time battalion commander, command sergeant major, and most of the primary staff also participate in this training. As a general rule, most E-5s and above also perform an additional ten days per year of training. The additional training is necessary to prepare properly for command-and-control responsibilities during drill or annual training periods.

Units collectively, however, usually conduct only thirty-nine days of training annually. As a function of available time, they can therefore accomplish only a finite number of tasks to standard. If converting to digitized systems increases the amount of training task prerequisites, fewer total tasks are completed in the same length of time. Time constraints also produce several additional training challenges.

Noncontinuous Training

To properly relate their training to that of active-duty units, consider that national guard units spend approximately 90 percent of their annual drill days training on mission-essential tasks. However, those same units train for two days, take more than twenty days of leave, train for two more days, and so on through a training year.

An active-duty unit might complete a Tank Table VIII gunnery qualification for an entire fourteen-tank company in two days' time. This follows a good two weeks of preparatory gunnery training designed to meet prerequisites for qualification. Active-duty units have the benefit of consecutive training days to accomplish their tasks with little to distract them from their missions. They would never dream of conducting some of the training and then letting soldiers go on mass leave for three or four weeks before completing the rest of the mission.

Inherently, the national guard does not work that way. Some mechanisms must be placed into the training system in order to bridge this time gap and help retain learned proficiencies.

Training at Lower Echelons

Guardsmen must train at lower echelons than their active-duty counterparts. This is, once again, primarily because of the amount of training time available. The national guard, however, completes like tasks to the same standards as active-duty units. A 1st Cavalry Division tank crew conducts Tank Table VIII qualification on the same tasks, conditions, and standards as a crew in the Louisiana army national guard. Likewise, the same standard exists for Louisiana army national guard platoon tactical task training as for 1st Armored Division platoons.

Most national guard units, however, do not go much beyond platoon level in a training year. Tankers in the 1st Cavalry and 1st Armored Divisions will train annually at the company team, battalion task force, and brigade combat team echelons. National guard units might train at these echelons once every three or more years.

Fewer Iterations

Time also becomes a factor in the number of training task iterations a unit conducts. It is a fact in learning that repetition builds proficiency. My active-duty counterparts have the privilege of visiting a combat training center such as the National Training Center approximately every two years during their time in service. In each rotation they conduct approximately five battles against the vaunted Opposing Force (OPFOR). Each battle includes days of jabbing and punching to gain intelligence by each side prior to a pitched battle lasting several hours. In each battle, soldiers learn many lessons about field craft that they could not otherwise learn without engaging in direct combat.

In a six-year enlistment, an active-duty tanker may duel with the OPFOR some fifteen times, learning a wealth of war-fighting skills. The multiple iterations of battle and the knowledge gained from these struggles produce a skilled warrior.

In an average six-year national guard enlistment, a tanker may get one-third of that experience. Most of the tanker's enlistment is spent fighting battles at the platoon level, where the lowest unit echelon is organized. There can be no doubt that guardsmen would benefit from more iterations of training tasks to reinforce war-fighting skills.

Civilian and Military Job Compatibility

Time is not the sole factor that produces an asynchronous effect. I have yet to see a want ad in the Sunday paper seeking a tank commander. The civilian job market just does not use M1A1 Abrams tanks in normal day-to-day business. This is not to say that a national guard tanker does not learn management and leadership skills in the course of training, but the tanker's military and civilian specialties do not have similar applicability. This is also true of the other combat arms branches, such as infantry and artillery.

Some guard specialties, such as engineering, transportation, and logistics, do use skills that directly translate to the civilian workplace. These soldiers and their units take less time to come up to speed once in uniform than tankers, infantrymen, and artillerymen, who function with a completely diverse set of working skills between the two modes of their lives.

Digitizing the national guard is not a simple question of providing units with the proper equipment. Thirty-nine or more days of noncontinuous training per year produce an asynchronous effect that can influence the guard's ability to train with these systems. If the guard makes the digital transition, the factors that produce this asynchronous effect must be attacked directly by unit training plans. Otherwise, these conditions can affect mission accomplishment adversely.

The National Guard Mission

What is the national guard's training mission? To state the obvious, different units have different missions. For simplicity's sake we will examine only the track of a tank battalion within an enhanced brigade of the national guard. This example is relevant to the digitization issue, however, because digitization would affect every soldier in this type of unit.

Enhanced tank battalion training is focused by two primary training regulations. One is Forces Command (FORSCOM)/Army National Guard (ARNG) Regulation 350-2. The other is the Department of the Army Pamphlet 350-38 (Standards in Weapons and Training—STRAC). Together these publications provide guidance on minimum training requirements and levels of resourcing. To meet army premobilization training goals, enhanced national guard armor units annually conduct the tasks listed in Table 1 on the following page.

In addition to what was listed previously, guardsmen are required to complete appropriate professional development schooling to advance through the ranks. Whenever possible, professional development schooling is done in addition to normal unit training requirements.

Guardsmen look at the guidance from these two regulations and conduct whichever requirements are the most restrictive. Some interpolation is required. FORSCOM/ARNG Regulation 350-2 provides training guidance for an entire battalion. The STRAC provides specific guidance for tank crew through platoon levels and no resources for training tasks above that level. The language in Table 1, taken directly from the two publications, allows for some unit in-

Unit	FORSCOM/ARNG 350-2 [3]	STRAC[4]
Individuals	• Individual weapons qualification • Annual physical fitness test	
Tank Platoon	• Crew gunnery proficiency • Platoon maneuver	• Bi-monthly Conduct of Fire Trainer (COFT) exercises • Gunnery Table IV semiannually • 85% of assigned crews annually qualify TableVIII • Annual platoon FTX
Tank Company Tank Battalion	• Conduct sustainment and Command and control Functions from a tactical Configuration using tactical Procedures and systems at the Level organized	
Tank Battalion	• Training for commanders and Staffs include multi-echelon Training to develop (warfighting) skills • Coordination of Annual Training allows realistic Combined arms training	

Table 1 – Pre-Mobilization Training Goals

terpretation. For instance, training staffs "at the level organized" in many brigades means, in effect, conducting orders drills and command-post exercises and deploying all elements to the field during training events. The number of times these tasks are conducted is a function of time, resource availability, training funds, and the approved training plan.

In a nutshell, an enhanced tank battalion must annually produce qualified tank crews; platoons that can move, attack, and defend; and companies and a battalion command group that can command, control, and sustain their elements in the field, employed in a realistic combined-arms manner. This is an enhanced combat arms unit's contract with the army and ensures that it can deploy in a timely fashion. From years of experience in fitting training tasks to available time, I can tell you that this is the most appropriate expectation level that still ensures that guard soldiers conduct training to army standards.

In the case of an armor unit, however, it is not as simple as conducting the primary tasks listed in Table 1. Army Field Manuals 17-12-1-1 and 17-12-1-2 dictate training prerequisites for crew gunnery proficiency that are only touched on by the publications previously mentioned. The current official gunnery training strategy requires extensive preparatory training before crews conduct live-fire qualification.

All crewmen must complete preparatory gunnery training (including such tasks as tank and radio maintenance) and a Tank Crew Gunnery Skills Test (TCGST). Tank commanders and gunners conduct eighteen to twenty-seven hours of exercises in the Conduct of Fire Trainer (COFT). And entire tank crews complete another eight to twelve hours of Abrams Fully Integrated Simulation Trainer training.[5] Finally, crews must successfully complete Tank Table IV using simulation devices such as the tank weapons gunnery simulation system (TWGSS).

After all of these tasks are successfully completed, crews advance to live-fire gunnery. These prerequisites can take from four-and-a-half to six drill weekends to complete. It then takes another two to four weekends to complete qualification gunnery. With additional intermediate gunnery tables, another one to two drill weekends per company are added to complete individual crew qualification. A crew that begins training in August is theoretically capable of completing qualification some time in the February to July annual training timeframe.

If the unit conducts annual training in July, as many as four drills are left to prepare for tactical training. Conducting tactical training requires some preparatory leader instruction, the briefing of members on the unit's plan, and some form of rehearsal before execution. These prerequisites require about one drill period to accomplish, followed by another drill to execute the task. A highly proficient unit can therefore potentially execute two platoon-level training tasks prior to annual training. These tasks would most likely be the platoon mission "move" (in which platoons learn the fundamentals of formations, techniques of movement, and basic battle drills) and either "attack" or "defend." Platoons can potentially arrive at annual training needing to complete only their tactical tasks to meet premobilization training goals.

There is a hitch, of course. If the unit conducts annual training in July, August is usually a month of recovery for maintenance and administrative responsibilities and the unit's annual physical fitness test. November or December drills may include a day set aside for a holiday celebration with families; the other day may be used for annual individual weapons qualification. A unit may also have a requirement to train for natural disaster and/or civil disturbance relief. And it might have to undergo a maintenance, mobilization, or readiness inspection.

Although these tasks are not devoid of relevance, none of them help the unit in meeting the active-duty army's premobilization training requirements. These national guard, state, and immediately higher headquarters' requirements can remove up to four drills from the premobilization training picture. So we return to possibly having only preparatory gunnery requirements completed prior to annual training.

To glimpse across the horizon, a national guard unit that makes a transition to either M1A2 or M1A1-D tanks in the future can expect preparatory gunnery training to take an additional one to two drill periods. Both of these tanks have digital command-and-control components that require additional preparatory and sustainment training. For example, the tank commander must use the onboard digital reporting systems to report the crew's status after each gunnery engagement. This is also likely to be a future requirement for digitally equipped Bradley Fighting Vehicle gunnery. Paladin-equipped field artillery units' digital reporting systems increase training requirements from the number of digital systems already on hand.

If you are a self-taught Windows 95 user and then take formal Windows 95 training, you quickly learn how much of the program you have never used. You also tend to forget tips, tricks, and shortcuts from class if you do not put them into practice. A digital tanker who does not mount a tank for three to four weeks per month is likely to experience the same kind of skill decay. The tanker may need a short operator's refresher course when he or she first climbs on board each month.

The crewmen are not the only ones affected. When does the staff complete its training? Staffs conduct required training parallel to crew preparatory gunnery training. During this time, tank-specific training is conducted at or below the company level, so battalion command and control are not required. The battalion must still provide logistics support to its units, but execution of support tasks does not consume the staff's entire drill. This would be the prime time for digital staffs to conduct proficiency training on the digital software and hardware systems inherent to their operations centers.

Leaders are in an entirely different predicament. A tank company commander fights from a tank, so that commander must train with the company's crews while simultaneously executing command responsibilities. The executive officer is a tanker and the unit's head logistician, and therefore also multitasks. The unit's first sergeant and support elements must come to each drill prepared to provide help with maintenance, logistical, medical, and administrative needs. When do these soldiers complete their predrill leaders' training?

The usual answer for leaders is that they are self-trained. After attending mandatory professional development training, they continue to read, study, and plan at home to make unit drills successful. Home study, however, is normally unstructured and requires no small amount of dedication, since jobs and families require time and attention. As mentioned in this chapter's introduction, leaders' training could use a more solid structure that is unit-training mission-focused. It will be a boost to morale if this training does not require additional time away from home at the unit armory.

So in addition to the challenges created by the very nature of guard training, preparatory and additional requirements serve to limit the number of tasks a unit can successfully complete. Any plans for digitization of the guard must fight these factors if units are to continue to meet premobilization requirements without significantly increasing the required number of unit collective training days. The extensive use of simulations can make this a reality.

Live or Simulated?

Before we can discuss the use of simulations, we must describe how the army defines that training. It is key to know that the army logically thinks of simulations training as a toolbox available to trainers. Within this toolbox are three simulation tools: live simulation, virtual simulation, and constructive simulation.[6] There is also a rational method of training with these three tools based on your echelon of focus and your desired outcome.

Live simulation is a hands-on event using assigned equipment with some form of simulators for weapons systems. An example of a live simulation would be a field maneuver using the newest army laser transmitter/detector sets. In a live event, units at any echelon put tactical vehicles, food, fuel, soldiers, and other necessary resources in the field to conduct training. There is no better training than placing a unit in the field with vehicles that break down, support that arrives late, and units going left when they should have gone right. It is through these adversities—Karl von Clausewitz's "friction"—that leaders are challenged, stressed, and molded. For this reason, evaluating a unit's ability to maneuver is best done in the live mode. If there is a drawback, it is that live simulation is the most expensive and time-consuming event the army conducts in peacetime.

Virtual simulation places individual soldiers and crews in simulators that replicate actual combat vehicles and allow them to "fight" as if they were in the field.[7] The current generation of virtual simulators uses second- and third-generation graphics that allow soldiers to fight on computerized desert (at the National Training Center), woodland (in the central United States and Germany), and soon mountainous (in Korea) terrain. Virtual training is used at various echelons up to and including the battalion level to teach skills such as fire distribution, tactics, techniques and procedures, and command-and-control principles.

Without burning fuel, firing live ammunition, or producing vehicle wear and tear, crews and units learn skills necessary to coordinate their actions in combat. There is also the added benefit of allowing commanders to stop the scenario at any point, dismount the unit, provide its members with constructive feedback about task execution, and then place them back in simulation for more mission training. This can all be done with a few strokes on a computer's keyboard. Virtual training, for its cost, realism, and number of training iterations, is excellent for preparing units to conduct live training missions.

Constructive simulation is usually identified with large-scale computer simulations that replicate units at or above the battalion level.[8] Instead of soldiers crawling into simulator crew compartments, they view their units as icons or game pieces on computer screens. They fight from air-conditioned rooms with good battlefield vision. There is no mud, rain, snow, or heat to deal with. Often, soldiers in constructive training get more rest and therefore suffer less stress than they would in live simulations.

Constructive simulation is best suited for training leaders and staffs in tactical concepts such as how to employ or command and control units in the field. Constructive training requires less powerful and complex computer systems than virtual training, so it is the least expensive method of the three. Many will argue that you get what you pay for, however. Constructive training is not often conducted below the leader level.

These three simulation tools are used differently at diverse echelons. They should also be used creatively in the future. At the individual level, for example, routine tasks and cognitive skills such as tactical decision making can be conducted or trained for by using simulations and computers. The unit administrative and training documentation can be placed on unit computers and made available to individuals with the proper permission. If individual and unit information is placed on a server, any request to change or access it can then be completed by a soldier from his or her home computer.

After the proper software and hardware is purchased or issued, training meetings can be conducted via remote conferencing prior to drills in order to coordinate unit activities. Online components for all of the army's professional development courses can be completed prior to attending a course to reduce the amount of time a soldier is away from his or her home station. Computer-based constructive simulations can be used to train staff officers and enlisted soldiers on battle tasks. Virtual and constructive training matrices can be constructed, as with the Captain Simpson example at the beginning of this chapter, for executing leaders' training tasks, again via conferencing software. And matrices can be developed for leader and staff proficiency training similar to tank crews' use of the army's computerized COFT.

This thought pattern would be of greatest assistance to a national guard M1A1-D or M1A2 tanker. Individual skills such as proficiency in the use of the Intervehicular Information System (IVIS) could be trained for on a home computer using additional peripherals that would provide the look and feel of an actual component. Based on the information already given here, the additional one-to-two drills of M1A2 preparatory gunnery training could theoretically be done at home. Using these technologies, all soldiers could work to dispel the asynchronous nature of time between drills.

At the crew level, virtual simulations using several devices are currently in place at unit armories. A look at current army publications, however, indicates a desire to embed simulations within combat vehicles.[9] This is the best training solution once soldiers arrive at their armories. Wherever there was a tank, a crew would only have to mount up and log on to conduct virtual maneuver, gunnery, and driver's simulations. This would be true even when they were deployed overseas and preparing for missions. However, this training is not best when conducted on home computers; it is important that crews use their combat vehicles physically to learn how to operate in a synchronized manner.

At echelons above the crew level, leaders already conduct constructive training on tactical events at a military installation's simulations center. There is a move afoot, however, to provide constructive simulations capability at unit armories. This would allow for distributed training by units spread within or across state borders desiring to collectively conduct command-post exercises from dispersed locations. A temporary network connection would be established and training would be executed.

Theoretically, this training could be carried down to the individual home personal computer. The question is whether one would want to do this. Digital war fighting will naturally disperse units across more territory. But decisions will still be made based on a staff's input to its commander, and the commander, in turn, will want to look his or her subordinates in the eye before they cross the line of departure. Taking a conservative bent, I cannot back the idea of logging on for every drill activity as opposed to conducting the traditional monthly muster at unit armories.

The active army, because of declining budgets, has taken to using simulations for live training event preparation. The premise is that you should make your mistakes in the simulator before you expend fuel, bullets, and spare parts in a live environment. In a typical training year, the active army uses a combination of virtual and constructive training for most of three quarters, and live training the rest of the time.

Your army national guard does not train in this fashion. Most guard training is in the live mode. With less time to execute tasks, more training benefit is gained from live training. This trend is diminishing, however, as shrinking dollars in national guard coffers tighten belts each year.

A Future Built on Simulated Preparations

If guard units digitize and still expect to maintain the same level of premobilization training, they must use more simulations. A combination of virtual and constructive training from the home will also be necessary to maintain proficiency in digital war-fighting tasks. What might a future digital national guard tank battalion's training year look like?

The year is 2010. You command a national guard enhanced tank battalion with M1A1-D tanks. Your battalion has three fourteen-tank companies, one six-vehicle scout platoon, one four-vehicle mortar platoon, and a staff. It is the time of year when you must determine your next year's training plan.

As has become your custom, for training you intend to directly address the problems of noncontinuous training, training at low echelons, and fewer training iterations resulting from time constraints. Whenever possible, primary training events such as gunnery will be conducted during continuous training days. Maneuver tasks will infuse multiechelon training whenever possible. And to increase repetitions in maneuver training, the unit will conduct several preliminary maneuver tasks in a combination of virtual and constructive environments.

Your training missions, most of which must be done within the required thirty-nine-day limit, include:

1. Military occupational specialty (MOS) training: initial entry and advanced individual training; subsequent and professional development training for tankers, scouts, mortarmen, and the staff.
2. Individual training requirements and administration: pistol/rifle qualification, physical fitness, and administrative tasks.
3. Tank/scout crew gunnery qualification/mortar platoon qualification.
4. Live tank/scout/mortar platoon maneuver (attack and defend tasks).
5. Staff proficiency training.
6. A combination virtual and constructive mission conducted in conjunction with an active-component unit rotation at the National Training Center.
7. If possible, live company-level maneuver training (attack and defend tasks).
8. Support for integrated training with the unit's forward support company.

Your number-one priority is to ensure that soldiers receive proper MOS training. As has been standard practice, all soldiers and officers attend initial MOS training in residence at the appropriate army school or training center. However, subsequent professional schooling has evolved during the last decade and a half. A good portion of officer and noncommissioned officer school is now conducted through a combination of online and distance learning in the unit's distance-learning center.

For the last three years your unit has had a technician run the center from 12:00 P.M. to 8:00 P.M. Tuesday through Friday, and from 10:00 A.M. to 6:00 P.M. on Saturdays of nondrill weekends. Soldiers, their families, and their employers all prefer that they stay at home more than in the past as they conduct this training. (Most of the schools only require two to four weeks of training in residence.)

Individual training requirements such as the annual physical fitness test and weapons qualification require one drill to complete, but individual administration tasks are all conducted online. From their home computers, soldiers dial in to their Internet service providers, connect to their unit servers, access their personal record files, and fill out the digital forms that update these records as necessary. Soldiers can complete myriad routine tasks over the Internet, including ordering new equipment, updating shot records, and forwarding change-of-address information.

Each company or specialty platoon has its own Web page to provide updated personnel, training, or logistics information. Also, the leaders and staff training matrix (LSTM) is posted to a unit application server. The LSTM consists of computer-driven or interactive vignettes that train leaders to make tactical decisions and staffers to conduct orders-planning or battle-tracking tasks properly within the context of tactical situations. A benefit of modernization through the Reserve Component Automation System in the late 1990s, this now-routine occurrence provides several unit benefits: soldiers no longer sacrifice training time for the sake of administrative paperwork; the unit stays abreast of the latest information between drills; and leaders and staff continue to train via the LSTM so that proficiencies are not lost when they are away from the armory.

Some time after the turn of the century, although it was understood that guardsmen would still drill for only thirty-nine days per year, old conventions of "one weekend a month and two weeks in the summer" disappeared. Such is the case in your unit for the sake of garnering continuous training days.

Gunnery is your main training effort. It includes your most technically challenging tasks and takes the most concentrated time and effort to complete successfully. It is because of gunnery requirements that your unit's tankers drill year-round in a more or less conventional fashion. There have been some changes from the conventions of twentieth-century training, however.

Preliminary gunnery training on the M1A1-Ds' drivers integrated display (DID) and IVIS is conducted outside of drills on home computers. (Peripherals that provide a realistic M1A1-D interface are issued to tankers to take home and attach to their PCs. As with the LSTM vignettes, they connect to the training applications server via the Internet and download appropriate training exercises; the server records successful completion of assigned tasks.) Soldiers also conduct the armored fighting vehicle and ammunition-identification tasks of the TCGST online prior to the hands-on portion of the test. This still leaves six months of preliminary gunnery training prior to live-fire qualification. Gunnery requirements for your scouts and mortarmen are less intensive, allowing more time for maneuver.

Maneuver is your secondary training effort. Because of digitization, your unit plans for and executes missions faster. Also, even though the platoon level is your echelon of emphasis, you conduct platoon attack and defend missions under company- and battalion-level command and control. With concentrated maneuver training, you can train on more tasks than you normally could have prior to your digital conversion.

This is required because the army's Force XXI training program mandates an annual national guard and active component integration exercise. Your unit must conduct a simulation that is fully integrated with your affiliated active-duty brigade's rotation at the National Training Center. This exercise, called a Synthetic Theater of War Exercise (STOWEX) consists of your tankers, scouts, and mortarmen in virtual simulators, your staff in their Tactical Operations Center (TOC), and your cohort brigade in the field at the National Training Center.

Your soldiers' virtual simulators are run by small mainframe computers and are tied in to digital systems in your TOC, the active-component brigade's TOC, and the National Training Center operations group. Your soldiers, reinforcing a brigade hasty attack, will fight a virtual enemy that is an extension of the opposing forces' unit at Fort Irwin. As far as the brigade is concerned, they will be fighting with three battalions against a larger-than-normal opposing force. Within another two to three years, you are told, you will have the capability to conduct these exercises using embedded simulations from your unit's M1A1-Ds.

Your yearly training calendar worksheets look like this.

4th Quarter, TY10

Month / Element	JULY	AUGUST	SEPTEMBER
Tankers	Annual Training II	**COs A & B (Home):** Prelim Gunnery Training (DID and IVIS) **COs A & B (Drill):** TCGST/COFT (2 days) **CO C (Home):** LSTM vignettes **CO C (Drill):** Prep for virtual attack (1 day)	**COs A & B (Home):** Prelim Gunnery Training (DID and IVIS) **COs A & B (Drill):** On-board Tank Tables I-II/COFT (2 days) **CO C (Home):** LSTM vignettes **CO C (Drill):** Virtual attack exercise (2 days)
Scouts	Annual Training II	Individual Weapons Qualification and Physical Fitness Test (1 day)	**Home** – LSTM exercises **Drill** – TY11 coordination meeting (1 Day)
Mortars	Annual Training II	Individual Weapons Qualification and Physical Fitness Test (1 day)	**Home** – LSTM exercises **Drill** – TOC Exercise (1 Day)
Staff	Annual Training II	Individual Weapons Qualification and Physical Fitness Test (1 day)	Support virtual attack (1 Day)
Forward Support Company	Annual Training II	Fueler/maintenance Support	Fueler/maintenance support

August and September – Preliminary training for gunnery/maneuver for Fall 2010; Home preparatory gunnery training is via S3 server; LSTM training is via S3 Applications server; COFT matrix and on-board Tank tables I-II training is embedded training on unit tanks; virtual Attack exercise is embedded training on unit tanks; individual weapons qualification is on local firing ranges; staff support of the virtual Attack mission is constructive simulation from the distance learning center and home station TOC vehicles.

1st Quarter, TY11

Month / Element	OCTOBER	NOVEMBER	DECEMBER
Tankers (Cos A&B - 5 days) (Co C - 5 days)	**COs A & B (Home)**: Complete Preparatory Gunnery Training (DID and IVIS) **COs A & B (Drill)**: On-board Tank Table III/COFT (2 days) **CO C (Home)**: LSTM vignettes **CO C (Drill)**: Prep for virtual defend (2 days)	**COs A & B (Home)**: Virtual Tank Table IV **COs A & B (Drill)**: Tank Table IV/COFT (2 days) **CO C (Home)**: LSTM vignettes **CO C (Drill)**: Virtual defend (2 days)	**COs A & B (Home)**: Virtual Tank Table VIII **COs A & B (Drill)**: On-board Tank Table VIII/Family Day (1 Day) **CO C (Home)**: LSTM vignettes **CO C (Drill)**: Virtual exercise retraining (1 day)
Scouts (4 days)	Preparatory Gunnery Training (1day)	Scout Table IV (2 days)	Preparatory Gunnery Training/Family Day (1 Day)
Mortars (4 days)	Mortar Gunners' Exam (1 day)	Mortar Live Fire Exercise (2 days)	Mortar Gunners' Exam/ Family Day (1 Day)
Staff (3 days)	**Home** – LSTM Exercises **Drill** – TOC Exercise (1 Day)	Support virtual defend (1 day)	Family Day (1 Day)
Forward Support Company	Fueler/maintenance Support	Fueler/maintenance Support	Support Battalion control

October, November and December - Preparatory gunnery training is via S3 server; LSTM training is via S3 applications server; COFT matrix and on-board Tank Table III and VIII training is embedded training on unit tanks; Tank Table IV is fired via live simulation (TWGSS) at the unit's local training area; on-board TTVIII is embedded training on unit tanks; Scout Table IV/mortar live fire exercise are live fire at the unit's mobilization station; TOC exercise is constructive simulation at the unit distance learning center; staff support of virtual Defend mission is constructive simulation from distance learning center and home station TOC vehicles.

2nd Quarter, TY11

Month / Element	JANUARY	FEBRUARY	MARCH
Tankers (Cos A&B - **18** days) (Co C - **10** days)	**COs A & B (AT I)**: Tank Table VIII Qual (3 days drill; 7 days AT) **CO C (Home)**: Prelim Gunnery Training (DID and IVIS) **CO C (Drill)**: TCGST/COFT (2 days)	**COs A&B (Home)**: LSTM vignettes **COs A&B (Drill)**: Prep for virtual attack (1 day) **CO C (Home)**: Prelim Gunnery Training (DID and IVIS) **CO C (Drill)**: On-board Tank Tables I-II/COFT (2 days)	**Cos A&B (Home)**: LSTM vignettes **Cos A&B (Drill)**: Virtual attack exercise (2 days) **CO C (Home)**: Complete Prelim Gunnery Training (DID and IVIS) **CO C (Drill)**: On-board Tank Table III/COFT (1 day)
Scouts (**18** days)	Scout Table VIII/ support Mortar training/Patrolling **(AT I)** (3 days drill; 7 days AT)	**Scouts (Home)**: LSTM vignettes **Scouts (Drill)**: Virtual screen mission (2 days)	**Scouts (Home)**: LSTM vignettes **Scouts (Drill)**: Virtual area recon mission (2 days)
Mortars (**18** days)	Mortar Platoon Evaluation **(AT I)** (3 days drill; 7 days AT)	Mortar Battle Drills training (2 days)	Mortar Gunner's Exam (2 days)
Staff (**6** days)	**Home** – LSTM Exercises **Drill** - TOC Exercise (1 day)	**Home** – LSTM exercises **Drill** - TOC Exercise (1 day)	**Home** – LSTM exercises **Drill** - Support virtual attack (1 day)
Forward Support Company	AT I Support Package	Fueler/maintenance Support	Fueler/maintenance Support

January, February and March – Cos A&B **AT I** is total of 10 days at mobilization station [Tank Table IV refires via TWGSS, Tank Table VII (Modified) and TTVIII are live fire]; After **AT I**, Cos A, B & C reverse training cycles from previous months; Scout **AT I** is total of 10 days at mobilization station [Scout Table VII (Modified) and Scout Table VIII are live fire; support of mortar training is with call for fire exercise; patrolling training is live simulation and live fire]; Scout LSTM training is via S3 applications server; Scout virtual screen and area recon training is embedded training performed on unit scout vehicles; Mortar platoon evaluation is a total of 10 days at mobilization station (dry- and live fire maneuver); Mortar battle drill training is live simulation retraining in local training area; the Forward Support Company provides a support slice for **AT I**; TOC exercise is constructive simulation at the unit distance learning center; staff support of virtual Attack mission is constructive simulation from distance learning center and home station TOC vehicles.

3rd Quarter, TY11

Month / Element	APRIL	MAY	JUNE
Tankers (Cos A&B - 24 days) (Co C - 24 days)	**Cos A&B (Home)**: LSTM vignettes **Cos A&B (Drill)**: Prep for virtual defend (2 days) **CO C (Home)**: Virtual Tank Table IV **CO C (Drill)**: Tank Table IV/COFT (2 days)	**COs A&B (Home)**: LSTM vignettes **COs A&B (Drill)**: Virtual defend (2 days) **CO C (Home)**: Virtual Tank Table VIII **CO C (Drill) (AT I)**: Tank Table VIII Qual (3 days drill; 7 days AT)	AT Prep (2 days)
Scouts (24 days)	**Scouts (Home)**: LSTM vignettes **Scouts (Drill)**: Virtual zone recon mission (2 days)	**Scouts (Home)**: LSTM vignettes **Scouts (Drill)**: Patrolling training (2 days)	AT Prep (2 days)
Mortars (24 days)	Mortar Live Fire Exercise (2 days)	Mortar Gunner's Exam (2 days)	AT Prep (2 days)
Staff (10 days)	**Home** – LSTM Exercises **Drill** - TOC Exercise (1 day)	**Home** – LSTM exercises **Drill** – Support virtual defend (1 day)	AT Prep (2 days)
Forward Support Company	Fueler/maintenance Support	AT I Support Package (-)/fueler & maintenance support	Support Battalion control

April, May and June – Tank gunnery and maneuver training is per similar events in previous months; Scout LSTM training is via S3 applications server; Scout virtual zone recon training is embedded training performed on unit scout vehicles; Scout patrolling is live simulation training in local training areas; Mortar live fire exercise is live fire at the unit's mobilization station; Staff TOC exercise and support of virtual Defend mission is per similar events in previous months; Forward support company provides a small support package for Co C **AT I**; AT prep is standard leader and soldier personal and equipment maintenance.

4th Quarter, TY11

Month / Element	JULY	AUGUST	SEPTEMBER
Tankers (Cos A, B &C - 39 days)	**ALL** – Maneuver AT (**ATII**) (2 days drill; 8 days AT) : - Platoon Battle Drills - Company Attack - Company Defense	**ALL** – STOWEX (3 days)	**COs B & C (Home)**: Prelim Gunnery Training (DID and IVIS) **COs B & C (Drill)**: TCGST/COFT (2 days) **CO A (Home)**: LSTM vignettes **CO A (Drill)**: Prep for virtual attack (2 day)
Scouts (39 days)	**ALL** – Maneuver AT (**ATII**) (2 days drill; 8 days AT) : - Platoon Battle Drills - Zone/Area Recon - Screen	**ALL** – STOWEX (3 days)	Individual Weapons Qualification and Physical Fitness Test (2 days)
Mortars (39 days)	**ALL** – Maneuver AT (**ATII**) (2 days drill; 8 days AT) : - Platoon Battle Drills - Support Attack - Support Defense	**ALL** – STOWEX (3 days)	Individual Weapons Qualification and Physical Fitness Test (2 days)
Staff (10 days)	(**AT**) – Staff training & maneuver support (9 days drill; 15 days AT): - Support/C2 maneuver training - Constructive NTC rotation	**ALL** – STOWEX (3 days)	Individual Weapons Qualification and Physical Fitness Test/ TY12 prep (2 days)
Forward Support Company	ATII Support Package	Fueler/maintenance support	Fueler/maintenance support

July, August and September – AT II is all live maneuver at unit mobilization station; entire Forward Support Company drills with the battalion; Staff constructive NTC rotation is conducted from distance learning center and TOC vehicles and is linked to cohort brigade headquarters at the NTC; STOWEX is virtual and constructive training from unit mobilization station simulation center and TOC vehicles and is linked to live cohort brigade at NTC for hasty attack (continuous with Staff's **AT** period); September training is similar to August 2010 training with Co A as the unit beginning maneuver training and Cos B & C beginning with gunnery training; individual weapons qualification is live fire on local ranges.

After reading through the worksheets, you might wonder how much of what is offered is fiction. Currently, there are no established plans to digitize the national guard. It is a funding issue; M1A2 tanks cost almost twice as much as the nondigital M1A1s, for instance. The active army does not even know whether it can afford to digitize past the initial corps that is planned in the early twenty-first century. Although there are rumors of efforts to field M1A1-Ds to the national guard, digitization must become a reality if we are to field a truly seamless force.

Conducting portions of professional development schooling via the Internet or distance learning is a reality. Guardsmen and active-duty soldiers deployed for a peacekeeping rotation to the Sinai in the mid-1990s conducted the primary leadership development course via distance learning with Fort Bliss, Texas. In addition, the reserve component armor officer advanced course went online for two phases, with only two weeks in residence, beginning in October 1998. This is but a beginning to what I believe will be the norm within a decade.

The practice of guardsmen drilling one weekend per month and two weeks in the summer is currently the prevailing technique. But if leaders were to think unconventionally, they would see that changing this technique would provide what would in effect be extra continuous training days. This would be highly beneficial for a staff that needs continuous training days to achieve proficiency in operational planning and execution and is not needed to command and control crew-level training.

Splitting everyone's annual training periods into distinct gunnery and maneuver iterations would allow for concentrated training on each event. In addition, there would be potential for less training asset strain with a unit's mobilization station. And employers and family might be able to do better without their soldiers for shorter spans of time. As a bottom line, this concept is nothing more than a technique that could be employed by any unit at any time.

Home training via the Internet and unit servers could happen today. In fact, many units already have informational Web pages for their soldiers to access. The missing ingredients to conduct this training, however, are (for some) unit and personal computer hardware, training matrices, and peripherals that replicate digital command-and-control components. Although computer prices have declined sharply during the last year, hardware is still cost-prohibitive for some. As the reserve component automation system brings computers and servers to units, however, this training can be a reality. Training matrices need only be developed at the appropriate training centers. Peripherals necessary to conduct home training may be as simple as software interfaces and joysticks of some kind.

Embedded training in combat vehicles is a process currently under development. When it is completed and in use, tremendous cost savings will be realized through the placement of simulations inside a vehicle instead of on several different expensive platforms. The linking of live, virtual, and constructive training is also progressing. It can be accomplished in a limited fashion right now. However, the training goal of making linked events seamless with those in training is not yet a reality. Mark my words: units will one day conduct STOWEXs as discussed previously. You will even find elements that are preparing to rehearse their missions and synchronize their actions via STOWEX simulation on the digitized terrain where they are destined to fight.

Conclusion

The entire army must digitize to support the "one team, one fight, one future" concept. This undertaking is costly. While the army steadily shrinks, you would think that more money would be available to build a digital force. One need only read the annual arguments from commanders at budget time, however, to understand that cost savings actually only allow them to do more of the required tasks they have had to stave off. If we are to digitize the entire force, we have to find more initial capital outlay for new equipment.

At a time in history when we seem to have found the correct expectations for national guard training, digitization potentially adds additional requirements to an already full training plate. For the guard to modernize successfully, the aforementioned challenges that conspire to produce an asynchronous training effect must be attacked at every turn. That means leaders must continue to work more than their normal thirty-nine collective days of training to meet requirements.

However, using current off-the-shelf technology, additional requirements can be met at home from a soldier's computer.

Throughout this transition, a liberal dose of simulations training will be conducted to save money and buy back time at all events. Simulators are already in wide use to conduct training on many tasks. A healthy mix of online and embedded simulations training will one day work to teach the basic building blocks necessary to properly execute live training and missions in the field.

The entire process may require commanders to think out of the box and conduct the national guard's thirty-nine annual days of training in unconventional ways. Our prevailing goal should be to produce continuous training days. This is especially pertinent for technical ground tasks such as tank gunnery and for higher-echelon synchronization tasks for staffs.

I must say that in my time in uniform, I have never known anything worthwhile to be simple. Digitizing the national guard is no exception. But it is a leap well worth taking to build a force that deploys in a coordinated and coherent fashion alongside its active-duty counterparts. When we make the decision and commit the resources to do so, we will truly have one team, one fight, and one future.

Author's Note

I would like to acknowledge the men and women of the 256th Infantry Brigade with whom I now train, and may one day fight; the troopers of 1st Squadron, 124th Cavalry, who raised me from a new lieutenant to a junior captain from 1984 to 1991; the motivated troopers of 2-1 Cavalry from Reforger '87 and 1-4 Cavalry from Reforger '88; the outstanding soldiers of 1st Brigade, 3d Armored Division, who went to Hohenfels as OPFOR in August 1989; and the men and women who make the National Training Center the training ground it is today. These patriots have all had a hand in molding me as I have progressed in my career. I would not be the officer

I am without the experiences I have shared with them in the past and hope to experience in the future.

Lastly, I have to acknowledge my four-year-old nephew, Austin Scott Pryor. I need only a few minutes in his delightful presence to remember why I swore to protect and defend the Constitution of these United States. I will bear any sacrifice to keep him from ever displaying the terror and anguish carved deeply into the faces of children in war-torn countries across the seas.

Notes

1. Gen. Dennis J. Reimer, *One Team, One Fight, One Future* (Washington, D.C.: Office of the Chief of Staff of the Army, 30 June 1998).

2. Personal experience.

3. Department of the Army, *FORSCOM/ARNG Regulation 350–2 (Reserve Component Training in America's Army)* (Fort McPherson, Ga.: Headquarters, U.S. Army Forces Command; and Washington, D.C.: National Guard Bureau, 1 January 1994), 27–29.

4. Department of the Army, *Standards in Weapons Training* (Washington, D.C.: Headquarters, Department of the Army, 3 July 1997), 3–5, 18.

5. Department of the Army, *Field Manual 17–12–1–2 [Tank Gunnery (Abrams)]* (Fort Knox, Ky.: U.S. Army Armor School, 5 May 1998), 13–6, 13–8, 13–9, 13–23.

6. National Simulation Center, *Training with Simulations* (Fort Leavenworth, Kan.: Combined Arms Center, November 1996), 34–35.

7. Ibid.

8. Ibid.

9. Claude W. Abate, Hubert A. Bahr, and John M. Brabbs, "Embedded Simulation for the Army After Next," *Armor* (July-August 1998): 41–44.

Daniel P. Bolger

Colonel Dan Bolger (Ph.D.) is a professional infantry officer. His service has taken him to units across the globe within the U.S. light infantry community. These assignments qualify him to offer a unique perspective on how these elite units might face the future. He is the author of several books, including *Death Ground: America's Infantry in Battle* (1998), *The Battle for Hunger Hill* (1996), *Savage Peace* (1995), *Americans at War* (1992), and *Dragons at War* (1989). He also penned the novel, *Feast of Bones.* As a recent graduate of the U.S. Army War College, his professional credentials are complete.

In this essay Bolger examines the course and direction of digitization as it applies to the light infantry. Looking into the near future (the next ten to twenty years), Bolger places before us an absolute best-case scenario and then brings us back to reality as he sets out the most probable course of equipment capabilities and budgetary realities. Because these observations deal with the funding and purchase of equipment and organizational change, they are strategic in nature. These hard observations, earned as only a soldier can earn them through years of experience, suggest that many of the projections of the techies are likely to be more dream than reality. Bolger shows us the possible, as well as the probable, in what we might expect to get for our high-tech dollar.

The Electric Pawn: Prospects for Light Forces on the Digitized Battlefield

Admiral Motti: This station is now the ultimate power in the universe. I suggest we use it!

Darth Vader: Don't be so proud of this technological terror you've constructed. The ability to destroy a planet is insignificant next to the power of the Force.

Admiral Motti: Don't try to frighten us with your sorcerer's ways, Lord Vader. Your sad devotion to that ancient religion has not helped you conjure up the stolen data tapes or given you clairvoyance enough to find the Rebels' hidden base (uh, argh . . . (choking)

Darth Vader: I find your lack of faith disturbing.

—From the motion picture *Star Wars*[1]

The CV-23 Owl tilt-rotors descended swiftly, their awkward outlines black on black, dimly silhouetted against the restless tropical night skies. Two hot yellow sparks lanced out from one hovering gunship, their dull reports masked in the growing roar of the arriving tilt ships. With that double shot, the blue taxiway lamps and harsh white terminal complex floodlights blinked out, leaving the largely empty runways and parking ramps as black as the clouded heavens. And out there, unseen but felt like the hot breath of death, the Owls came down.

The CV-23s dropped neatly, touching in pairs and fours at various points around the unlit international airport. Each buglike tilt-rotor disgorged some two dozen black-clad men, themselves insectlike with their bulbous nightscope helmet rigs and deadly mandibles spitting unseen bullets. Invisible to the naked eye but bright as stars to the black bug-men, auto-rifle laser spotters painted scrambling defenders. Some of these surprised opponents shot back wildly, but the black warriors scythed them down, knocking them off roofs or out of windows with unerring accuracy. The airbase fighters sprayed a lot of bullets to little effect. The insect warriors from above needed only a few, but all of those counted.

Within minutes many of the airport's security force had fallen, gunned down before they even saw who shot them. The bulk of the others dropped their submachine guns and raised their arms, stunned, cowed, and utterly finished in less time than would be used for the average network television commercial break.

To onlookers, most notably a fortuitously placed news camera crew in the main passenger terminal, it all happened incredibly fast. On the film the entire operation went by in a flash: twin explosions, lights doused, a whirl of Owl rotors, the rattle and bark of small-arms fire, and then those lithe, relentless, black soldiers, seemingly conjured out of the night shadows.

Even in slow motion with a voiceover and halts, the video record breathed speed—purposeful velocity aimed right where it needed to go. Impotent control tower, abandoned generator/power rooms, confused terminals, darkened hangers, unmanned workshops, inert radar platforms—every key facility changed hands in minutes. Indeed, the entire sprawling airport went over just as rapidly. One minute it belonged to the regime. And then it became property of Task Force Eagle, U.S. Army. Long columns of prisoners, hands on their heads, lined up in range of the news crew. The videotape ground on, a long postgame show after a brutally effective one-round knockout.

Groping for terms to address what the unblinking camera so ably depicted, the reporter on the scene gestured over his shoulder at a pair of killer bug-men moving through the television picture frame. "It's like they knew exactly where to land, exactly where to go, and exactly where to shoot."

Exactly.

Digitization: What Can We Really Expect?

Digitization of U.S. forces promises to use modern information technology to share a common picture of friendlies, foes, and the environment. Instead of casting about to reel in wandering armed comrades, struggling to match up maps and compasses with unfamiliar ground, or hunting over hill and dale in search of bad-tempered, sneaky opponents, it all just comes in courtesy of microchips and data bits. All knowledge, all the time; and sure of themselves, U.S. forces can act quickly and shoot surely. What Third World enemy can hope to compete with that kind of military?

Digitization is a typically American solution, pioneered by the country's sea and air forces. Faced for decades with numerically superior Soviet foes, the U.S. Navy and U.S. Air Force decided to emphasize early detection and target discrimination to sort out the various implements winging, pinging, and zinging their way. Surface naval ships and naval aircraft have long shared the big picture, epitomized by the Aegis cruisers and destroyers and the E-2C Hawkeye airborne warning and control system (AWACS). Similarly, Air Force E-3C Sentry AWACS planes routinely direct today's flying circuses.

Since the joint service initiatives of the 1980s, the U.S. Navy and Air Force have talked to each other via digital streams, sharing their views of the air and sea situations. Right now over Iraq and the Balkans, U.S. Navy and Air Force AWACS can see every friendly, neutral, or hostile device in the skies. The friendlies blip back with encrypted transponders, saying, "Shoot me not," among other things. Neutrals and enemies can be identified by other means, such as characteristic radar signatures, with some degree of confidence. Tied into satellites that track hot missile exhausts and computers that plot trajectories, the Americans can truly claim that when it comes to bad guys, if it flies, it dies, and fast.[2]

Of course, all those transponder links and radar eyes get kind of mixed up when you get near the ridges and valleys. The flyboys call it "ground clutter." The U.S. Army and Marine Corps call it home. Organizing all of that confused, intractable ground clutter amounts to the purpose of digitization. If the United States pulls it off, then the technology of AWACS will extend all the way down to the rifleman, and everyone will be able to see the same broad, dynamic view.

Never averse to pumping up the volume, brigades of eager manufacturers and regiments of energetic contractors sell some snake oil along with the Gatorade. Jumping on the digital bandwagon and scenting big dollars, various firms promise a transparent battlefield (luckily only for our side). Certain visionaries assure us that constant awareness of our own positions will do much to smooth out the friction so characteristic in all human conflict. Some people claim that digital hookups can blow aside the fog of war that shrouds the terrain and the foe. Extreme advocates even propose that future digitized soldiers will know so much more than their opposition that they will be able to smash them in a single calculated attack with very limited damage to nearby innocents.[3] All knowledge, all the time—to echo Dick Vitale, "Awesome baby!"

Well, maybe . . . if it were so. But it's not quite that good a deal, all slick brochures and PowerPoint slide shows to the contrary. You see, we already know what this will look like when it works. And no, based on what we have seen, digitizing ground units does not revolutionize land warfare. But it gives an edge to the guy who has the technology and knows how to trust and use the stuff. In a game of inches, we'll take a few however we can get them.

How do we know what to expect? The U.S. Army digitized the battlefield at the National Training Center at Fort Irwin, California, in 1985. Virtually every tank, helicopter, truck, and rifle squad got a transmitter to beam its location to a central collection station. At that time, it was done to facilitate training. The information went to a neutral operations group that controlled the action between visiting brigades and the local opposing force regiment. The group used the data to depict battles during postclash after-action reviews (AARs).[4] With thousands of soldiers engaged on rough desert ground, sorting out who went where, who shot John, and why it happened all became a challenge. Digitizing the player forces was the solution.

Participants often remembered events differently than they had actually happened. Who could blame them? You only see so much of a two-hundred-vehicle scrum from your own tank turret; it's like watching the Super Bowl through a soda straw. To ensure that the soldiers at the AARs truly understood what had happened in their mock fights, the operations group officers and noncommissioned officers replayed parts of their displays. Fascinated commanders watched little red and blue icons motor about and swap simulated rounds. More than a few wondered what it might be like to see that picture before and during the battle, not just in the AAR process.

The impressive graphic light shows hid some frictions. Even at the National Training Center, not all vehicles or soldiers got digitized. Lots of things and lots of people went through Fort Irwin rotations without ever showing up on anyone's computer monitor. In addition, only about 80 percent of the stuff with transponders could be tracked at any one time.[5] Tanks went down in crevasses, soldiers went behind ridges, and radio waves did not transmit through hot rocks. Black boxes broke. The friendly screen proved a bit blurry, a bit frayed, and maddeningly incomplete. We can expect as much with any future systems. It's that damned ground clutter again.

Speaking of ground clutter, the National Training Center terrain and weather data proved pretty good. Because the U.S. Army had been at the post since 1942, mapping and surveying accurately depicted most key terrain. Some details got missed on the maps or even the satellite photos, hidden by shadows, blowing dust, and outright mistakes. As for the desert climate, well, even computers cannot reliably predict all forms of weather. The digitized environmental knowledge at the National Training Center approached a 90 percent correct reading, but that last 10 percent could drive strong men to their knees. Sometimes they literally stumbled into unexpected ditches or breasted unanticipated sandstorms.

And that's in a place we have used for more than fifty years. It won't go so well in the unpleasant garden spots that become U.S. battlegrounds. Mapping and surveying, even by satellite, are least complete in some of the very places the United States may someday go to fight in Africa, South America, and the Asia/Pacific region. Maybe we should plan on an 80 percent correct image of the turf and weather at our eventual destination and be glad for that.

That relatively high degree of confidence in environmental information will not extend to information about active opposing forces. Because the enemies at the National Training Center responded to the local U.S. Army chain of command, they too kept about 80 percent of their fighters online at any given instant. That suited the trainers there quite well, but real foes will not play along. Even allowing for the great intelligence downlinks possessed by the United States, bad guys will hide and deceive. Those countermeasures will work some of the time.[6] Showing the enemy with 50 percent certainty would amount to pretty good work.

Thus, our National Training Center experience points to what we can count on for digitized ground combat: 80 percent accuracy for ourselves, 80 percent for the environs, and 50 percent for the opponents. You can debate the precision of the resolution, but given all the variables, that's probably as good as it gets.

The Digitized Light Fighter: Toward Checkmate

Even with an 80/80/50 degree of knowledge of self, land, and enemy, U.S. forces can definitely begin to garner the benefits of vastly improved situational awareness. To date, most of these efforts have focused on heavy formations in major conventional combat—just what you would expect from an initiative born from Soviet-driven AWACS developments and the armored conflicts of Fort Irwin's National Training Center. But what about the light forces? How can they benefit from this technology?

By light forces, we mean the infantry-based contingents of the U.S. Army and Marine Corps. They are characterized by speed of deployment, measured in hours in many cases. Most can blast their way into a hostile country, some from nearby bases, others directly from their stateside garrisons. Their biggest weakness involves staying power. Though arguably elite in personnel selection and tactics, they lack powerful armor and robust service support. If they are strongly opposed by a foe with lots of tanks and lots of guts, it could get ugly. Digitization might assist in that equation.

Army light units include the ranger, airborne, air assault, and light infantry organizations, each featuring distinctive organization, training, and mission profiles. All parachute-qualified, the rangers field a three-battalion regiment (about twenty-two hundred soldiers) and conduct special operations including raids, runway seizures, and supporting missions for elite counterterrorist units.

Army airborne units focus on transcontinental forced entry, conducting night parachute assaults from U.S. Air Force transports. They compose the 82d Airborne Division (some seventeen thousand soldiers) and separate parachute battalion task forces (up to eight hundred soldiers each) in Italy and Alaska.

Army heliborne outfits reside in the 101st Airborne Division (air assault—about eighteen thousand soldiers), with a pair of battalions in the 2d Infantry Division as well. These forces concentrate on long-range vertical envelopments of up to ninety miles of hostile positions, deep raids, and forced entry assaults from regional staging bases.

Finally, the U.S. Army's light infantry forms into two divisions, the 25th (roughly eleven thousand soldiers) and the 10th Mountain (about nine thousand soldiers), and the 172d Infantry Brigade (approximately two thousand soldiers). These highly trained light fighters specialize in night fighting, dominance of urban and rough terrain, and saturation patrolling. They specialize in long foot infiltrations over allegedly impassable ground.[7] In recent years, army light forces have deployed for combat as battalions, brigades, and divisions, always bringing in a combined arms team including light artillery, aviation, engineers, signal, logistics, and usually a small armored backup team.

The U.S. Marines field three divisions: the 1st (some twenty-four thousand), 2d (closer to twenty thousand), and 3d (about twelve thousand). Marines fight by divisions and regiments in major wars such as World War II, Korea, Vietnam, and the Gulf War. But more often, marines deploy in U.S. Navy amphibious shipping as marine expeditionary units (special operations capable), or MEU (SOC). An MEU (SOC) includes an infantry battalion reinforced with a few tanks and light armored vehicles and a battery of six-towed-155mm howitzers, plus engineers, signalers, and the like. An aviation squadron of up to thirty aircraft also goes along to form the inseparable marine air-ground team made famous in World War II Pacific fighting and perfected since.

To keep the marine riflemen shooting and the marine airmen flying, the MEU (SOC) also includes a service support group with a full fifteen days worth of supplies, all optimized for over-the-shore delivery. Among other capabilities, an MEU (SOC) can make an opposed forced-entry beach or port landing, pull out endangered U.S. citizens (a common task), or launch a raid from the sea. On most days, three of these MEU (SOC) formations steam along the fringes of foreign shores.[8]

Digitizing such light forces means putting reliable compact transceivers on every truck, every aircraft (so far, so good), and every rifleman (uh oh). That final requirement is the heart of the matter. In light forces, hundreds or thousands of individual soldiers and marines on foot represent the ultimate arm of decision. To make digitization work, each trigger puller must share the same big picture—all knowledge, all the time. If the military can pull that off, the results could be very significant.

Although friction will not be eliminated or even substantially reduced, and the fog of war will continue to drift hither and yon, there will be some noteworthy advantages available to trained light fighters. Digitization offers three crucial enhancements for forces only too used to being outnumbered and sometimes outgunned. Each one helps a lot.

First, the unit with situational awareness can better maintain its bearings in urban warrens, congested jungles, and convoluted mountain outcroppings, not to mention under cover of darkness, all the preferred fighting arenas of U.S. light contingents. Right now such fights consume infantry by the gross because we have a hard time finding the enemy. When we do, we then have too many soldiers out of place, and they tend to get shot up as they struggle to march to the sound of the guns—no easy task in constricted, twisting streets or forests choked with undergrowth. Despite all the great night-vision devices, it still gets dark at night, and a fuzzy telescope stuck to your face does not daytime make.

When we can share a fairly good view of ourselves and the ground, and at least a common agreement about the emerging picture of the other side, then we can move out and fire away in any terrain, day or night. The few minutes or even seconds gained on the opposition may well make all the difference in the world.[9] If you turn a corner or enter a room and know that the armed men you see are not your buddies, you come up firing, likely while the badniks are still taking their weapons off "safe." It's hard to put a price on that bit of knowledge, but it surely separates the quick from the dead. Currently, we rely on training alone to give us that edge.

The second benefit relates to the first and again gains time, widely acknowledged to be the most valuable currency of combat.[10] If a relatively accurate common battle map is available, subordinate leaders can continue to fight, shoot, and move with better assurance. Right now units must hold up to get oriented as they enter new city blocks or cross into unfamiliar wooded areas. How many squads have been ambushed while checking soggy maps or debating whether to go right or left?

With a heads-up display portraying friends and terrain pretty well, young noncommissioned officers and lieutenants will have much more opportunity to keep up the pressure rather than backing off to await orders. In addition, units will be less likely to run off on their own or "split from the herd," a worthy thought in a complex, three-dimensional, house-to-house firefight. Knowing where you are is important, but so is knowing where you are not. After all, there may be enemies, and that's always worth knowing.

Finally, a digitized light unit can more quickly recover from the confusion that usually accompanies its inaugural events: an airborne, air assault, or amphibious forced-entry operation. In such circumstances, the side that gets unscrewed first will win. Right now U.S. units have to land right on their targets, or pretty close, to ensure that enough combat power shows up intact to do the job. It's simply too hard to get organized for follow-on missions anywhere but in the local neighborhood.[11] If U.S. troops could immediately locate most of their comrades and figure out where they were on the ground, with a partial read on the enemy, then matters would improve a great deal. Effort could go toward defeating the foe rather than assembling squads and platoons. Again, this would be an edge of minutes, or an hour or so at the most, but it could make a hard job easier for our people.

These advantages accrue to a trained, disciplined force that adds them to well-honed close-combat skills. They are not magic wands that guarantee victory when wielded by any guy dragged in off the street. No, to open these slight windows of opportunity—and to have the combat savvy to exploit them—you need trained experts, probably more so than ever. When made available in bulk, digitization promises to turn today's light force knife fight in a dark alley into a bloody game of human chess. We'll see the board as a whole, even though our opponent will try his hardest to beat us. If we do this right, we'll increase the chances that we win by checkmate most of the time.

Rocks in the Rucksack: Stalemate

OK, this all sounds great—if it works. U.S. soldiers and marines have heard this story before, and yet somehow it always comes down to a man with a rifle banging into an unexpected opponent full of bad attitude. More than a few previously advertised wonder weapons have not exactly panned out as hoped. What are the challenges that endanger today's attempts to digitize America's light fighters?

Clearly, we have to raise legitimate concerns about the size, weight, and durability of information hardware. We are not there yet—not by a long shot. The present prototypes are heavy, bulky, and fragile and eat equally heavy, bulky, and fragile batteries like a fat man on a junk food binge. Industry claims it can reduce and harden the devices and points to examples from other lines of work. True, you can fix up a gray wolf tracking collar that weighs an ounce and traces the critter uphill and down, but nobody expects to tell Mr. Wolf to do anything, let alone to have him talk back.

The proposed U.S. Army Land Warrior weighs more than forty pounds and does all kinds of great digital tricks, but that forty pounds comes in addition to the other hundred pounds or so a rifleman already carries. Imagine carrying another guy on your back forever and you get the idea. You cannot fight like that no matter how much physical training you do.[12] It does no good to gain minutes or seconds when you cannot move fast enough to benefit from them. Some skinny guy in a T-shirt with an AK-47 will have his way with you.

Worse, the boxes go on the blink a lot. Troops can be hard on their tools. Pentium computer chips were never designed to absorb the compression of parachute-landing falls or the passage of jagged grenade fragments. Plus, as any laptop owner knows, when it goes out, it goes out completely. "Abort, retry, fail?" are not good options to have on your eyepiece screen when somebody is shooting at you.

The cost of these items cannot be overlooked. The heavy, finicky systems in testing cost about $167,000 per soldier, roughly the price of a nice family home. Even under the most optimistic contemporary plans, only a fraction of our soldiers and marines will be outfitted with Land Warrior kinds of rigs.[13] (And who wants to talk about our less affluent allies?) By not digitizing the entire frontline force, we tell our enemies where to strike. The foe only sees targets—the softer the better. For our part, we put a lot of non-trigger pullers in peril because they will not show up on anybody's screen. That 80 percent friendly readout may drop precipitously; no good news there. This is one of those cases in which doing part of the job may be worse than doing none of it at all.

Finally, there is a psychological dimension to this endeavor. We may fool ourselves into thinking that what shows up on our eyepieces is reality. It will always be only a part of reality—probably more than we know, but by no means complete. We may get 80/80/50. We may get more. We may suffer with less. But whereas today riflemen rely on their God-given senses alone, future U.S. ground fighters will need to compare and contrast conflicting inputs from electronic sensors and their natural eyes and ears. The greater the dissonance, the slower they will be to sort it out, and the less sure their resulting actions and reactions will be.

Oddly enough, an incomplete or inept conversion to digitization promises more task loading for already busy soldiers and marines than if we never tried it at all. Once again a nimble teenager with a rusty Kalashnikov may blow gory holes in our putative starship troopers. Low technology might not be elegant, but it kills you just as dead.

The Road Ahead: Ground War with and Without Bill Gates

The U.S. military has been more open to technological advances than most. In this we mirror our society, always hungry for the newest and the latest. The digitization initiatives now under way represent the latest cycle of the military's infatuation with the fruits of science and engineering. Given the promises and challenges of digitizing our light fighters, what can we expect to see during the next decade or so?

Money problems granted, it is a fair bet that we will digitize some of our heavy forces. Armored warfare has always had some similarities to naval and air combat, if only in the limited number of platforms engaged at any one time. It's at best a cast of tens or hundreds, not thousands. Inspecting the inside of an M1A2 Abrams main battle tank suggests more than a passing resemblance to a contemporary fighter jet cockpit or a cruiser fire control center. They are kindred metal souls, all right.

That is where ground digitization has already begun and where we will see its initial prospects fulfilled or frustrated. The funding slope is painfully slow, with the experimental 4th Infantry Division (Mechanized) set to complete conversion in 2000, its brother 1st Cavalry Division in 2004, and the entire III Corps in 2006. That accounts for two of the ten active U.S. Army divisions, neither of them light fighter types.[14] Just getting things running at that languid pace has required tremendous moral courage and tough decisions by senior army leaders, who have learned a few things about squeezing fiscal blood out of stones and turnips.

Even when the U.S. Army gets its initial digitized lineup, the entire force will not be equipped. In each division, only one-third—one fighting brigade—will make the full leap. Another one-third will make do with the appropriately named appliqué systems: off-the-shelf commercial computer gear strapped onto nondigitized tanks and trucks. Imagine sticking your laptop inside a rumbling, bouncing tank, and you get the idea of how well that works. Worse than the appliqué crowd, the third divisional combat brigade and its supporting arms will keep nondigitized legacy weaponry—essentially the same stuff they used in the Gulf War of 1990 to 1991.[15] And that, folks, represents the best case. We could get much worse.

Grim as things may be in the U.S. Army, they are positively rosy compared to prospects for the perennially parsimonious U.S. Marine Corps. Marine efforts have turned primarily toward targeting for long-range jet, helicopter, naval gun, and artillery fires. The marines expect to gain some discrete useful improvements as a result of their ongoing ground combat experiments with situational awareness tools, some conducted jointly with the U.S. Army.[16] Frankly, aside from borrowing appropriate U.S. Army vehicle and aircraft information transceivers, the marine corps must hope that its soldier brothers can cook up a workable Land Warrior suit at a reasonable price.

That appears to be a tall order. If the design freezes today in accord with traditional procurement practices, our light fighters will be saddled with devices that are too heavy, too big, too unreliable, and way too expensive. Worse, only some of our dismounted troops seem likely to get these systems. It sort of reminds you of buying twenty tanks back in 1939—better than none, but you need two thousand, or you get an expensive set of novelties, not blitzkrieg. In the same way, a few thousand starship trooper rigs will not digitize the United States' light forces. Indeed, the items may just serve to complicate and confuse an already dangerous and overly busy battlefield. Nobody wants that outcome except our enemies.

This is one of those things that must be done right across the entire light force or not tried at all. Otherwise the improvements will be marginal at best. Information technology improves daily, so waiting for smaller, cheaper, and sturdier hardware would mean recognizing today's positive trends. Constrained defense dollars may well drive us toward spot experiments and force-wide patience whether we like it or not.

That said, the digits are here to stay. The intelligence and fire support worlds have long used primitive information-exchange devices to speed shells toward the right targets. During the next few decades, as this technology becomes more useful and more widely issued, we can be certain that digitization will change the framework of warfare.

It will not, however, change the face of battle. War remains a highly emotional, deadly clash between human wills. We must never forget that we face thinking enemies out there. Regardless of what we show up wearing, they will not be impressed. Rather, you can be sure that the bad guys will do their level best to kill all of us in the most gruesome way possible. In the words of current U.S. Army Chief of Infantry Maj. Gen. Carl F. Ernst, the rifleman's fight remains "close, personal, and brutal."[17] With or without digitization, some things never change.

Notes

1. Laurent Bouzerau, *Star Wars: The Annotated Screenplays* (New York: Del Ray Books 1997), 115–16.

2. James F. Dunnigan and Austin Bay, *From Shield to Storm* (New York: William Morrow, 1992), 195–96.

3. For the friction of war, see Karl von Clausewitz, *On War,* ed. and trans. Michael Howard and Peter Paret (Princeton, N.J.: Princeton University Press, 1976), 119. For the fog of war, see Clausewitz, *On War,* 117–18, and Bernard Brodie, "A Guide to Reading *On War,*" in Clausewitz, *On War,* 649. Brodie notes that the term "fog of war," though affiliated with Clausewitz's view of intelligence lapses, was actually applied by others.

4. Anne W. Chapman, *The National Training Center Matures, 1985–1993* (Ft. Monroe, Va.: U.S. Army Training and Doctrine Command, 1993).

5. Ibid.

6. For excellent examples of the limits of contemporary U.S. intelligence means during the Gulf War, see Michael B. Gordon and Lt. Gen. Bernard E. Trainor, U.S. Marine Corps (Ret.), *The Generals' War* (Boston: Little, Brown, 1995), 424–26, 429–30, 497–98.

7. Department of the Army, U.S. Army Office of Infantry Proponency, *The Office of Infantry Proponency* (Ft. Benning, Ga.: U.S. Army Infantry School, 15 June 1998), 2–5.

8. U.S. Marine Corps, *FM 1–2: The Role of the Marine Corps in the National Defense* (Washington, D.C.: Headquarters, Marine Corps, 21 June 1991), 4–7 to 4–9, C8. See also GySgt. Bob Newman, U.S. Marine Corps, *Marine Special Warfare and Elite Unit Tactics* (Boulder, Colo.: Paladin Press, 1995), 13–14.

9. For a good discussion of the value of speed of action in close-quarters combat, see Department of the Army, *FM 90-10-1: An Infantryman's Guide to Combat in Built-Up Areas, Change 1* (Washington, D.C.: Government Printing Office, 3 October 1995), K-2.

10. Lt. Col. Robert R. Leonhard, U.S. Army, *The Art of Maneuver* (Novato, Calif.: Presidio Press, 1991), 82. In support of the value of making optimum use of time in war, Leonhard quotes the renowned Napoleon Bonaparte and Russian commander Aleksandr V. Suvorov.

11. Lt. Gen. Edward M. Flanagan, Jr. (Ret.), *Battle for Panama* (McLean, Va.: Brassey's, 1993), 171–76. This section describes the 82d Airborne combat jump in 1989 and the follow-up operations. Issues related to the 82d's combat parachute assault imposed delays on all three subsequent heliborne missions. These attacks occurred in daylight rather than under the cover of darkness. These frictions have typified most parachute landings since the birth of airborne warfare in World War II.

12. Col. S. L. A. Marshall, U.S. Army Reserves, *The Soldier's Load and the Mobility of a Nation* (Washington, D.C.: Combat Forces Press, 1950), 70–73. Marshall cites compelling evidence that a soldier fights most effectively when carrying weight equal to or less than one-third of his body weight.

According to Sandra I. Meadows, "Infantry System Turns Soldier into High-Tech Urban Warrior," *National Defense* (April 1997): 24–25, the U.S. Army's Land Warrior system weighed seventy-five pounds in its 1995 prototype, which was substantially the same as the present model. Based on informed comments by procurement officers, Meadows speculated that the weight could be reduced to as little as fifteen to twenty pounds. The rig is not there yet. In fact, the system displayed at the 1998 Infantry Conference weighed more than forty pounds—that to be added to the other poundage already carried by dismounted riflemen. Assuming an infantryman stripped to bare essentials of water and ammunition, minus a rucksack, we are in the 100-pound range, or up to 150 pounds when you add a sustainment ruck load. Because recruitment of 300–450–pound soldiers seems unlikely, it appears that a high-tech Land Warrior rifleman will far exceed Marshall's long-accepted ideal soldier's load of one-third of the soldier's body weight.

13. Department of the Army, U.S. Army Infantry Center, *Infantry Programs and Projects, 3d Quarter FY 98* (Ft. Benning, Ga.: U.S. Army Infantry Center, 1998), A-7. This project forecasts procurement of only 20,256 Land Warrior ensembles at a total cost of $3,382,700, or a unit price of $166,997.43. Not surprisingly, the Infantry Center considers funding the major issue confronting the program.

14. Gen. William Hartzog, U.S. Army, *Keynote Address and Presentation to the Infantry Conference* (Ft. Benning, Ga.: U.S. Army Infantry School, 9 June 1998), 3–11.

15. Jim Tice, "How Will You Fare in XXI?" *Army Times* (22 June 1998): 12, 15.

16. Maj. John F. Schmitt, U.S. Marine Corps Reserves, "A Critique of the HUNTER WARRIOR Concept," *Marine Corps Gazette* (June 1998): 13–19. This insightful article analyzes one key experiment in the overall Sea Dragon series.

17. Maj. Gen. Carl F. Ernst, U.S. Army, *The State of the Infantry: A Presentation to the Infantry Conference* (Ft. Benning, Ga.: U.S. Army Infantry School, 9 June 1998), 1.

Robert R. Leonhard

Lieutenant Colonel Robert Leonhard (M.A.) is an infantry officer. He is probably the United States' foremost military theorist of this age. In numerous articles and several books he has slowly changed the way that many professional warriors of all services think about the phenomenon of war. His previous books include *The Art of Maneuver* and *Fighting by Minutes*, as well as a new work published in 1998 titled *The Principles of War for the Information Age*.

In late August 1805, the Grande Armeé of France under the personal command of Napoleon Bonaparte stood upon the French coast along the English Channel. Hundreds of miles to the south and east, the land forces of the newly formed Third Coalition, primarily the armies of the Russians and Austrians, started to assemble in preparation for war with the hated Napoleon. In early September one Austrian army under the command of Archduke Ferdinand and General Mack marched into Bavaria to the town of Ulm with fifty-five thousand men. This was roughly eighty miles west of Munich. They had covered no more than two hundred miles total.

Napoleon broke camp along the channel on 26 August 1805. He crossed the Rhine River starting on 25 September 1805.

On 6 October 1805 the lead elements of the Grande Armeé crossed the Danube River northeast of Ulm. On 11 October there were two entire French corps in the vicinity of Munich, with the rest spread to the north and west, moving south and east.

In a series of small but sharp engagements Napoleon made his presence in Bavaria known. On 14 October Archduke Ferdinand opted to leave Mack and the twenty-six thousand Austrians remaining at Ulm to their own devices. Mack, unaware until these last moments that Napoleon was even in the area, was encircled.

Faced with an untenable position and overwhelming odds, on 20 October 1805 General Mack became "The Unfortunate General Mack." He surrendered the entire twenty-six-thousand-man Austrian army remaining under his command at Ulm without firing so much as a shot. French maneuver won the day. The tally at the end of the campaign was roughly two thousand French dead. The bill for the Austrians was four thousand dead and roughly sixty thousand taken prisoner.

Napoleon's men moved four hundred miles in less than sixty days, entirely on foot. Some corps moved an average of eighteen miles per day in the last stretch between the Rhine and the Danube. This is speed. Yet speed is useless without guidance. Military forces need velocity, a vectored quantity that consists of speed and direction.

The motivation, leadership, and movement formations of the Grande Armeé created the speed. The personal genius of Napoleon (as well as his intelligence-gathering apparatus) allowed him to visualize the operational environment far better than his opponents. He provided the direction. Thus the French could capitalize on their velocity to conduct a turning movement against the Austrians and force them to surrender before they could reposition or escape.

In this chapter Leonhard explores the potential future of digitization and suggests that the true revolution available to digital forces is not in the capabilities of the individual systems. Rather, he suggests that it is in the abilities that computers and digital communications give us and how we might use them to create greater velocity that we will see the greatest payoff.

A Culture of Velocity

FROM: Alexander323@aol.com
TO: Thejones@aol.com
SUBJECT: I'm okay!

Dear Mom and Dad,

Sergeant Wilcox told us we can send only a few lines. I am fine, and we have been given peacetime rules of engagement, which I think means the war is over. We have flown over 500 miles in the last few hours, and when we hit the enemy, it was over before it started. I shot a few rounds, but all I hit was an abandoned supply dump. SGT W is yelling, so I gotta go. No official word on when we will return, but I am hopeful it will be soon.

Love,
Alex

Since 1994 the U.S. Army has been digitizing the battlefield. Through a focused application of computer science, position-location technology, and the latest communications improvements, the army has poked its nose into the twenty-first century. The digital battlefield has been born, but with what result? There is no question that the technologies being applied to war-fighting units—both in the army and in the other services—are revolutionary. Yet the doctrines and concepts that attend this modernization effort are still fumbling around at Industrial Age speeds. The U.S. Army desperately requires a culture of velocity.

In this chapter, we will see why the most immediate product of digitization should be an enormous leap ahead in velocity. We will look at the truncated vision the U.S. Army currently has toward the commodity of speed. And finally, we will postulate how increased velocity and the information advantage should result in new fighting techniques.

Hiyo, Silver, Away!

Digitization should be analogous to a hunter who reaches down and unleashes his bird dog. Suddenly unfettered by the traditional restraint of pervasive ignorance, the army should dash into the future of military operations. Instead we are inching forward, unsure of ourselves and unaware of the potential for velocity that we now have.

During the past half-decade, the U.S. Army has conducted extensive experimentation with what is known as situational awareness technology. Essentially, situational awareness is brought about by equipping combat units with onboard computers, position-location devices, and digital communications capability. Through this combination of technologies, each platform—whether it is a tank, a fuel truck, or a foot soldier—can instantaneously and continuously answer three questions that have befuddled soldiers since the beginning of human history:

Where am I?
Where are my buddies?
Where is the enemy?

A moment's reflection on the history of military art and science will confirm that battles, campaigns, and wars have turned on these three questions. For the last four or five millennia, soldiers and leaders have acquiesced in their fundamental ignorance of the battlefield. As a result, the received wisdom we have concerning the art and science of warfare must be suspect. Military doctrines ranging from the revered *Principles of War* to our latest army field manuals are based on a pervasive, immovable blindness. Generals, captains, sergeants, and privates—steeped in pre–Information Age truisms based on the fog of war—can conceive only of an uninterrupted ignorance in battle. Thus constrained, they cannot envision or summon a different future.

The purpose of this chapter is to free ourselves, at least momentarily, from the received wisdom of the past and instead conceive of a radically different future for military operations—a future built around information and velocity.

From 1996 through 1998, I was privileged to participate in the most advanced war-fighting experimentation in the history of our nation. The U.S. Army, under the supervision of Training and Doctrine Command, conducted two major experiments, along with numerous supporting tests and analyses, on the subject of battlefield digitization. In March 1997, the 1st Brigade Combat Team, 4th Infantry Division (Mechanized), stationed at Fort Hood, Texas, deployed to the National Training Center at Fort Irwin, California. This Experimental Force was equipped with prototype situational awareness technology as well as other enhancements (seventy-two initiatives in all). The Experimental Force then fought against the world-renowned professional Opposing Force for more than two weeks in the most rigorous war-fighting environment available to army forces.

The results of this experiment, termed the Task Force XXI Advanced Warfighting Experiment (TFXXI AWE), were controversial even before the experiment ended. In a disappointing display of the ineffable conservatism of soldiers (both retired and active duty), the army proceeded studiously to miss the entire point of the experiment, instead focusing its analytical scrutiny on innocuous details and irrelevant mathematics.

Task Force XXI did not cover itself with glory if the observer looks at the statistical results. This digitized brigade combat team, equipped with experimental technologies that at times were just days out of the laboratory, experienced both grave defeats and startling successes, but mostly just indecisive attrition against the Opposing Force. Because the legions of army analysts who attend such experiments are thoroughly untrained in anything but ham-handed statistical analysis, their focus remained fixed on crude numbers of tanks destroyed and maintenance performance. As a result, many sincere students of the experiment believed that situational awareness yielded, if anything, only inconsequential advantages.

Later that year, in November 1997, the next step in experimentation took place: the Division XXI Advanced Warfighting Experiment (DAWE). This experiment was a completely different enterprise than the TFXXI AWE, because in place of actual tanks, infantry fighting vehicles, and soldiers maneuvering against each other, the DAWE featured a computer war game between the 4th Infantry Division (Mechanized), stationed at Fort Hood, Texas, and the army's World Class Opposing Force, stationed at Fort Leavenworth, Kansas. The purpose of the DAWE was to see how digitization and situational awareness would affect division- and corps-level operations.

Once again, the results were disappointing. Analysts and critics gravitated to the most inane levels of inquiry, as water seeks the lowest point. Rather than focusing on how Information Age technology might launch us into a whole new approach to warfare, the analysts probed for failure and measured according to their aged rule of attrition. As in the TFXXI AWE, testers and statisticians painstakingly examined the minutiae of death: How many tanks were killed, how many aircraft were shot down, and how efficiently each side spilled cyberblood.

To date, we have utterly failed to remove the veil and peer into tomorrow. The collective lack of imagination and vision of the leaders, soldiers, and analysts in these experiments can be explained only by the extreme conservatism of the military establishment and the overpowering influence of command hierarchy in suppressing new ideas. In short, we missed the point by a country mile.

Situational awareness is the most revolutionary technology in the history of warfare. It is more important and far-reaching than the invention of the wheel, gunpowder, or the internal combustion engine. Once harnessed by intellect and vision, situational awareness will give birth to a whole new way of warfare—a method of conducting military operations that will be unlike anything we have seen in the past.

The most important vision we must capture is that situational awareness should result in a tenfold increase in velocity. Why is this so? How can the addition of computers, digital communications, and position-location technology increase the speed of our units? Unless we replace our heavy combat vehicles with aircraft, is it reasonable to suppose that we can move significantly faster than armies of the past?

The answer is a resounding Yes!

Digitization of the friendly force is aimed at producing an information advantage over the enemy. The point of all this technology is to enable the commander, the troop leader, and the soldier to understand the locations of themselves, their supporting forces, and the enemy. Although in practice there are innumerable challenges related to this technology, by and large the idea behind it is valid, feasible, and accurate. We can dissipate the fog of war even if we cannot remove it totally.

The great question remains: What will we do with this information advantage? What will U.S. commanders do when they have a disproportionate amount of usable information at their fingertips?

The answer so far is that they will convert that information into targeting data. In the experiments mentioned previously, the commanders of the Experimental Forces chose to forego the tremendous potential for increased mobility that information technology offered and instead use the data produced merely to feed their artillery more targets at which to shoot.

As a result, both experiments revealed an enormous increase in the logistical demand for more ammunition. Suddenly able to perceive, track, and identify literally thousands of targets, Experimental Force commanders reclined in their natural tendency toward caution and long-range fires. Information Age warfare degenerated into a turkey shoot.

In the resulting simulations, both at the National Training Center and in computer war games, army officials pushed beyond rational limitations on available ammunition and allowed the Experimental Forces the freedom to blast the enemy into nonexistence at extreme ranges to their hearts' content. Realistic limitations on transportation, ammunition, and the ability to fire into inhabited territory were tacitly ignored. The simulated enemy enthusiastically and obediently cooperated with the cybercarnage, stupidly charging into terrain that was easy to target, unit after unit, never learning and never adapting to fires like a real enemy would.

By the end of the experiments, we had retrained ourselves in our beloved attrition theory: Warfare was ultimately about killing the enemies with battlefield fires faster than they could kill us. The army continues to insist that the best way to defeat an enemy in war is through long-range destructive fires. (Yet we likewise keep insisting that only the army can deliver such fires—not the air force.) How disappointing! Handed the most exciting, most revolutionary military technology in history, we collectively opted to shy away from reality and bury ourselves in McNamara-esque attrition games.

Digitization, if we will simply permit it, will allow us to move ten times faster than before. We need only understand the theory behind why it leads to such a dramatic mobility advantage so that we can shape our experiments toward the reality of flesh-and-blood battlefields instead of the fiction of simulated loss-exchange ratios.

To begin with, digitization and the situational awareness it produces eliminate irrelevant or counterproductive movements. By providing commanders, soldiers, and weapons platforms with digital mapping, position locations, and fast communications, we virtually eliminate the simple problem of getting lost. As a lieutenant, when I made a wrong turn, I could take myself and my troops out of the fight for hours or days. With situational awareness I can probably avoid becoming seriously disoriented, and even if I do stray, my boss will see the error almost immediately and correct it.

During the TFXXI AWE at the National Training Center, an almost totally ignored incident occurred that should have pointed to this phenomenon. At issue was a piece of difficult, undulating terrain known locally as "the washboard." Consisting of rough ridges that inhibit both movement and vision, the washboard is traditionally viewed as "no-go" terrain—in other words, terrain that units avoid. In the history of the thousands of mock battles fought at the National Training Center, units have often become lost, disorganized, and disrupted merely by trying to traverse the washboard, even apart from enemy action.

However, during the TFXXI AWE, a mechanized infantry company team entered the washboard and came out on the other side intact and cohesive. Situational awareness enabled the commander, platoon leaders, and troops to navigate, move rapidly, and keep tabs on each other even when operating on some of the worst terrain in the desert. Military analysts, interested only in glorious tank fights, missed this event entirely.

Students of future warfare must take heed! Battles throughout history have been won or lost when units unexpectedly traversed difficult terrain. From the Romans' crossing into Sicily to disrupt Carthaginian siege operations to Scipio's dramatic taking of New Carthage, from Frederick's crossing of the swamps at Zorndorf to the Wehrmacht's attack through the Ardennes, armies that could create mobility across difficult terrain have obtained a decisive advantage over their enemies. Situational awareness technology creates mobility where mobility did not exist before.

Secondly, because situational awareness technology allows the army's intelligence apparatus to sense, analyze, and report enemy locations and activity rapidly, friendly units are able to much more accurately base their battlefield movements on where the enemies are and what they are doing, rather than on often faulty estimates. Military history records countless marches against foes who weren't there, defenses in mountain passes that the enemy never intended to use, and sudden maneuvers to intercept nonexistent enemy attacks. All this useless diversion of combat power has reduced operational tempo and at times threatened otherwise well-conceived concepts of operation. Situational awareness allows us to replace the wastefulness of mass warfare with the extreme economy of precision warfare.

The large-scale application of computer technology to tactical units and their staffs likewise confers upon units a dramatic leap ahead in the ability to perceive the battlefield, decide what to do, and issue orders. In the not-too-distant past, division, brigade, and battalion commanders would routinely assemble their subordinates and issue oral orders, using a paper map to explain their intents. With digitization, commanders can address their subordinates without physically assembling them, disseminate complex orders over a network of digital communications, and even rehearse execution over a virtual map without the loss of time inherent in face-to-face orders. This aspect of digitization alone saves hours during each operation.

In addition, digitization obviates the need for repetitive questions and answers between the battle staff and the fighting commanders, which have for so long plagued officers in battle. When voice radio communications were the primary means of passing information, most radio traffic concerned not orders but questions: Where are you? Where is the enemy?

With situational awareness, the staff officer tracking the battle in the tactical operations center does not need to constantly ask for updates about unit positions. Instead, that officer simply looks at his or her computer screen and watches a near-real-time display of friendly maneuver, as well as an up-to-date estimate of enemy locations. Likewise, the commander does not need to constantly question the staff, because he or she can also watch and supervise the action on a screen.

The result of all these advances should be a direct tenfold increase in operational tempo. That we have not yet seen such an increase points to a failure to grasp the intellectual aspects of digitization. To date, we have been shy about exploiting situational awareness, primarily because we have been distracted by the favorite question of critics.

What If It Doesn't Work?

The digitization of the U.S. Army is as much a cultural revolution as a technological one. There has been and will continue to be great dissension in the ranks concerning the wisdom of our modernization effort. In some respects, this resistance to change is natural and unavoidable, regardless of the context of the late twentieth-century United States. However, much of the aversion to modernization results from concurrent post–Cold War cuts in the military budget. Downsizing the military was inevitable once the Berlin Wall came down, but the simultaneous move toward digitization has permitted modernization to become synonymous with force cuts. Modern soldiers are afraid to embrace digitization partly because it could cost them their jobs.

This identification of modernization with downsizing is a shame, because it has given rise to a sustained insurgency within the army against digitization. The strength of the army hierarchy has suppressed much of the open debate, but e-mail and informal seminars more than compensate, becoming a forum for almost open revolt against modernization. I have witnessed fanatical hostility toward the latest technological advancements from people ranging from retired senior officers all the way down to active-duty lieutenants and sergeants. Much of their discontent is justified. The extreme budget cuts of recent years, in conjunction with ever-growing commitments abroad, have left the army without the funds or personnel to train for war. Still, the ancillary hostility toward digitization is founded largely upon a lack of imagination and unjustifiable conservatism.

The great question that everyone is asking is, "What if it doesn't work?"

This fundamental question manifests itself in many ways. Some people, supported by the innocuous analytical results of the AWEs, openly suggest that digitization, situational awareness, and information dominance confer no real advantage upon the force. Others allow that the advantages are real, but say that information technology as a whole is extremely vulnerable to enemy disruption. Still others remain fixated on the ultimately small-scale technological shortcomings of prototypical, experimental initiatives. In short, all of these dissenters endlessly reiterate the thematic question, "What if it doesn't work?"

If we—as an army and as a nation—are to advance, we must answer this question. As to the contention that information technology does not lead to an advantage, all experimentation as well as common sense suggest otherwise. Even the most dyed-in-the-wool attritionists admit that information dominance leads to moderate advantages in the application of firepower. Even those who militate openly against modernization agree that units with information technology experience a general increase in awareness of where the enemies are and what they are up to. In short, to believe that information technology is worthless, one must resort to personal bias and ignore the facts.

The concern about the susceptibility of information technology to enemy disruption is more well founded. There is no doubt that the introduction of digital technology into the force brings with it new vulnerabilities. Armed forces in the future will face threats of viruses, equipment failures, faulty software, enemy intrusion, casual hackers, data theft, and so forth. Digital communications may be jammed. Communication pipes may be overloaded and shut down. The enemy may overrun headquarters and seize computers. In short, there are many ways in which reliance upon information technology creates vulnerability.

However, digital vulnerabilities, as with any new technology, can be overstated. It is a curious phenomenon of the Information Age that critics have an affinity for what we might call collapse theory. The idea—from which many excellent movies and novels have sprung—is that computer technology lends itself to a sudden, catastrophic, widespread collapse across a network. Thus, if the collapse theory is accurate, future U.S. armed forces might fall prey en masse to a teenage hacker who infiltrates our tactical Internet.

It's all hogwash. In all of our experimentation, the army plans and conducts attacks against our own networks. During the most recent war-fighting experiments, we conducted a rigorous campaign of jamming our digital networks, reconnoitering our networks for weaknesses, and trying to hack past our network defenses. The results? As expected, we found some vulnerability. It is conceivable that future attackers, including even casual hackers, might be able to degrade our networks to some degree. But collapse does not happen—even when we try to make it happen. As digital networks proliferate, the sudden, catastrophic collapse idea retreats back into the world of fiction.

There is no end of cynics and critics who envision a cybernetic doomsday, but the practical reality is that digital networks are no more vulnerable than any other element of the combined arms force. Given the right conditions, we could isolate and destroy a tank, a jet fighter, or even an aircraft carrier. In real life, we protect ourselves effectively through combined arms operations, an offensive fighting doctrine, and a reasonable amount of security.

As to the contention that information technology is too immature, we must review the army's Force XXI experimentation philosophy. When the army began experimenting in earnest in 1994, senior leaders deliberately structured a campaign that would be more dynamic and productive than the slow, methodical combat-development process of the Cold War era. To that end, the generals described a "leap into the future." Everyone applauded the words and the intent, but they forgot about the ramifications of leaping ahead.

To conduct truly futuristic experimentation, we must develop and rapidly field prototype technology. What is prototype technology? It is partially developed, advanced technology that might be effective on tomorrow's battlefield. The drawback of prototypes, however, is that they are still developmental. It is a foregone conclusion with any developmental technology that the prototypes will be fragile and prone to breakdowns.

Nevertheless, when we began serious experimentation, the analysts wrote voluminous reports documenting—and lamenting—the fact that the prototypes were not reliable. It was as if it surprised these observers that breadboard, partially developed, untested models might break down or experience less-than-perfect performance. Shortly after the experiments in 1997, I personally read reports of more than nine hundred pages that detailed minor, innocuous equipment failures—all the while completely missing the more germane questions about Information Age warfare. It became evident to me that to conduct futuristic experiments, it is mandatory that we train the observers and analysts in what to look for. For the most part, they missed the boat entirely.

Prototypes will break down. Developmental software will have glitches. Hackers will occasionally break into networks, just as in the old days the enemy would sometimes capture maps and plans. Technologies will sometimes prove themselves irrelevant or even detrimental. This is all a natural part of experimentation and modernization. It must not become an excuse for an army to collectively whine, "What if it doesn't work?" For there is a far more fundamental and weighty question we must face.

If we are to advance and take hold of the revolution in military affairs, the question we must boldly face is: What if it *does* work? What if information technology truly delivers even partially on its promises? What if we can really get at the fog of war and roll it back considerably? To answer that question, we must have courage, character, and a whole lot of unfettered imagination. The answer to the question will strike to the very heart of our perception of war.

Velocity + Information = A New Way of Fighting

It is a terrible shame, but the dominant theme of army concepts and doctrine is that nothing has changed. In reading the thousands of white papers, concepts, and field manuals available today, one can easily detect the frustration of an army that lacks imagination. We are culturally unable to perceive something new, and we are politically suppressed from doing so. The frightening truth is that everything has changed, but we are waiting for our future enemies to reveal it.

We know intuitively that speed is good, but we are largely ignorant as to why it is good. As a result, the Army After Next (AAN) forum—the army's large-scale effort to conceptualize the future—has resurrected and sustained a fatally flawed vision of the purpose of speed: to cross "the deadly zone." The great shortcoming of the AAN is that the concepts about the future that flow from it are totally based on simulation results. The AAN process features a continuous series of war games—tactical, operational, and strategic—which serve to stimulate ideas for both future concepts and future requirements. Although such efforts are praiseworthy, AAN participants take their war games too seriously. The attrition-based computer models that support the war games are programmed only to input and output attrition ideas. Human factors, though fundamental to real conflict, play no significant part in AAN war games.

As a result, the well-intentioned officers and civilians thinking about the role of velocity in the future have hit upon the only possible use for speed in attrition gaming: to reduce the time that the friendly force spends moving in the range of enemy weapons. This is analogous to World War I armies dashing across no-man's-land. The idea is to move as quickly as possible to engage the enemy so that he has less time to shoot at you.

This is total nonsense. Dashing across no-man's-land is not the point of high-velocity operations in the Information Age. We are fixated upon this attritional interpretation of speed only because we are untrained in realistic conflict theory. Because we have collectively remained ignorant about the phenomenon of perpetual unreadiness, we can conceive of no logical reason to move fast—except as a way to nudge the attrition dynamics in our favor. We must do better than that.

In 1918 Ludendorff was fascinated with the idea of hurrying across the deadly zone in France. His vision of agility and speed foundered on the central tactical problem of World War I: crossing no-man's-land. Hence, just like our army today, he failed to think more broadly and to envision and plan for success. His operational plan for the Spring Offensive of 1918 was simply to achieve a penetration. The naïve assumption was that a small-scale tactical achievement would somehow metamorphose into strategic success. It didn't in 1918, and it won't in 2018.

The need for velocity is much more profound than simply scooting past the enemy's field of fire—and our conceptual basis for modernization had better be deeper than achieving a superficial tactical advantage. To get into the future, we must think beyond no-man's-land.

There is, buried beneath all the superficial platitudes about speed, a greater truth. The purpose of velocity is to unlock the door to the enemy's perpetual unreadiness. What is perpetual unreadiness? Simply stated, this refers to the fact that armies at war remain unready for combat almost all of the time. Even military forces on the front lines of battle suffer from perpetual unreadiness. Human nature, the complexities of military operations and logistics, and the intricacies of terrain create unreadiness. Units are most often moving through suboptimal terrain, facing the wrong way, unaware of the enemy, resupplying, resting, planning, or refitting. They are only rarely ready to shoot at the bad guys.

Perpetual unreadiness, although completely absent from our doctrine, is a simple battlefield concept. It is intuitively understood even by the most dense and conservative generals. The problem is that because we have never expressed the concept clearly, we have failed to study it in a disciplined fashion. As a result, we do not perceive how velocity can give us a decisive advantage in the future.

If armies at war are perpetually unready for conflict, why do battles occur at all? Why does the bulk of military history describe opponents who are ready for battle? When we think about war, why do we automatically imagine an enemy in good terrain, in proper formation, well supplied, morally strong, well led, fighting with proper tactics, its flanks secure, and so forth? The reason is that when opponents in war move with equivalent velocity, neither can move fast enough to take advantage of the other's unreadiness. By the time one side begins to maneuver to exploit the vulnerability of its enemy, that enemy detects the threat and prepares to receive the attack. Thus, both sides appear to be perpetually ready for a fight.

What happens, though, when one side has a clear advantage in velocity and/or information? Inevitably—almost without exception—that side attacks an unready enemy. Velocity is the doorway to the enemy's perpetual unreadiness. When velocity is married to an information advantage, the entire nature of warfare changes. In place of symmetrical battles of firepower and attrition, we fight asymmetrical battles between cohesive, fast-moving friendly forces and unready, disrupted enemy forces. All this leads to a style of warfare that we can term preemptive warfare.

Preemption is turning the time flank of the enemy. It occurs when a friendly armed force acts against an opponent that is not yet ready for a fight. It is mandatory that we as a nation look seriously into this style of warfare. To start us down this thoroughly unexplored path, let us consider how preemption is defined at the three levels of war.

At the strategic level, preemption targets the enemy's political processes. That is, the preempting armed force acts to affect political decision making rather than directly attacking an enemy armed force. This can take the form of simple troop deployments to act as deterrents, or it can include the seizure of political figures or facilities. The Wehrmacht's remilitarization of the Rhineland in 1936 was a good example of strategic preemption. Without a shot being fired, Hitler presented the world with a fait accompli. Had he stopped there—or even in 1938—it is likely that he could have avoided war with the Western powers.

Operational-level preemption targets the enemy's mobilization processes. In this form of conflict the opponent has already decided to oppose friendly intentions but has not yet mobilized its combat power fully. The preempting armed force enters the theater of operations and destroys or disrupts mobilization centers, rail lines, supply dumps, communications, and so on to impede or stop further preparation of hostile combat power. The intent, naturally, is to convince the enemy that it has been rendered incapable of armed resistance.

Tactical preemption focuses on the enemy's combat processes. This type of preemptive warfare aims at engaging, destroying, or defeating the unready portions of the enemy's deployed combat power. Typically, such attacks take the form of deep, highly mobile raids against forces that are moving through bad terrain or are otherwise ill disposed for fighting. Tactical preemption also includes attacks against logistical infrastructure, command posts, and so on.

The army had better start thinking seriously about preemption or stop investing in situational awareness and digitization. Preemption—a form of high-velocity warfare—is the natural offspring of information technology on the battlefield. If we try to shy away from velocity in favor of attrition dynamics—overuse of battlefield fires, or high-velocity operations aimed at small-scale tactical advantage—we will never see a return on our investments. Further, as we downsize the army, we will risk catastrophic defeat if we continue to favor heavyweight boxing with a featherweight force. A smaller, digital army can prevail in the future—but only if it takes advantage of its potential velocity.

Characteristics of High-Velocity Warfare

I have been disappointed with the lack of vision displayed in army experiments. The senior leaders of the army have chosen to cast away all the advantages of digitization in favor of reinforcing the demonstrably inapplicable power of long-range fires. Fascinated by fireworks, our generals have missed the much greater potential of high-velocity warfare.

Frustrated with their conservatism, I began to investigate the other implications of digitization myself. Using commercially available simulation software, I conducted a series of experiments to answer the question: What happens on the battlefield when one side has a significant information and velocity advantage over the other?

To look into this matter, I ran a series of control-group scenarios in which the opponents in various battles and campaigns possessed relatively equivalent operational tempos. After recording the results, I proceeded to replay the scenarios, this time giving first one side and then the other a twofold advantage in information and speed. The results—some expected, some not—are provided following. The intent is not to suggest that the conclusions are absolutely valid. Rather, they should be viewed as hypotheses for further experimentation.

1. As a general rule, high-velocity armies can conduct more effective and less risky disruption operations against their enemies.

Disruption operations are those aimed at deceiving, delaying, and diverting the enemy prior to a major battle. The commander conducting disruption operations attempts to break the forward momentum of the enemy, disorganize its formations, and dislocate its combined arms integration prior to fighting the main action. In the past, the equivalent velocity of opponents made such actions a highly risky affair. Disruption operations—economy-of-force actions—put small friendly forces into hostile territory without significant supporting arms. As a result, when such operations were attempted, they most often accomplished little while sacrificing the friendly force.

When there is a velocity and information advantage, such actions become much more effective. Disrupting units can advance securely and quickly into unoccupied key terrain and ambush enemy lead elements or raid enemy vulnerabilities in the rear. When the enemy reacts, high-velocity units can retreat quickly and elude capture. In the scenarios I observed, high-velocity disruptive forces continued to prevail against much larger but slower opponents, at times making it nearly impossible for the enemy to advance as a cohesive force.

2. As a general rule, when one side has a velocity advantage over the other, there are fewer large-scale battles.

The reduced number of battles comes about simply because although the friendly (high-velocity) side can choose to engage the enemy at will, the enemy cannot force a fight on the friendly side. When threatened with superior concentrations of combat power, the friendly force moves away rapidly. The exception to this is when the enemy attacks to seize critical terrain that the friendly force must defend and retain. Even in such situations, velocity gives the friendly force an advantage because it can concentrate faster than the enemy can. Still, these types of encounters resulted in the most friendly losses.

3. High-velocity warfare results in more small-scale engagements in previously unused portions of the area of operations.

One of the unexpected results of the experimentation was that in place of massive battles fought on traditional battlefields, high-velocity warfare resulted in multiple small-scale engagements in obscure places. This phenomenon resulted from the high-velocity force sensing enemy dispersed movements and accelerating its marches to intercept such movements, which led to ambushlike skirmishes. The high-velocity force, rather than acquiescing in hammer-and-anvil clashes of massed combat power, inflicted a thousand stings on an enemy unready for combat.

This sustained result in experimentation suggests that a velocity and information advantage must change the way we analyze terrain. Traditional approaches to choosing engagement areas that favor large friendly concentrations must give way to small-scale interception and ambush opportunities in bad terrain.

4. Enemies tend to mass and slow down when faced with a high-velocity friendly force.

These experiments pointed clearly to the tension between the competing goals of concentrating combat power and maneuvering combat power on the enemy side. A high-velocity friendly force makes enemy maneuver a risky affair. As enemy forces attempted to distribute combat power in a flanking movement, friendly forces propelled by knowledge and great agility would routinely intercept, surround, and destroy such movements. As a result, the enemy adapted by refraining from risky maneuver and instead keeping combat power massed.

5. High-velocity attacks led to the large-scale dislocation of enemy strength.

When the friendly force attacked enemy defenses, its advantage in knowledge and speed allowed the friendly commander to surround, isolate, and destroy vulnerable aspects of the enemy force, leading to a rapid general defeat of the enemy. In these types of engagements, traditional attrition dynamics were not manifested. Velocity created great asymmetry.

6. High-velocity forces can get themselves into trouble faster.

The balancing truth about high-velocity operations is that knowledge and speed do not always replace firepower and security. On occasion, particularly in the earlier runs of the test scenarios, high-velocity forces raced into trouble. Underestimating enemy resilience, willpower, and even agility, friendly forces sometimes got themselves surrounded and destroyed. When these setbacks occurred, they tended to happen to only small portions of the force—mainly because the high-velocity force did not often have the need to concentrate. The lesson learned was that although the friendly force accrued decisive advantages through information dominance and velocity, a resourceful enemy could still inflict pain if friendly vulnerabilities were exposed.

Conclusions

We have much to unlearn and much prejudice to set aside. Imagination and unfettered experimentation are the keys to success. We must turn our attention to the study of high-velocity armies of the past in order to see the asymmetry that results from a disparity in speed and knowledge. More importantly, we must be ready to challenge every assertion, every principle, and every hallowed precept of symmetrical warfare.

The most palpable roadblock to the development of a culture of velocity is our simulations and analysis. Simulations pervade all aspects of the army—training, materiel development, leader development, and doctrine. The problem is that our family of simulations is long on attrition dynamics and short on human factors. These simulations cannot, in their current state, simulate perpetual unreadiness or vulnerability to dislocation. Simulated enemies in today's army do not rout, surrender, or get demoralized. Their logistical problems are assumed away, thus removing the most valuable target for friendly maneuver. Their command-and-control systems invariably work perfectly, thus disallowing the disruptive effects of a high-velocity campaign. In short, modern army simulations make a culture of velocity impossible.

The solution is a renaissance of simulation, modeling, and analysis within the armed services. Incremental improvements to existing hardware and software will avail us nothing, because the simulations are founded squarely upon attrition equations despite their total irrelevance to modern warfare. If the army desires to get serious about Information Age warfare, the first step will have to be fundamental simulation reform.

The path to success, both in our Information Age doctrine and on the battlefield, is balance. The ideas in this chapter are aimed at moving the debate, not predicting the end state. To exploit the potential of digitization, we must get past traditional ideas and think seriously about high-velocity warfare. However, in each stage of experimentation and development, we must also recall that warfare is a dynamic process. The enemies will not cooperate with our intentions, and they will adapt to our successes. Tomorrow's leader must strive for an asymmetrical advantage—and be ready for a symmetrical threat.

John A. Antal

This may prove the most contentious chapter in this book. Although several of the others include ideas that are not universally accepted, in this chapter Antal heads straight for the throat of the issue currently debated. The questions are: Does the digital revolution obviate the need for maneuver? Have fires or firepower delivered by indirect means advanced to the point where they are now the dominant element in the future of warfare? Is this less an issue of command and control and more an issue of the rise to supremacy of precision-guided munitions?

The U.S. Air Force certainly seems to believe the latter. In the wake of Desert Storm countless articles have been published by airpower advocates that in one form or another reach the same unstartling conclusion: Douhet was right. (Guillermo Douhet was the post–World War I Italian airpower theorist who started the intellectual argument that nations might be subjugated through the application of airpower.) Although the phenomenon of war reaches across a wide spectrum, these authors contend that precision munitions delivered from the air may dominate the future.

Indeed, even in the army, among those who spend most of their time around helicopters and really big guns (the aviation and artillery groups), the belief appears to be that this is a revolution dominated by the effects of precision-guided munitions. The true change, as they see it, is in the ability of computers and digital communications technology to collect and disseminate precise information about the location of the enemy, thereby changing the enemy's status from "projected" to "targeted."

The major problem with this theory, applied by either the air force or the army branches that specialize in stand-off weapons, is that precision may be a chimera. Despite the application of NATO airpower in Bosnia, the conflict has not ended in areas where NATO has not applied ground combat forces. Similarly, it appears unlikely that Mohammed Farah

Aideed, the Somali warlord whom the United States pursued in 1993, would have felt terribly threatened by the specter of Tomahawk cruise missiles. They just don't apply, especially in a situation that is something less than war and something more than peace.

Finally, there is a demographic factor that many of the stand-off firepower advocates fail to address. The population of the planet continues to increase. The implication of this for militaries around the world would seem to be that there will probably be more fighting in built-up areas in the future. Does firepower applied from a distance work in this situation?

Monte Cassino, an Italian monastery bombed into rubble by U.S. firepower during World War II, actually became a better defensive position for its German defenders thereafter. Precision was moot as an element in this case, because the structure was hit time after time through massive air strikes by U.S. bombers. U.S. artillery bounced the rubble some more. Yet the German defenders did not retreat, did not stop fighting, and turned the rubble into a quagmire of death for the attackers. For reasons that apply to the political level of war, it is unlikely that the United States would apply similar firepower against an enemy in any event that came short of declared war.

Precision Tomahawk strikes against terrorists may continue, yet it appears that terrorism will as well. U.S. Air Force and Navy fighter-bombers may keep up their punitive strikes against limited targets, but the fighting in the Balkans continues. So long as the United States operates in an environment in which political opinions matter, it is doubtful that firepower will truly reign supreme. Antal takes this issue head-on. It is up to the future to decide the validity of his argument.

The End of Maneuver

I believe we're at the threshold of a major change for the combined arms team—the ascendancy of fires. What that means is that we, as a nation, will fight conventional battles using firepower of all kinds from longer ranges, much of it indirect—not eyeball-to-eyeball using direct fire. We'll use long range fires as the spearhead of the attack to the extent that the ground maneuver forces may only need to mop up after the fires. That's a totally different concept of operations. This concept aims at achieving decisive results while minimizing the usual high casualties of the direct fire battle.

— Glenn K. Otis[1]

A central mission of the U.S. Army is to fight and win sustained land combat conflicts. Army doctrine establishes five elements to accomplish this: dominant maneuver, precision strikes, protecting the force, winning the information war, and projecting and sustaining combat power. The emerging revolution in the accuracy of firepower and the requirement to win future wars quickly, decisively, and with minimal friendly casualties are challenging this balanced approach.[2] Some proponents argue that precision strikes have ushered in the ascendancy of fires, a new paradigm for ground combat that will transform the role of precision strikes into the "decisive element of land combat power."[3]

The U.S. Army has historically overwhelmed its enemies "with sheer weight of firepower."[4] The new precision-strike technologies promise to destroy the enemy throughout the breadth and depth of the battle area with long-range fires and appear to be a high-technology extrapolation of this old method. High-technology distant punishment promises to minimize the exposure of friendly forces and win the battle without the requirement to physically dominate the enemy. According to Glenn K. Otis, "The fundamental tenet of the construct is that we not expose our forces to enemy fires any more than we have to."[5] Proponents of this construct believe that precision strikes have created a condition of interchangeability, in which firepower can substitute for maneuver on the modern battlefield.[6] In essence, precision-strike advocates predict the end of maneuver.

Will precision-strike systems obviate maneuver?

This is an important question that will decide the future shape of the U.S. military. The battlefield dynamic of simultaneous attack throughout the depth of the battlefield hinges on detection of enemy locations, near-real-time reporting of this information, and near-real-time engagement by friendly weapons. To make this concept work we will have to grid the battlefield and know the location of every target, potential target, and point of interest. Can we afford the cost of an army dominated by a doctrine devoted to precision strikes?

If Force XXI is a "forcing function," designed to make the U.S. Army figure out how to design, train, and fight a future force, then we need to understand what happens to armies whose doctrines do not balance the elements of combat power. The quintessential example of the value of doctrine and the lure of the promise of fires' ascendancy is the story of the French army of 1940.

France 1940

Firepower dominated the battlefields of World War I, slaughtering much of a generation in the blood-soaked trenches. After the war, reducing casualties became a prime directive for the French military. As a result, the French army "devoted considerable effort to create the best possible and most modern doctrine. It organized a complex and sophisticated system for considering new ideas and new technologies."[7]

The result of its detailed studies was clear: Overwhelming firepower, centralized control, detailed planning, and fixed defenses would reduce casualties. Enemy penetrations of the defensive line would be slowed, worn down by attrition, and ground to dust by well-placed, overwhelming firepower. In the French army, the ascendancy of fires replaced maneuver. Highly accurate cannon fire placed in the concrete and steel bunkers of the Maginot Line would provide all the elements of victory.

The best minds of the French army attacked the new battlefield equation with vigor and initiative. Tactics, techniques, and procedures were developed to employ new technologies in an intricate system that maximized firepower. The artillery set the tempo and rhythm of the attack, and detailed preparation and synchronization were emphasized. The system required that plans leave nothing to chance—let alone human error—and the standard of discipline therefore became rigid. To avoid fratricide in a firepower-intensive environment, everyone had to act according to a detailed, well-rehearsed plan. The French "gridded" the battle area in front of their guns and accepted as certainty the mathematics of destruction. "The attack is the fire that advances, the defense is the fire that halts the enemy," became the motto of the French army.[8]

The French doctrine that evolved from this intense study was called methodical battle, or *battaille conduite.* As laid down by French army regulations, methodical battle was a step-by-step process of tightly controlled movement and rigid timetables designed to generate the maximum amount of firepower to destroy the enemy. The development of methodical battle "represented the best available thought on what would usually work best on the battlefield"[9] and came from a strong belief in the decisive effect of "the destructiveness of firepower."[10]

The power of ideas is sometimes frightening. Methodical battle not only seized the minds of the French army's leadership—setting their thinking at the pace of their cannons—but it also shaped the procurement of weapons, dramatically altered the organization of the force, and set the command style.

By 1940 the French army was considered a premier, world-class, well-knit fighting force "which had devoted two decades to preparing for the possibility of a future war."[11] Unbalanced with all the best intentions, the French felt confident that their doctrine—their system of systems—was the superior method of war fighting. They expected to fight by their game plan, "a carefully controlled, highly centralized battle" based on preserving lives through the lavish employment of firepower.[12] The thinking of that time has a curiously familiar ring to it: "The new weapons of greater firepower . . . had made the battlefield much more lethal than in the past."[13] Under this framework, decisive maneuver became merely the ability to move firepower forward.

The Germans, on the other hand, acknowledged the value of firepower but also understood the need for a balance between firepower, mobility, and protection. Out of the desperate necessity of their geopolitical and economic position, the Germans selected an asymmetrical approach to make French firepower and twenty years of French preparation irrelevant. In Gen. Erich von Manstein's words, "The aim of the offensive must be to achieve decisive results."[14]

As noted French military historian Col. Robert Doughty has observed, in this effort German doctrine played a decisive role: "German doctrine, in short, emphasized the advantages of one continuous battle, ultimately leading to the complete rupture of the hostile defenses and the defeat of the enemy, while French doctrine accepted the possibility of a successive series of methodical battles. The Germans believed this continuous battle enabled them to retain the initiative and to achieve victory. And this belief existed long before German panzer forces or the blitzkrieg were created."[15]

The story of the Battle for France in 1940 is well known. The German attack through the weakly defended Ardennes forest, however, was not a simple drive through the woods by German panzers. It was a skillful fight by a well-balanced force fighting with superior doctrine. German infantry, engineers, artillery, and close air support were as critical to the French defeat as the fast-moving panzers.

The story of this battle is not only that of the inexorable drive of the tanks supported by shrieking, dive-bombing stukas, but also that of the clash of two diametrically opposed doctrines. The fact is that before the battle, the two sides were closely matched—except in the realm of their ideas. The difference lay in the way the two sides thought about warfare. The French overemphasized the elements of firepower and protection, while the Germans emphasized a balanced approach of combined arms and applied firepower, maneuver, and protection as the situation demanded.

The German method permitted strength where strength was needed at any particular instant. In all cases the involved German forces retained sufficient reserves and supplies. This in turn created flexibility in their operations—flexibility to drive the operations in the direction that they desired, at their own pace, and in the places of their choosing.[16]

In May 1940 the Germans dominated the battlefield, risking all in a determined attack to win decisively. The Germans emphasized four characteristics at the tactical, operational, and even strategic levels. These were boldness, speed, shock action, and firepower.[17] Methodical battle dominated the French response. Unprepared mentally to respond to the battle's fast pace, the French army suffered defeat in only six weeks—but the battle was decided in the first seven to ten days. As Doughty states, "Few defeats have been as unexpected or as sudden. . . . France simply could not respond to the type of fighting thrust upon her. The resulting debacle swept her from the first rank of world powers."[18]

Battlefield Dominance

Several important lessons from the French defeat in 1940 are valuable to today's development of the Army After Next concept. The first lesson is the significance of doctrine. Doctrine's dominance appeared clearly in May and June of 1940.[19] The French developed a sophisticated, unbalanced doctrine that aimed at preserving French manpower by substituting firepower for maneuver. The French system of systems was based on the idea of interchangeability embedded in the Maginot Line. Unfortunately for the French, interchangeability failed catastrophically in 1940.

The second lesson is that the ability to use available technology effectively is more important than the technology itself. The Germans had a high degree of congruence between their weapons and their method of fighting.[20] Their doctrine aided this congruence and was an essential element of victory. A vivid example of congruence was the use of the radio as an information system. Every German tank had a radio. Radios were demanded by a doctrine that emphasized maneuver and combined arms. Few French tanks had radios, because they were not as necessary to fight precise, preplanned, methodical battles.[21] French agility was as severely hampered by the mindset that doctrine imposed as by the lack of informational systems.

This doctrinal influence on equipment usage was so pronounced as to prompt historian Len Deighton to observe, "The vital role that radio played in the technique of the blitzkrieg . . . was entirely due to the way in which German commanders were prepared to change plans minute by minute in the face of enemy opposition. It is extremely doubtful if such radio contact would have made much difference to the French or the British Army, which had trained to fight in set-piece battles."[22]

Third, for all the right reasons, the French tried to reduce warfare to a science based on the mathematics of destruction. The human element was considered secondary to the need to mathematically assure victory at minimal cost to friendly forces. Fire support is easily reduced to a science—processing target information, selecting the target and the engagement system, and developing the order to fire—especially in the age of the microchip. The science of methodical battle, however, disregarded the idea that the first requirement in war is decisive action, not just the physical destruction of the enemy's forces. When events cascaded faster than the firepower of methodical battle, the French system of systems was paralyzed.

Today, U.S. Army doctrine states that combat power is created by combining the elements of maneuver, firepower, protection, and leadership. The 1993 version of the army's capstone doctrinal manual, Field Manual 100-5 (*Operations*), is explicit on this when it states, "Overwhelming combat power is achieved when all combat elements are violently brought to bear quickly, giving the enemy no opportunity to respond with coordinated opposition."[23] Without maneuver, the most effective precision strike is indecisive. A determined enemy can always endure the fire, as the British did in the Battle of Britain, and will eventually develop asymmetrical ways to respond to precision-strike forces—as the North Koreans have with their hardened artillery sites. Precision strikes that are not backed up with a continuous battle of decisive maneuver are merely artillery raids set out to punish, not defeat, an opponent.

Force XXI and the Army After Next

To prepare for the future, the U.S. Army has launched a two-pronged attack. The main attack is Force XXI, which will become Army XXI. The supporting attack is the Army After Next. The Force XXI concept envisions an army that can overwhelm the enemy, win quickly, sustain minimum casualties and loss of material, and produce decisive victory—a tall order for an army that is smaller than the force fielded in 1940.

The central idea behind Force XXI is that digital communications technology will provide battlefield commanders with a comprehensive view of the battlefield. This information dominance will enable units to be smaller and yet more lethal. Digitization's impact during exercises was impressive. Spot reports reached the battalion in five minutes, as compared to nine under conventional communication means. Spot reports under conventional means required repeating the message about 30 percent of the time, as compared to only 4 percent when digitized. Digitized spot reports save time and can rapidly synchronize direct and indirect fires. This provides Force XXI with the ability to shoot quickly and place accurate and overwhelming direct and indirect fire on the enemy.

Digitization brings attack helicopters into the fight faster and makes them more effective killers by providing better enemy and friendly situational awareness. Improved battlefield awareness allows faster digitized command and control. Maps, overlays, and orders can be transmitted quickly. Operation orders and especially fragmentary orders can be published and distributed in minutes as opposed to hours. In war, these minutes saved can be decisive.

The Force XXI concept is expected to achieve force coherence through shared knowledge delivered by advances in weapon systems and information technology. The army's vision is that all elements within the force will share a common perception of the battle space simultaneously. It is hoped that the synergy possible in a digital framework will increase the efficiency and organization of the force and that through the free sharing of information leaders will be able to organize the battlefield and control the operational tempo.[24]

The army is well on its way to creating Force XXI, with digital information systems playing a similar role to that of the radio in the blitzkrieg of 1940. In 1940 the key concepts upon which the success of the German blitzkrieg rested were surprise, speed, and concentration. Moreover, all of these concepts relied on the presence of the others to achieve success.[25] For Force XXI the terms have been changed to precision strike, dominant maneuver, and information dominance.

Within the parameters of shrinking budgets, can the army maintain the balance that these interdependent principles require? Can we provide the exact, secure, and constant flow of intelligence information required for precision strikes to work? Some people doubt that we can achieve any significant gains in this area. Military theorist Edward Luttwak has gone so far as to say, "Even satellite observation, modern aerial photography, and more advanced communication would not change matters greatly, as the evidence of recent war has shown. As soon as movement begins, so does the fog of war."[26]

The mission of the Army After Next is to determine the future of warfare in about 2020 and predict what operational, organizational, and informational changes the army will need to win on future battlefields. The vision of the Army After Next sees a future army of small, extraordinarily lethal, and highly mobile units, dispersed to protect against weapons of mass destruction and capable of rapidly detecting and eliminating large numbers of fast targets, down to the individual soldier level.[27]

Brilliant weapons will increasingly define the nature of war on the ground. Long-range, autonomous target acquisition, and hit-and-kill-capable brilliant munitions will enhance the abilities of maneuver forces by setting the conditions that make dominant maneuver possible. The enemy may see U.S. forces maneuvering against it, but it will not be able to react in time because of the accurate pinpoint destruction of their critical combat capabilities. Precision strikes will pin the enemy to the battlefield while dominant maneuver forces move to decide the issue. The effectiveness of brilliant munitions, however, is contingent on information dominance. We cannot expect firepower to destroy enemy capabilities with pinpoint accuracy if we do not know the exact location of enemy and friendly forces.

The reality of 2020 may well be painfully different from the dreams of the visionaries of the Army After Next. As Jack Weible has observed, "The gap between reality and dreams can seem a mile wide, but when it comes to the shortfall in the Defense Department's equipment modernization account, it can be measured in dollars: about $15 billion a year."[28] In addition, it is estimated that Congress may have to trim the $1.3 trillion allocated for defense spending over the next five years by $55 billion to meet budget requirements.[29] Something's got to give, and the most likely candidate will be the high-technology systems of the future force. Today's soldiers may find that the battlefield of 2020 looks surprisingly like battlefields of today, with many of the same old weapon systems still in use.

What will be important to the changing nature of warfare is what you will not see. The art of warfare is expanding as new means of conducting war emerge at the dawn of the twenty-first century. Although most soldiers and theoreticians consider this a revolution, it is in fact an evolutionary development of the cascading disruption of the twentieth century. It is only revolutionary in a relative sense, especially since few, if any, commanders in the past have had a technological advantage over their opponents in the methods of dislocating the enemy through manipulation of information.

Interchangeability did not succeed in the twentieth century, and the cost of providing a system of systems that will make interchangeability work in the twenty-first century is problematic. In spite of the fantastic, precise destructive effects of brilliant munitions, the requirement to maneuver direct fire to physically dominate the enemy remains. If Force XXI must be prepared to conduct quick, decisive, highly sophisticated operations and also be ready to execute limited, possibly protracted operations against low-technology enemies, then battlefield dominance will require forces that possess maneuver, protection, and firepower—not firepower alone. As a recent army pamphlet reminds us, "Overwhelming, decisive power is not solely firepower."[30]

Preparing for the next war is always a riddle. France's pre–World War II expenditures dwarfed those of Germany. The Maginot Line was so costly that "few dared to suggest spending equally vast sums on a newer, more mobile military machine that would have rendered the line obsolete."[31] The Germans, unburdened with such a massive expenditure, searched for asymmetrical means to overcome the brilliant defenses of the French.

The great cost and effort of the Maginot Line forced an imbalance in French military thinking that was codified in their doctrine of methodical battle. To win with mathematical certainty on the gridded battlefield required huge concentrations of firepower and the creation of the Maginot Line—a post–World War I "silver bullet" solution to war. The French put their faith in concrete and firepower. The Germans put their faith in training and the maneuver of a balanced, combined arms force.

The April 1997 *Annual Report to the President and the Congress* by the Secretary of Defense, William S. Cohen, emphasized that the first major concept of the new revolution in military affairs is "that long-range precision strike weapons, coupled with very effective sensors and command and control systems, will become the dominant factor in future war."[32] With insufficient funds to procure new maneuver systems, the U.S. Army has decided to buy a "limited number of new, high payoff weapons."[33] Maneuver systems are paying for the revolution systems and precision strikes. In a recent Army After Next simulation the following was learned:

> The major lessons learned from the first war game [Army After Next], held Jan. 27–Feb. 6, was that the United States' increasing reliance on satellites could become a fatal vulnerability. In the war game, set in 2020, Russia launched a nuclear attack in space that destroyed almost every satellite circling the globe, knocking out much of the United States' technological advantage in one fell swoop."[34]

The 1997 Quadrennial Defense Review, the latest attempt at military reform, was primarily an attempt by the Department of Defense to "insist that rapidly aging weapon systems built in the 1970s and 1980s needed to be replaced."[35] Are we in the process of creating an information warfare Maginot Line?

Conclusion

The ability to win bloodless victories through firepower alone is a siren's call—an idea with the best intentions that has historically produced bad results. War is a complex event, and combat solutions are rarely purely technological. The ascendancy of fires and the dominance of precision strikes in U.S. Army doctrine are a dangerous case in point.[36]

The aim of our future land power strategy should be the rapid and simultaneous dislocation of the enemy, not its total destruction.

Victory through precision strikes is too costly and will bankrupt the forces' ability to train and negate systems required to dominate the maneuver battle. Dislocation, as shown by the Germans in 1940, can win a decision with minimum bloodshed.

Battlefield dominance requires balanced forces that possess maneuver, protection, firepower, and leadership. In 1918 battles were fought by masses of men and artillery that aimed for the destruction of the enemy's personnel; in 1940 blitzkrieg was waged with mobile units of men and tanks supported by artillery and combat aviation aiming at the destruction of the opponent's combat cohesion as embodied in its command and control.

In 2010 battlefield dominance will be generated by small, self-contained, mobile combined arms forces maneuvering simultaneously with the support of land, sea, and air precision strikes to defeat the enemy rapidly. The combination of mobile-strike forces and precision-strike forces will place the enemies on the horns of a dilemma—killing them with precision-strike forces if they venture out of their defenses and smashing them with quick-moving, lethal maneuver forces that inexorably conduct a continuous battle, disrupting and dislocating their ability to resist.

Our efforts to discuss Force XXI operations today are sowing the seeds that will bear the fruit of tomorrow's victories. The simultaneous application of precision strikes with dominant maneuver offers the U.S. Army a method to dominate future opponents much as the German army dominated the French army in 1940. General Dennis Reimer put it this way:

> For the Nation to be decisive in war, our enemies must be presented with complex military problems beyond their ability to solve. We must maintain an adequate balance between our capabilities to assure that adversaries cannot and will not solve the military puzzle that we pose. Precision strike is important but it isn't adequate. Balance between precision strike and dominant maneuver is required."[37]

It seems that everyone agrees to balanced forces, but the spending figures point in the direction of precision strikes. It seems that with regards to the army's budget, General Otis is right: "In all of modern warfare, the biggest killer on the battlefield has always been artillery. I only see the role of artillery ascending."[38]

High-technology methodical battle must not be allowed to shape the procurement of weapons and the command style of Army XXI or the Army After Next. The U.S. Army must avoid the siren call to become dominated by firepower as the French were by their doctrine of methodical battle. Army XXI and the Army After Next should not become a moveable fortress—a high-technology version of methodical battle.

The most significant problem in warfare today is the need to produce the correct balance of firepower, mobility, and protection to create a force that can apply decisive action. Decisive action in the twenty-first century will require precision strikes and the ability to achieve dominant maneuver on the battlefield. Our doctrine, training, and procurement must reflect a balance in which precision-guided munitions provide maneuver a greater freedom of movement. Contrary to the wishes of many, the close fight may never disappear from future battlefields. With this in mind, dominant combined arms maneuver, enabled by precision strikes, still offers the greatest probability for decisive action in the twenty-first century.

Notes

1. Glenn K. Otis [General, U.S. Army (Ret.)], "The Ascendancy of Fires, The Evolution of the Combined Arms Team," *Field Artillery Journal* (June 1995): 18–19. An interview of Glenn K. Otis, retired general, former commander of NATO's Central Army Group, and commander-in-chief of U.S. Army Europe.

2. The most obvious way to defeat U.S. policy is to dramatically increase the number of U.S. casualties. U.S. policy in the last twenty years has been changed more dramatically after significant U.S. casualties have been inflicted than by any other means. Beirut and Somalia are key lessons in point. Employing systems that limit friendly casualties is one of the strongest arguments for interchangeability.

3. Lowry A. West, "Field Artillery in the 21st Century," *Military Review,* Vol.LXIX, No. 8, August 1989: 21. See also Maj. Gen. Fred Marty's comments in "Deep Operations," in *Field Artillery* (Fort Sill, Okla.: U.S. Army Field Artillery School, April 1993), 1. "The traditional view of ground combat focuses on the close fight. Our organic precision strike capabilities now join air assets in extending the land commander's [LOC] options for decisive victory."

4. Russell F. Weigley, *History of the United States Army* (Bloomington, Ind.: Indiana University Press, 1984), 475.

5. Otis, 19.

6. Robert R. Leonhard, *The Art of Maneuver, Maneuver Warfare Theory and AirLand Battle* (Novato, Calif.: Presidio Press, 1991), 178–183.

7. Robert Allen Doughty, *The Seeds of Disaster, The Development of French Army Doctrine 1919–1939* (Hamden, Conn.: Archon Books, 1985), 5.

8. Doughty, *The Breaking Point, Sedan and the Fall of France* (Hamden, Conn.: Archon Books, 1990), 28.

9. Doughty, *Seeds of Disaster,* 6.

10. Ibid., 3.

11. General Franz Halder, the chief of the German army's general staff, noted in his diaries: "Techniques of Polish campaign no recipe for the West. No good against a well-knit Army." See Doughty, *Breaking Point,* 19; and *Seeds of Disaster,* x.

12. Doughty, *Breaking Point,* 325.

13. Doughty, *Seeds of Disaster,* 3.

14. Field Marshal Erich von Manstein, *Lost Victories,* ed. and trans. Anthony Powell (Novato, Calif.: Presidio Press, 1982), 121. Von Manstein was responsible for developing the German plan for the Battle of France.

15. Doughty, *Seeds of Disaster,* 109–10.

16. John Strawson, *The Battle for the Ardennes* (New York: Charles Scribner's, 1972), 12.

17. Colonel T. N. Dupuy, *A Genius for War, The German Army and General Staff, 1807–1945* (Englewood Cliffs, N.J.: Prentice-Hall, 1977), 257.

18. Doughty, *Seeds of Disaster,* ix–x.

19. Ibid.

20. Dupuy, *Understanding War, History and Theory of Combat* (New York: Paragon House Publishers, 1987), 103. The concept of congruence is explained on 216–18. In addition, Dupuy explains on 216: "The Germans won through a superior strategy and by applying the Principles of War, and not through better technology or a larger force. . . . No conventional weapon has been as important to battle success as have been the troops employing the weapons . . . and there is not a lot of evidence or logic to suggest that technology will become more important than the troops in future warfare."

21. As remarkable as it may seem, the commander of the French army, sixty-eight-year-old Gen. Maurice Gamelin, considered one of the world's most brilliant commanders in 1939, had no radios and only one commercial telephone line at his headquarters in the Chateau de Vicennes, near Paris. Gamelin said that the use of radio might give away the location of his headquarters. By his own admission it usually took forty-eight hours to issue orders from his headquarters. See Len Deighton's *Blitzkrieg* for more detailed information.

22. Len Deighton, *Blitzkrieg, From the Rise of Hitler to the Fall of Dunkirk* (London: Jonathan Cape, 1979), 175–76.

23. Department of the Army, FM 100–5, *AirLand Operations* (Washington, D.C.: Department of the Army, 14 June 1993), 2–9.

24. TRADOC Pamphlet 525–5, "Force XXI Operations" (Fort Monroe, VA: U.S. Army Training & Doctrine Command, 1994), chapter 3.

25. Strawson, *The Battle for the Ardennes,* 10. Strawson goes on to say, on pages 10–11: "Speed was only made possible by surprise and concentration. Surprise itself was achieved principally by concentration and speed. Concentration could only reap decisive results if in conjunction with speed and surprise it tore open the enemy's front, penetrated deeply behind it, paralyzed opposition, and led to a battle of annihilation. Suddenness, violence, blitzkrieg schnell—these were the very nuclei of blitzkrieg. But there was something more. Once this violent all-destroying thrust had got going, it must never stop until the battle is won. If it halted it would be found, checked and attacked. To maintain momentum, night and day, was everything. The forces engaged must penetrate ever deeper, ever broader, and so bring about the absolute disruption of enemy positions, reserves, headquarters and supplies. The key to it was a never-ending flow of mixed panzer groups constantly supported and supplied by fire power and transport aircraft of the Luftwaffe. Thus the two indispensable agents of blitzkrieg were still Panzer and Stuka. Nor should it be forgotten that each was helpless without fuel."

26. Edward Luttwak, *Strategy; The Logic of War and Peace* (Cambridge: Belknap Press, 1987), 106.

27. Jeff Erlich and Robert Holzer, "Smaller Units Wave of Future/21st Century Fighters Seen Grouped in Lethal, Highly Mobile Bands," *Army Times,* 1 June 1995.

28. Jack Weible, "Cash Scramble Spurred on by Aging Weapons," *Army Times,* 5 January 1998.

29. Rich Maze, "Military May Have to Shoulder Budget Shortfall," *Army Times,* 5 January 1998.

30. TRADOC Pamphlet 525–5, "Force XXI Operations," Chapter 3.

31. Noel Barber, *The Week France Fell* (New York: Stein and Day, 1976), 71.

32. William S. Cohen, Secretary of Defense, *Annual Report to the President and the Congress* (Washington, D.C.: Government Printing Office, April 1997), 70.

33. Cohen, 251.

34. Sean Naylor, "Force XXI, Army After Next Brought into Focus," *Army Times,* 5 January 1998.

35. Weible.

36. P. A. J. Cordingley, "Armored Forces and the Counter Stroke," in *The British Army & the Operational Level of War,* ed. J. G. Mackenzie and Brian Holden Reid (London: Tri-Service Press, 1989), 97–98. "As J. F. C. Fuller puts it, 'we see these three principles of war [firepower, mobility, and protection] must be combined, that is work together like the parts of a machine.' It took the Israelis three days to realize that reliance on the Bar Lev Line and the invulnerability of the tank was not going to win the Yom Kippur War in 1973 and only return to a balanced army would counter the threat of the anti-tank guided weapon. Earlier history also supports this view. Hannibal offers an outstanding example of inferior but balanced forces overcoming forces that were both larger and better equipped. He had no new weapon and his troops were inferior in quality and training to the Romans. His amazing string of successes resulted from his ability to use combined arms and then focus on maneuver."

37. Gen. Dennis J. Reimer, chief of staff of the U.S. Army, 20 November 1996 in an e-mail message relating to his comments on "The Army: An Instrument of National Power—Today, Tomorrow and into the 21st Century," at the 1996 Fletcher Conference on the subject of "Strategy, Force Structure and Planning for the 21st Century."

38. Otis, 19.

Douglas A. MacGregor

Colonel Douglas MacGregor (Ph.D.) is an armor officer. In 1997 he shook the establishment and earned himself a full-page profile in *U.S. News and World Report* as the author of the book *Breaking the Phalanx*. Former national security adviser Brent Scowcroft wrote that his book was "exactly the sort of thing that should be preoccupying us all." Currently, MacGregor is assigned to NATO headquarters in Belgium.

MacGregor has never been known as an officer who shied from controversy. In some cases that means he has put pen to paper and recorded some thoughts that many consider unpleasant. Our profession sometimes is unpleasant, and hard truths are still truths. Through his writing MacGregor invites and creates a discussion on the course and direction of the profession of arms, the primary indicator of a healthy organization.

In this essay MacGregor addresses organizational structures for command and control. One of the assumptions made here is that defense budgets as they apply to force levels will continue to decline. This is not an unreasonable assumption given the recent history of the United States as well as the projected abilities of digitized ground forces. As a result, this chapter looks beyond the effects of individual weapons (a tactical application) and asserts that whatever the effects may be, military forces must organize themselves within a logical joint multiservice command structure designed to maximize the strengths of the combat forces remaining.

Perhaps the best thing about MacGregor's writing is that he not only identifies problems; he offers solutions. In this chapter he sustains that reputation. Where the U.S. military goes in this arena in the future is open to debate. We now have at least one blueprint in addition to the option of maintaining the status quo. Options are never bad.

A version of this chapter appeared as an article in *Joint Forces Quarterly* in 1999.

Command and Control for Joint Strategic Action

Nearly ten years after the dissolution of the Warsaw Pact and a series of defense policy reviews, the most important question in U.S. defense policy remains unanswered: What kinds of U.S. armed forces, military strategies, and resource commitments will be needed for the future?[1] This is no accident. A 30 percent reduction in the defense budget since 1989 and service reluctance to adopt any plan that does not reaffirm traditional roles and force structures have combined to obstruct meaningful change.[2]

In fact, the budget "top line" imposed by defense reviews and Congressional legislation has intensified interservice rivalry and prompted senior military leaders to stress the validity of existing single-service doctrine, organization, and tactics rather than embracing change. As a result, the United States risks wasting opportunities to steal a dramatic march on the rest of the world's armed forces. This is because revolutions in military affairs occur whether senior military leaders encourage them or not. The only real choice is whether the United States becomes the beneficiary of the current revolution in military affairs or its eventual victim.

Evidence for the current revolution's developing impact can be seen in regional settings where potential nation-state adversaries, disintegrating states, and groups dispossessed by modernization[3] are all trying to acquire the capability to strike decisively in crises and conflicts with weapons of mass destruction.[4] U.S. military strategists must assume that future adversaries will possess not only some form of weapons of mass destruction, but also a limited supply of precision-guided munitions, as well as access to electronic intelligence and satellite imagery provided by third powers.[5]

Armed with these capabilities, future opponents will attempt to outpace the U.S. response and present the United States with a strategic fait accompli. Moreover, by confronting U.S. forces with the prospect of fighting a war of attrition or a war in which U.S. battlefield successes are avenged with the use of weapons of mass destruction, future opponents will aim to eliminate U.S. political resolve in order to forcibly reverse our aggression.[6] This strategy deserves Western attention. If U.S. and allied forces do not move beyond contemporary single-service operational concepts and war-fighting organizations, this strategy can potentially defeat any mix of U.S. and allied forces today or in the future, regardless of technological superiority.[7]

Part of the solution to this twenty-first-century dilemma involves projecting U.S. ground forces into the unified commands much more rapidly and with greater mobility, firepower, and force protection. To cope with these new dynamics, fundamental changes in the way U.S. ground forces organize to deploy and fight are essential. Army ground forces must become more expeditionary in character and orientation. Marine ground forces must adapt to a world in which an island-hopping campaign reminiscent of World War II is no more probable than a future defense of the Fulda Gap. Both forces will have to organize to cooperate closely with each other, as well as with U.S. airpower, in order to exploit the United States' growing arsenal of air- and space-based capabilities. All of these points suggest that U.S. land power in coming decades must be an amalgamation of army and marine forces and capabilities within a more agile, operational joint framework.[8]

Changes in military strategy have always been equal in importance to successively acquiring the ability to fight new kinds of war.[9] With this point in mind, this essay builds on concepts introduced in *Breaking the Phalanx: A New Design for Land Power in the 21st Century* and argues for a top-down transformation of the joint force land component command (JFLCC) concept.[10]

The idea is to take advantage of new technology, new operational concepts, and new war-fighting organizations to more rapidly project and jointly employ U.S. ground forces. By building on the foundation of experience in the U.S. Army and Marine Corps structures, the changes in concept and execution sketched here in outline are designed to achieve a flatter, less hierarchical command structure that can reduce the time it takes ground forces to deploy and begin combat operations.[11] As the reader will soon discover, effecting this transformation involves establishing joint operational command-and-control structures for deploying tactical ground forces that are subordinate to regional unified commands.[12]

Adjusting to New Dynamics

When the Spartans were at the height of their military fame and glory, they sent a deputation to the oracle at Delphi and demanded arrogantly: "Can anything harm Sparta?" The oracle answered: "Yes, luxury."[13] Today, in answer to the same question about the U.S. armed forces, the oracle might say: "Yes, bureaucracy." Ever since the collapse of Soviet power in eastern Europe gave the United States unprecedented military dominance, the ratio of command, control, and support to fighting forces has grown without any resulting increase in combat power or flexibility at the level where it is most needed: on the battlefield.

This is interesting because the opposite is true for U.S. business. Corporate headquarters in the private sector continue to shrink. Partially as a result of this paring of the top-heavy management hierarchy, U.S. productivity and economic growth continue their climb to record highs while exhibiting historically unique flexibility and agility. Downsizing, reengineering, outsourcing, and decentralization have cut the size of corporate staffs and the number of functions concentrated at corporate headquarters. Information technology is being exploited to reduce the need for frequent meetings and to create function-based organizations that share critical information.

Dr. Rosabeth Moss Kanter, an influential professor of business administration at the Harvard Business School, characterizes the private sector's response to change in the strategic environment of business in her latest book, *World Class*. In many ways, her words suggest directions for change in the way U.S. ground forces can be commanded and controlled.

> Across industries, forces for change are similar: industry consolidation, changing regulation, new technology, more de-

manding customers, and pressures for lower cost, higher quality, greater speed. The responses are also similar: a search for new markets (often internationally), acceleration of new product development, and implementation of a new organizational model, one that comprises fewer layers, faster processes, greater use of teams, employees educated to solve problems autonomously, deeper relationships. . . . Change is a matter not of failure, but of success. The most change is occurring in the most successful companies.[14]

Military progress tends to follow civil progress, though at a considerable distance. One reason for this time lag is that in the culture of the professional military, the burden of proof is on the advocate for change, not on the advocate for the status quo. Thus, for change to occur in military affairs, a change in the nature of conflict and warfare has to be widely recognized inside the military. In 1929, for example, there was still no sense in the United States' professional military that anything had really changed as a result of World War I. Opponents of mechanization and defenders of the horse cavalry in the U.S. Army went so far as to suggest, "An unfed motor stops; a starved horse takes days to die."[15]

There is not enough space here to debate the question of how much has changed. However, it is possible, against the backdrop of experience in Panama, southwest Asia, Somalia, Haiti, and Bosnia, to highlight a few critical observations about the direction of change as it pertains to U.S. ground forces in the current and future strategic environment.

- In the future, the requirement for rapid response to crises and conflicts around the world will clearly be much greater than the need for static, territorial defense of central Europe or northeast Asia.
- The question of how quickly a force can be deployed is no more important than that of how much force is necessary to assemble in a crisis or conflict. To obtain a real advantage from rapid deployment, ground forces must be capable of conducting operations (offensive, defensive, or peace enforcement)

almost immediately upon arrival in all regional unified commands.[16]

• Permitting future conflicts to drag on rather than rapidly crushing an armed opponent means risking failure.[17] The proliferation of weapons of mass destruction and the revolution-in-military-affairs technology to effectively employ them suggest that there is good reason to fear the danger to friendly forces created by delay.[18]

• The newer the technology or its application, the more important it becomes to design its use with the whole world in mind. Single-service, theater-specific remedies are features of the past, not the future.[19]

• The direction of the current revolution in military affairs points to the creation of a "system of systems" that literally encircles the earth and has global reach. It will be critical for ground forces to integrate seamlessly into the global-strike capabilities this system will make possible, both to exploit its potential and to guarantee the safety of deployed ground forces.[20]

Based on these points, the ability of CINCs to gain quick access to a pool of ready ground forces and to command and control these ground forces, operationally and tactically, will be decisive in twenty-first-century conflicts or crises.[21] In practice, this means that U.S. Army and Marine ground forces must be prepared to deploy on a phone call. Given the reductions in the size of the U.S. Army's active-component combat force since 1991 and the requirement for rapid force projection, these points also underline the need for a degree of command-and-control unanimity on the operational level of both form and function that transcends service lines. Thus, the U.S. Army and Marine Corps should take a hard look at streamlining their operational-level command and control within a joint framework.

In Force XXI, the U.S. Army is concentrating on developing a tactical command-and-control structure from the ground up, taking for granted all existing command-and-control nodes and echelons.[22] Its decades of service in Germany and Korea reinforce a preference for theater-specific army command-and-control structures. However, it is no longer possible to limit the scope of U.S. Army command and control to predetermined geographical locations with narrowly defined tactical missions. Deployments since the mid-1980s make it clear that future army missions necessitate a much more global approach to command and control.

Top-Down Versus Bottom-Up Command and Control

Jointness is a condition that exists when services develop mechanisms—operational and tactical structures, processes, and expertise—for bridging service differences and extracting strategic value from interservice cooperation. In this sense, joint command and control, or joint C2, is defined as a joint system of command links or nodes integrating maneuver forces and strike assets, informed by a variety of sensors (digital or other communication and data links). When viewed as a unified system, this conceptual structure provides information for the planning and execution of coordinated all-arms operations.[23] The critical step, however, is to create joint C2 structures on the operational level that assist war-fighting CINCs to respond quickly to events in regional commands. The question is how to do it.

One approach to developing joint C2 architecture for U.S. ground forces is to borrow from the experience of U.S. naval forces whose global mission focus has resulted in a different command-and-control evolution. In view of this global orientation, U.S. naval forces have tended to stress the importance of a top-down, rather than a bottom-up approach to command and control on the strategic and operational levels. This top-down approach has assisted U.S. naval forces in bridging the gap between the requirement for an efficient global command-and-control structure and the demand for tactical autonomy by emphasizing function-based organizations and the concept of modularity.

An example of this orientation can be found in the Marine Expeditionary Force. The Marine Expeditionary Force is the principal Marine Corps war-fighting organization, particularly for large crises or contingencies. Unlike the army's corps structure, which is essential to the division's war fight, a deployed Marine Expeditionary Force can vary dramatically in terms of size and composition depending on the requirements of the mission.[24] In fact, the Marine Expeditionary Force is designed to expand or contract to cope with the specific situation and may contain as few as five thousand or as many as fifty thousand marines.

At the heart of this expeditionary structure is the Marine Air-Ground Task Force. This task force is interesting in this context because it provides a potential model in microcosm for joint C2 on the operational level for both army and marine forces. The Marine Corps building-block approach to Marine Air-Ground Task Force organization is based on a simple formula that organizes marine forces in the task force into discrete command-and-control elements. At the top of the structure is the command element for planning and execution of operations.

There are three subordinate command-and-control elements: a ground combat element to direct ground combat operations; an aviation combat element to perform the functions of aviation—air-to-air combat, close air support, air reconnaissance, electronic warfare, and control of aircraft and missile systems; and a combat service support element to provide the full range of support functions from sea bases aboard naval shipping or from temporary bases ashore. The modular structure lends itself to rapid expansion into a larger force as the situation demands by adding forces as needed to the core units of each existing element.[25]

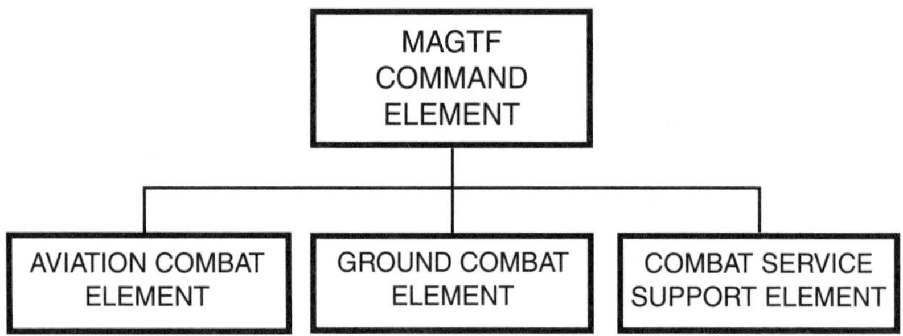

In theory, an effective joint C2 system on the operational level could mirror this simple, discrete, modular approach. However, to do so it would have to consistently provide the commander with useful real-time information in a form that would assist the commander in recognizing key events, formulating a response, and transmitting this response to subordinates in time for implementation. This is because the land component commander on the operational level of war must shape actions in a crisis or conflict environment through a combination of threatening targets and actually moving forces and striking them. In addition to thousands of movable subordinate entities, land force commanders must deal with the complexities of a thinking enemy reacting to their every move.

In this setting, the opportunity for information overload cannot be overstated. Consequently, the need for functional simplicity as seen in the Marine Air-Ground Task Force is enormous. Masses of information flowing through sensors and aggregated by computer power into preformatted messages will not reach the critical points of authority in time if the complexity of the command-and-control structure impedes the flow of information.

None of this is to suggest that new information technology will provide answers that have eluded commanders in the past. If a commander does not already know what is important, more information will not help. Still, provided the command-and-control structure is simple in organization, today's technology will deliver the information. This is a critical reason why using the close/deep/rear framework as the conceptual basis for command-and-control organization on the operational level offers significant advantages. Each military decision maker has a limited area of authority distinct from the others (modularity), commands pass in only one direction (a hierarchical structure), and each decision maker determines within the higher commander's intent how to execute commands from higher authority (operational autonomy).[26]

Extrapolating from the Marine Air-Ground Task Force structure to the operational level suggests a model for a new JFLCC structure with close/deep/rear functionality. The lieutenant general commanding the army corps-based or Marine Expeditionary Force-based structure has an independent mobile headquarters element and commands three separate, autonomous, mobile headquarters under general officers.

For reasons that will become clear later, in the notional JFLCC structure outlined here, major generals were selected to command the close/deep/rear headquarters. Depending on the crisis, conflict, or peacetime mission, one or all of these headquarters could be deployed. The numbers of officers and other ranks assigned to all three elements could total as few as five hundred. Ideally, these headquarters were configured for rapid deployability using strategic airlift, including wheeled armor, helicopters, and satellite communications.

OPERATIONAL COMMAND AND CONTROL IS POSITIONED IN THE UNIFIED COMMANDS TO FACILITATE RAPID DEPLOYMENT AND JOINT INTEROPERABILITY

LIEUTENANT GENERAL
(Joint Forces Land Component Commander)

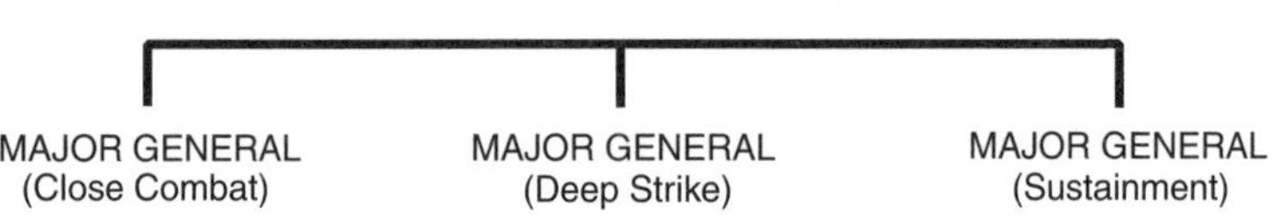

Within this conceptual framework, one major general within the JFLCC commands the close combat forces deployed to the JFLCC. These close combat formations could consist of army or marine armor, air-mobile infantry, or attack helicopters in support of the close fight. In some actions, for instance, marine infantry might cooperate closely with army armored and helicopter reconnaissance. In practice, this commander supplants the army or marine division commander and headquarters which would otherwise have to deploy from the United States. It should be obvious from both the strategic and operational levels whether the tactical maneuver formation is army or marine.

A second major general in the JFLCC commands deep combat operations. "Deep" in this context is a potentially misleading term. Time, target, and effect rather than just space separate the deep and the close fights.[27] Further, "deep" in land warfare is operational, not strategic in the sense of strategic air operations.

This is not to suggest that the advent of new precision weapons and dramatically increased firepower from short- or long-range rocket artillery and air power do not create the need for a joint command-and-control structure on the ground that can effectively exploit these capabilities. On the contrary, for a strategy of ground force maneuver to succeed, the means to employ these strike assets are critical. Sophisticated intelligence collection and targeting analysis are of limited value if the command-and-control structure to quickly exploit both information and strike capabilities does not exist.

With the emergence of a "system of systems" global-strike complex, the deep fight commander's links to the army and marine tactical formations as well as to the global-strike complex become pivotal. This structure becomes the critical link to the joint force air component commander, who will want to exploit the capabilities residing in ground-strike and maneuver forces to suppress or defeat enemy air defenses, as well as enemy missile attacks. For that matter, the theater antiballistic and cruise missile defense mission will also become an integral feature of the deep structure's focus and activity.

In the event that combat maneuver forces were assigned the mission to strike deep into enemy territory, this headquarters would also command these maneuver elements. This suggests that the deep headquarters instead of the close combat headquarters would control air-mobile formations operating in conjunction with attack helicopters to the front of advancing friendly ground forces. This deep command-and-control structure would be postured to harmonize air force and army/marine corps operations in the deep fight, ensuring mutual support and fratricide prevention. When the movement of forces changed the spatial disposition of ground forces, the close combat commander or even the rear sustainment commander could assume control of these elements.

Sustainment operations offer a rich field of opportunity for joint C2 under the third major general in the structure. In the short term, some specific weaponry and technology will remain service-specific, but there are many ways for the army and the marines to share logistics support. Some of these include cross-service equipment, supply transportation, storage, transfer, port-opening services, prepositioning afloat, and over-the-shore logistics. As seen during Desert Storm, rationalizing the conduct of sustainment operations within a joint C2 framework for ground forces simply institutionalizes practices that emerge under the pressure of war anyway.[28]

In the long term, the transition to progressively newer forms of warfare will reinforce the need for greater independence in tactical formations, as well as potentially eliminating the rear area, except as a communications zone.[29]

How this JFLCC structure could contribute to the formation of a mission-specific joint task force headquarters is equally important. The concept suggests three possibilities. In the simplest case of a large-scale crisis or theater war, the regional CINC could assume the joint task force commander (COMJTF) duties, and the army-marine JFLCC could be involved as a subordinate. One JFLCC could control as many as fifty thousand troops. If the ground force was larger, a second JFLCC from USACOM or a part of a CONUS-based JFLCC could be deployed as augmentation or reinforcement. For instance, a second close combat headquarters could be added to the existing JFLCC structure if the joint land component commander determined that the addition of more close combat formations would make the span of control too great for one close combat headquarters.

In the case of a three-star COMJTF, the regional CINC could designate the appropriate component commander as COMJTF. The COMJTF's component command staff would form the bulk of the joint task force staff, augmented by the other two component commands. A three-star U.S. Air Force joint task force commander could require the use of the deep fight JFLCC commander and that commander's headquarters if ground forces were needed to augment air force SEAD (Suppression of Enemy Air Defense) ele-

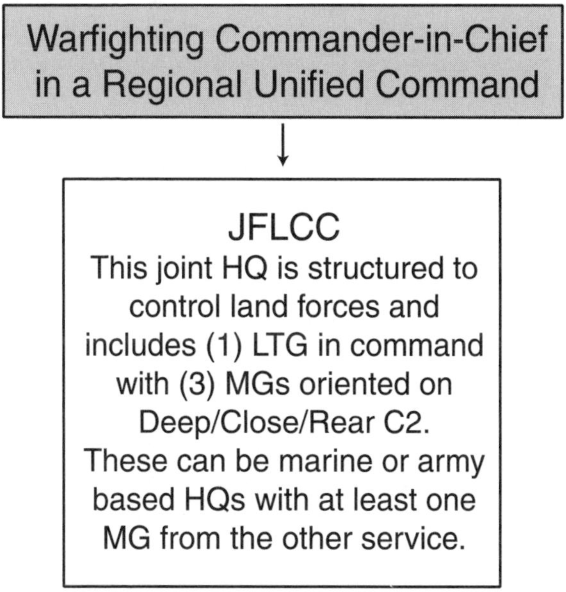

Warfighting Commander-in-Chief in a Regional Unified Command

↓

JFLCC

This joint HQ is structured to control land forces and includes (1) LTG in command with (3) MGs oriented on Deep/Close/Rear C2. These can be marine or army based HQs with at least one MG from the other service.

There can be two types of JLFCCs: Standing JLFCCs with assigned forces and Contigency JFLCCs without assigned forces. With embedded operational joint C4I, JTFs can be formed as needed for regional employment.

ments. In the Balkans, where the potential for conflict and crisis is acute, a JFLCC in the Mediterranean could be called upon to command and control up to fifty thousand troops in combat or peace-enforcement operations.

In the case of a smaller joint task force commanded by a two-star COMJTF from within the appropriate component command, that command would again contribute the bulk of the staff, augmented by the other component commands. An example of a two-star-commanded joint task force could be a disaster relief operation in a place such as Papua, New Guinea, which was recently struck by a tidal wave. One of the major generals with close, deep, or rear headquarters already assigned to the regional command could provide the core headquarters element and assume responsibility for this mission. This would help solve the problem of establishing joint task force headquarters that on the one hand are knowledgeable about the region and on the other hand are formed on short notice to cope with an immediate crisis.

An important question for the short term is how many of these JFLCC headquarters structures should exist and how they should be focused. The role specialization that this approach proposes could lead to the establishment in the regional commands of JFLCCs comprising designated army and marine commanders and joint staffs with responsibility for planning and executing operations within the close/deep/rear framework of land warfare. Land force commanders must integrate political directives and military power with a thorough knowledge of regional socioeconomic conditions, historical development, and political life. Experience in Vietnam, southwest Asia, Somalia, and more recently Bosnia all indicate that the use of military power can go awry without an appreciation for the context in which it is being exercised.

There is an acute need for operational command-and-control structures directly subordinate to the regional CINC to be focused on the regional contingencies in which they are likely to play a critical role. The world today is far too complex to suppose that an operational headquarters based in the United States can effectively go anywhere in the world and execute a broad range of complex military tasks with a minimum of notice. In view of these points, a possible distribution for JFLCC structures is shown in the illustration on the following page.

Scrapping many of the single-service component headquarters in the unified commands and at home in the United States would allow for the organization of future joint task forces around functional areas of responsibility. The resulting function-based joint forward deployed land force headquarters would then be positioned to replace the CONUS-based army division and corps headquarters that require many weeks, if not months, to deploy.

Tactical ground maneuver formations could then rotate on a regular basis to the regional commands to both exercise and execute forward presence missions in the same way naval forces rotate in and out of regional commands.

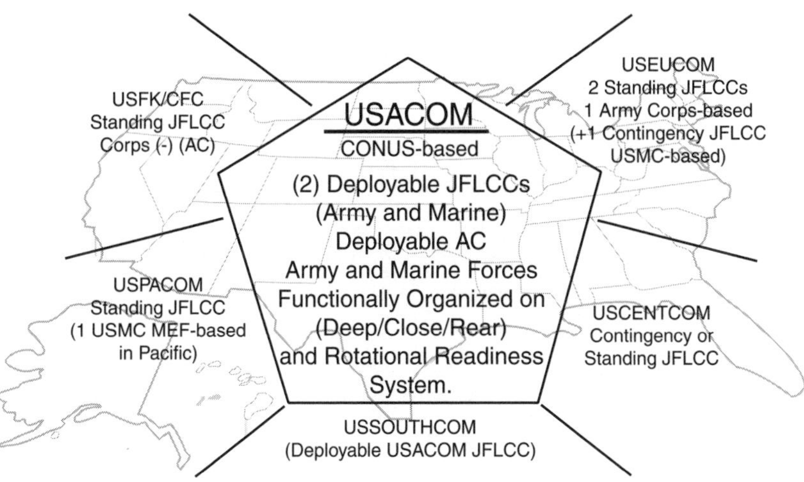

Similar economic measures could be applied to CONUS-based marine headquarters with the object of reallocating general officers and staffs to JFLCCs in the regional commands. These measures are not only critical to reducing the deployment times for army and marine forces; they also promise to save money. At the same time, change in the employment component of military strategy in land warfare has consequences for jointness in the force-development component of land warfare.

Command and Control for Strategic Responsiveness

Because of the threat of weapons of mass destruction and the fragility of alliance structures under crisis conditions, an extended preparation of U.S. ground forces for operations in close proximity to the enemy's forces is extremely risky. Moreover, the U.S. National Command Authorities will not want to grant an enemy time to organize its own forces or to disrupt the deployment of U.S. ground forces. It is therefore dangerous to concentrate combat power in any one region too early.

Subordinating joint C2 on the operational level to the regional unified commands creates the opportunity to package army and marine tactical forces for rapid deployment.[30] Without the enormous weight of administrative overhead in the Cold War headquarters structures, army and marine tactical forces could be configured to move much more rapidly from widely dispersed staging areas overseas and in the continental United States.

Today's theater, army, corps, and division structures were designed for World War II and the requirements of a mass-mobilization Industrial Age war. Laminating these structures with tons of electronic hardware and computer software is unlikely to simplify command arrangements, improve readiness, or reduce the response time for deploying ground forces. For example, brigades are still structured to deploy as part of larger divisions, and divisions in turn are structured to deploy as part of larger corps. A decision to deploy one without the other necessitates the selective removal and reallocation of mission-critical elements. As a result, the readiness of one or more of these formations to deploy and fight is inevitably degraded.[31] This condition is unresponsive to the demands of the current and future strategic environments.

Strategic responsiveness in the twenty-first century means organizing ground forces that can come into action before the peace is lost. Grouping ground tactical forces based on function—close/deep/rear—confers greater independence on tactical formations smaller than divisions, which can rapidly deploy and operate across the spectrum of conflict. When these forces are structured for joint C2, they provide an agile force mix that is capable of dominating maneuver and precision strikes within the framework of the joint task force. Packaging tactical forces on the deep/close/rear basis also creates joint and CINC visibility for critical army war-fighting assets such as rocket artillery, attack, and

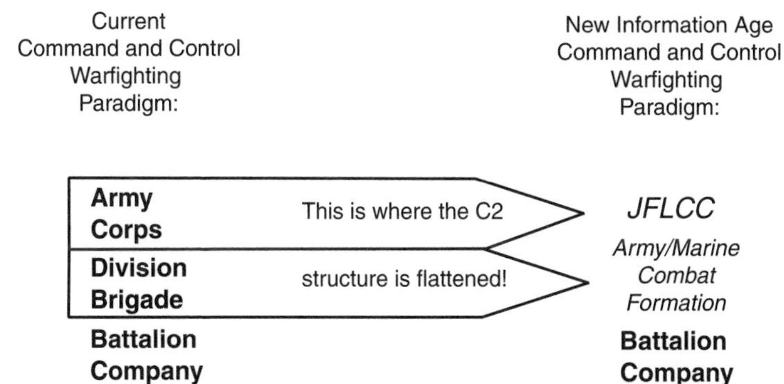

transport helicopters, which are currently submerged in the amorphous Cold War structure.

The JFLCC structure presented here is an attempt to address the urgent strategic need for rapid deployment and operational readiness of U.S. ground forces within a joint framework. As mentioned earlier, designating major generals to serve as close/deep/rear commanders would eliminate the need for division and corps headquarters to deploy from CONUS. At the same time, post commanders in the United States would focus on providing a training environment conducive to the readiness of tactical formations for rapid deployment to regional unified commands. These commanders would manage core competency training up to and including training center rotations.

This suggests a two-dimensional system. The system would contain an administrative logistical command structure to supervise and support training and an operational command structure subordinate to the regional unified commands to deploy ground forces in joint training or conflict within a particular unified command. The U.S. Navy currently employs a similar approach to training and organizing elements for deployment.

Such a top-down approach to organizing command-and-control and ground forces promises to result in a flatter command structure with the potential for more rapid decision making and strategic responsiveness. Most important, this concept recognizes that army and marine forces are likely to be combined into the core elements of most future joint task forces. These changes will also necessitate modifications to the way army national guard and reserve forces are structured for command and control. Although that subject is beyond the scope of this essay, the impact of disestablishing unneeded headquarters in the reserve components is no less important than in the active component.[32]

The potential for integrating information systems with the command-and-control process in support of the arrangements outlined here is limitless. Provided that the need for simplicity in command-and-control structures and the need for training, leadership, and equipment to achieve greater autonomy and dispersion on the tactical level are kept in mind, airborne and space-based sensors expanding coverage beyond line-of-sight will allow tactical commanders to exploit opportunities much more rapidly than in the past. It is no exaggeration to suggest that the old adage, "Give them artillery and you've made them independent," will soon be replaced with, "Give them unmanned aerial vehicles and joint C4ISR (Command-Control-Communications-Coordination-Intelligence-Surveillance-Reconnaissance) and you've made them independent."

Colonel Bob Killebrew describes the type of communications capability that could support the modular JFLCC envisioned here:

> Communications nets of all kinds can be lodged in space, with databases on the ground and data transferred over dense, redundant nets using virtually unlimited bandwidth. These changes can free maneuver units from dependence on bulky terrestrial systems that are easier to intercept and jam than those in space or near-space. The explosion of space-based commercial systems, now on the horizon, suggests that most, if not all, future military space-based communications may be carried by commercial vendors.[33]

Almost imperceptibly, personal computers have gone from unconnected to connected. Networked embedded processors are beginning to integrate diverse activities in the private sector to achieve greater adaptability and transparency.[34] This innovation must inevitably find its way into joint C4ISR systems. These points notwithstanding, how is the United States' professional military establishment ever to keep up with the maddening pace of change in communications? Commercial off-the-shelf technology is far more advanced than that fielded in the U.S. armed forces today.

Part of the solution to the problem of selecting joint C2 systems with the desired level of baseline joint interoperability is to lease operational and strategic C4I hardware and software from private-sector corporations such as Lockheed Martin and ITT. There is not much point in investing scarce defense capital in outright purchases of C4I equipment in the current and future environment. Technology is outpacing the defense research, development, and procurement systems. Contracts that lease these systems could include provisions for regular upgrades to guarantee state-of-the-art capability in the military sector—something that is clearly not the case today.

Closing Thoughts

Senior officers on the operational level of war are central figures in the drama that translates strategic goals into tactical action. These leaders must not only constantly engage in linking the strategic and tactical levels, but simultaneously comprehend the actions of their opponents in a similar context. How senior officers interpret missions and subsequently employ their armed forces dominates operations. This is why an integrative structure of multiservice command and control must exist on the operational level to induce military leaders to interpret information and military activity in ways that result in the exploitation of capabilities across service lines. This is the underlying purpose of the JFLCC structure described here.

This is, of course, only one of several critical steps that must be taken in the future. Joint training, doctrine, education, and, to the extent possible, modernization are also essential to the success of this endeavor. Based on progress in this arena, the JFLCC concept outlined here could be adapted to include senior officers from all of the services. Integrating army and marine leadership on the operational level is, however, a plausible starting point in this much longer process.

What U.S. ground forces need now is a joint war-fighting command-and-control structure on the operational level with joint C4ISR that facilitates the rapid deployment of tactical formations by strategic air and fast sea lift to the scene of action in the unified command. The JFLCC concept outlined here is designed to meet this need for speed and agility while simultaneously offering an alternative to the debilitating force structure cuts that too many appointed and elected leaders are still prepared to make. The JFLCC alternative promises to achieve long-term economy through the reallocation of human and materiel resources from the World War II war-mobilization headquarters structure to the regional unified commands, where the JFLCCs can be organized and positioned to contribute to joint task force headquarters establishment, ready for immediate joint strategic action.

As mentioned at the beginning of this essay, the bureaucratic and technological legacies of the United States' Cold War military establishment continue to distract attention from the dramatic influence of social, political, economic, and technological change in the strategic environment since 1989. Ambivalence about change in the strategic environment keeps U.S. ground forces from being prepared for it. At the same time the international situation is becoming more dangerous, and nothing is emerging to replace the earlier European world order.

This necessitates a reshaping of the U.S. military system toward an effective posture for conflict across the spectrum—across the globe.[35] In this regard, the concepts in this essay are part of an adaptive approach at the beginning of a revolution in military affairs that will allow army and marine land power to absorb emerging technologies. Ideally, a unified command should be selected for the purpose of examining these adaptive concepts in a joint operational environment.

Adaptation, however, is not just a function of technology. The Russian officer who witnessed Prussia's titanic victory over Austria at Koniggratz in 1866, Major General Dragomirov, dismissed claims in the newspapers of the day that new breech-loading rifles had been responsible for the Prussian army's success. He stated: "It wasn't the needle gun by itself that won the victories of 1866, but the men who carried it."[36] The French military attaché was probably more insightful when he noted that regardless of what technological advantage the Austrians might have possessed, it would not have changed the outcome in 1866; the war was won by the Prussian high command.[37]

For the army and the marines to adapt successfully to this new environment, a common view of what can work and what is necessary must shape the design and organization of U.S. ground forces. If the army and the marines cannot articulate a common, coherent vision, it is much more likely that the U.S. defense bureaucracy will supply the nation with the force structure it knows rather than the force structure the nation needs. Some of these changes involve the recognition that new surface ship design and better propulsion have not resulted in significantly faster surface ships and that U.S. Army and Marine combat forces can reach the scene of the action much more quickly from the air.

Judicious choices made now about modernization and the configuration of tactical ground forces for rapid deployment within the close/deep/rear joint framework will equip these forces with the operational reach, force protection, and mobility that today's army and marine crisis-response forces do not have in sufficient quantity or quality. At the same time, prudent requests for further additions to U.S. air and fast sea lift transport and prepositioning capabilities can augment the JFLCC's role in boosting land power's responsiveness on the tactical level.

Notwithstanding these points, the alternative approach—keeping headquarters that are no longer strategically relevant in their current form and relying exclusively on the infusion of new information technology to enable Cold War organizations to fight the last war better—will not transform the force. Moreover, this approach risks wasting real opportunities to steal a dramatic march on potential adversaries' armed forces. To paraphrase the oracle of Delphi, "Missed opportunities to make real and substantive change are luxuries that can harm the U.S. military in the twenty-first century."

The author is indebted to the assistance of Dr. Williamson Murray; Dr. Fred Kagan; Mr. Frank Finelli; Capt. Mark Fitzgerald, U.S. Navy; Col. Michael O'Neal, U.S. Marine Corps; and Lt. Col. Keith Self, U.S. Army.

Notes

1. Dr. John Hillen, *Future Visions for U.S. Defense Policy* (New York: Council on Foreign Relations Press, 1998), 7.

2. Rowan Scarborough, "Peace Dividend Apparently Paying Off," *Washington Times,* 9 March 1998. "Budget has fallen 30% since the Soviet Bloc dissolved."

3. Ralph Peters, "Spotting the Losers: Seven Signs of Non-Competitive States," *Parameters* (Spring 1998): 36–47.

4. Barbara Crossette, "Arms Inspectors Brief Diplomats on Iraqi Deception," *New York Times,* 4 June 1998; and Robert Whymant, "North Korea May Have Nuclear Bomb," *London Times,* 4 June 1998.

5. David A. Fulghum, "Improved Air Defenses Prompt Pentagon Fears," *Aviation Week & Space Technology* (6 July 1998): 22.

6. Jeffrey Record, "The Creeping Irrelevance of U.S. Force Planning," Strategic Studies Institute Monograph, (Carlisle, PA, U.S. Army War College, 19 May 1998), 2.

7. Memorandum for record; subject: *Strategic Concepts Wargame III* (Washington, D.C.: Office of the Chief of Naval Operations, Department of the Navy, 5 June 1995), 1.

8. Dr. Williamson Murray, "In Search of the Army After Next: Another Perspective," *Marine Corps Gazette* (January 1998): 71.

9. Julian Lider, *Military Theory: Concept, Structure, Problems* (Aldershot, U.K.: Gower Publishing, 1983), 341.

10. This paper builds on earlier concepts for reorganizing the U.S. Army in *Breaking the Phalanx: A New Design for Land Power in the 20th Century* (Westport, Conn.: Praeger, 1997), and outlines the contribution that a joint command-and-control structure for land power could make to U.S. military strategy.

11. Phillip Odeen, National Defense Panel chairman, *National Defense Panel Report* (Arlington, Va.: National Defense Panel, 1997), 49, 53, 71.

12. The boundaries of the levels of war and conflict tend to blur and do not necessarily correspond to levels of command. Nevertheless, in the U.S. system, the strategic level is usually the concern of the National Command Authorities and the highest military commanders; the operational level is usually the concern of theater

commands; and the tactical level is usually the focus of subtheater commands. *Essays on Air and Space Power,* vol. I (Maxwell Air Force Base, Ala.: Air University Press, 1997), 13.

13. Field Marshal Earl Wavell, *The Good Soldier* (London: MacMillan, 1948), 43.

14. Rosabeth Moss Kanter, *World Class: Thriving Locally in the Global Economy* (New York: Simon and Schuster, 1995), 149.

15. Charles Messenger, *The Blitzkrieg Story* (New York: Charles Scribner's, 1975), 58.

16. Douglas A. MacGregor, *Breaking the Phalanx: A New Design for Land Power in the 20th Century* (Westport, Conn.: Praeger, 1997), 129.

17. Nathan Leites, *Soviet Style in War* (New York: Crane Russak, 1982), xix.

18. "For instance, cruise missiles are attractive as strategic weapons. They offer both a first strike and retaliatory capability in crisis or conflict. They are relatively small and can be launched from a variety of platforms, including trucks, submarines and aircraft. And they are easy to hide and disperse." W. Seth Carus, *Cruise Missile Proliferation in the 1990s* (Washington, D.C.: Center for Strategic and International Studies, 1992), 45.

19. Senator Dan Coats, "Joint Experimentation: Unlocking the Promise of the Future," *Joint Force Quarterly* (Autumn/Winter 1997–1998): 13–15.

20. Adm. William Owens, U.S. Navy (Ret.), "System of Systems," *Armed Forces Journal* (January 1996): 8.

21. Col. (Ret.) C. Kenneth Allard, *Command Control and the Common Defense* (Hartford, Conn: Yale University Press, 1990), 250.

22. "Force XXI: Division Redesign," *Army Times,* 22 June 1998.

23. F. E. Littlebury and D. K. Praeger, *Invisible Combat: C3CM A Guide for the Tactical Commander* (Washington, D.C.: AFCEA International Press, 1986), xi.

24. *Expeditionary Organizations* (Headquarters, U.S. Marine Corps, 1998), chapters 3 and 5.

25. Ibid.

26. S. L. Brodsky, "Control Aspects of C2," in *Selected Analytical Concepts in Command and Control,* ed. John Hwang, Daniel Schutzer,

Kenneth Shere, and Peter Vena (London: Gordon and Breach Science Publishers, 1982), 56–57.

27. Suggested to the author in an April 1998 letter from Lt. Gen. Sir Rupert Smith, KCB DSO OBE QGM.

28. Comdr. Terry J. McKearney, U.S. Navy (Ret.), "Rethinking the Joint Task Force," *Proceedings* (November 1994): 54.

29. Alvin Bernstein and Martin Lubicki, "High-Tech: The Future of War? A Debate," *Commentary* (January 1998): 29–31.

30. MacGregor, *Breaking the Phalanx,* 149.

31. "Current Readiness Reports Do Not Fully Disclose Personnel Shortfalls," GAO Report to Congress, chapter 0:2, April 1998.

32. MacGregor, *Breaking the Phalanx,* 193.

33. Robert B. Killebrew, "Learning from Wargames: A Status Report," *Parameters* (Spring 1998): 133.

34. Stan Davis and Christopher Meyer, "We're Already Surrounded by Them. . . . What Happens When They Team Up?" *Forbes ASAP* (1 June 1998): 80.

35. Sam Sarkesian, *The New Battlefield: The United States and Unconventional Conflicts* (New York: Greenwood Press, 1986), 295.

36. Gordon Craig, *The Battle of Koniggratz: Prussia's Victory over Austria, 1866* (Westport, Conn.: Greenwood Publishers, 1964), 174.

37. Ibid., 174.

Don Vandergriff

Major Don Vandergriff is a professional armor officer, a former marine, and one of the most outspoken critics of the direction and thrust of the current army culture on active duty today. As a graduate of every professional development course available to his grade, he is well qualified to speak on most topics. His writings appear in numerous professional journals with regularity, all hammering on one main point: The U.S. Army needs to change its culture if it desires to fight the way that it claims it should.

Major Vandergriff looks at digitization from a broad angle. His essay is a detailed historical analysis of how the army got where it is today and an analysis of where it must go if it expects to fully utilize the proposed benefits of the digital age. As an examination of the culture of the institution as a whole, this is a strategic-level chapter in the broadest sense. It addresses one ominous potential result of our current personnel system. Specifically, if we create a generation of leaders unwilling to speak out and experiment, we will lose the potential that can come from information manipulation. Instead of the perfect tool for battlefield flexibility, it might become the perfect tool for micromanagement. The end result may be that we find ourselves fighting in the same old way, but using new and horrendously expensive hardware to do so.

Whether or not you agree with him, Major Vandergriff's chapter is one that should make every reader sit back and go, "Hmmm."

The Culture Wars

The late Col. John Boyd, U.S. Air Force (Ret.), the United States' most creative military thinker and theorist, was a self-taught mathematician and aeronautical engineer. His energy maneuverability theories have revolutionized the design of fighter aircraft since the 1960s. Boyd used to drill the message, "Machines don't fight wars, people do, and they use their minds," into the heads of his protégés ad nauseam.

Boyd's message is central to understanding the army's fascination with the theory of management science as applied to warfare, which now permeates the officer corps. His message was that technology is subordinate to and serves people. To understand which technologies work and do not work in war, one first has to understand how people think and act when the fog, fear, and chaos of combat inhibit vigorous activity.

More importantly, it is essential to understand that the very way the army accesses, develops, and promotes officers, as well as its focus on the individual, is outdated. The army's personnel system, which shapes the current officer culture, is based on an organizational model adopted between 1899 and 1904. The officer personnel system evolved from the need for rapid mobilization in order to fight the Soviets on the plains of Europe, beginning with the passing of the Officer Personnel Act of 1947 (OPA). This system needs to change dramatically for the army to be prepared to confront the challenges of the future.[1]

Today, nothing could be further from the army's cultural mindset than Boyd's common-sense wisdom. Technology is now an end in itself, not a means to an end. Doctrinal manuals and concept briefs even state that technology—especially highly complex, expensive technology—will revolutionize the conduct of war. The historical reliance on technology as a substitute for a truly professional army is ingrained in a culture that prides itself on leading the rest of the nation with its businesslike practices—especially in the way it manages its personnel systems.

The subordination of soldiers to machines has evolved during the last ninety-five years into seeing soldiers as individual parts of an ever-larger bureaucratic machine. The belief that machines fight wars and people are of secondary importance was exemplified by the official Department of Defense posters commemorating Armed Forces Day in 1996 and 1997. These extolled weapons and ignored the sacrifices and patriotism of our people. The high priests of technology in the Pentagon and industry (and their wholly owned subsidiaries in the media and think tanks) even have the temerity to construct a precisely defined vision of a high-technology world in 2010. It justifies today's obsession with "revolutionary" precision-guided weapons and all-seeing, all-knowing command-and-control systems.[2]

This chapter argues that the obsession with technology cannot be disentangled from a methodical attrition doctrine that is turning the U.S. Army into a contemporary variant of the French army of the 1930s.[3] Our heritage, dramatic events such as the Spanish-American War and the shock of preparing for World War II, along with simulation and modeling, are at the root of this problem. The application of technology through an authoritarian command style constricts flexibility and saps the initiative that is needed at lower levels to practice maneuver warfare in conventional war.[4] Most importantly, however, I will try to critique the limitations of the management culture that now permeates today's officer corps.[5]

This culture has evolved based on several complex factors, such as our tradition of improvisation in the face of war and the way in which the officer corps has conducted itself during peace. This led to and forced two dramatic organizational and personnel revolutions in the U.S. Army, transforming the army and its personnel system into a "technical system."[6] Two periods, Secretary of War Elihu Root's reform of the War Department in 1899 through 1904 and Gen. George Marshall's transformation of a scattered force occupying small posts into an army capable of fighting a global conflict from 1940 through 1947, are in fact what have prevented today's culture from achieving effective reform.

What must occur within the next few years is not a technologically driven revolution in military affairs, but a true cultural revolution in which thoughts, practices, and the environment mold the minds of officers who are prepared for third- and fourth-generation warfare, assisted, of course, by technology.[7]

Instead, our current culture upholds and practices second-generation warfare doctrine. This is a linear doctrine enhanced by information technology. The army's culture promotes centralized decisions and stifles subordinate independence and autonomy. Second-generation warfare advocates the use of massive firepower, calling for a strictly controlled battlefield outlined by detailed graphics. Both the divisional and corps graphics in Desert Storm and our emphasis on teaching checklists and lockstep procedures at our branch schools and combat training centers confirm this fact.[8]

Third-generation warfare evolved during World War I as a German idea-based reaction to the Allies' material superiority. It relies on groups of highly trained units led by well-educated leaders who are trusted to make on-the-spot decisions in order to bypass enemy strengths and attack enemy weaknesses. The key to the success of this tactical and operational approach for the Germans was that they already possessed a culture that emphasized decentralization and rapid decision making by its officer corps.[9]

Fourth-generation warfare is an extension of third-generation warfare with no limits to its depth and no front lines. It has no targets going beyond the traditional type, such as military units. Fourth-generation warfare consists of irregular war-fighting skills and capabilities in close-quarters combat and small unit operations among state or nonstate actors. In contrast to the U.S. Army's current second-generation-focused doctrine, fourth-generation warfare calls for a decreased reliance on firepower and attrition in ground combat. It also reduces reliance on deep strikes and strategic bombardment in air warfare.

The officers who operate in a fourth-generation warfare environment must become experts in fast-transient littoral penetration operations, information war operations, special force operations, political-military operations, and counterdrug, antiterrorist, and antinuclear operations, and they must be prepared for increased occurrences of urban or suburban combat.[10]

Future adversaries, driven by the moral forces of cultural and ethnic differences, are learning how to neutralize the technological advantages of industrial-strength firepower-intensive armies, particularly in irregular close-quarters combat in urban and suburban areas. In Chechnya, Beirut, and Mogadishu, front lines disappeared; the distinction between friend, foe, and noncombatant became vague to nonexistent, and simple handheld weapons (RPG-7s) used by well-disciplined, small irregular units turned armored vehicles and helicopters into coffins and conventional formations into death traps.

The *Intifada,* armed with stones and reinforced by CNN, bought more for the Palestinians than four conventional wars with Israel. The main weapons in the Ayatollah's arsenal when he overthrew the Shah were the moral strength of the committed and the audiocassette recorder. While fourth-generation warfare has roots reaching back at least to T. E. Lawrence and Lettow-Vorbeck in World War I, it is still evolving and is not yet well formed or understood. One common denominator, however, is beyond dispute: enhanced by information technology, the premium on individual initiative has grown.[11]

The type of revolution that must occur is not technologically but mentally driven, dealing with changes to the army's culture. Part of the revolution is most assuredly technological, but whatever technology offers us must be validated and vitalized by human nature. The army's culture is defined by the way it assesses, develops, and manages its officers. It enforces policies promoting the economic advancement of the individual at the cost of unit cohesion. Such practices have been passed down from generation to generation of personnel managers beginning with the management scientific revolution, or the "progressive era" at the end of the nineteenth century.[12]

This discussion is important and timely because the current culture uses the interaction of technology with itself to stifle initiative. The ideas of maneuver warfare, particularly Boyd's theory of operating inside the adversary's observation-orientation-decision-action loop, provide a way out of the dilemma that has evolved from two revolutions. These ideas can provide the army with the foundation for the right culture to prepare leaders and units to fight on future battlefields. Boyd's theories are grounded in an appreciation of how the mind and body act in conflict situations. Once we understand this, we can develop a personnel system using the superior engineering skills of the United States to match variable technologies to historically proven invariant human capacities.

The Past: The Amateur and the Militia

Four important periods have influenced today's officer culture. It is important to briefly describe their cumulative effect on today's culture prior to presenting the adjustments to the current culture that will be necessary to prepare the army for the synergistic twenty-first century. Also, it must be noted that the periods are not distinct or sequential; they overlap and influence one another.

The first period was characterized by the nation's and the army's reliance on expansion and improvisation to fight wars. The period occurred from the establishment of the Continental Army under George Washington up to the Korean War. The second period was Gen. Emory Upton's and Secretary of War Elihu Root's attempt to professionalize the army beginning after General Upton's visit to Germany in 1876, coupled with the near disaster as the army failed to mobilize effectively to fight the Spanish-American War in 1898.

The third period began with World War I. Remarkably, World War I left an implant on the officer corps that continues to affect today's culture. Furthermore, Gen. George C. Marshall's reactions to the expansion required by World War II influenced the third period, which saw dire results in Korea and Vietnam. The fourth period consisted of the army's reaction to the Vietnam War and its dramatic reforms in the 1970s and 1980s, which affected almost every aspect of the army except the officer personnel system.

A fifth period must occur at the turn of the twenty-first century that combines technology with the best lessons about how to prepare the leaders and soldiers of the army to fight in the next century.

The first period was significant because it has left the army with a rebuttal of the traditions of intellectualism and professionalism from the European model, and a belief that when war comes, the army will draw on its frontier roots and improvise to overcome the adversity created by a war crisis.

Ironically, at the end of the Revolutionary War, officers of the U.S. Army adopted the aristocratic tradition of Britain, their former adversary. Attempts to change this mold by none other than George Washington were met by resistance from both Congress and the people, who feared domination of the government by a professional class of officers.

Washington proposed forming a professional cadre of officers and regiments in a standing army. When Congress voted his proposals down in favor of state militias, Washington remarked, "the Jealousies of a standing army, and the Evils to be apprehended from one are remote, and in my judgment, situated and circumstanced as we are, not at all to be dreaded."[13] Based on this congressional decision, the army continued to react to wars as if they were unnecessary passing phases instead of acting as a professional force preparing for future conflicts.

U.S. Army officers continued to cling to aristocratic notions about leadership during the remainder of the eighteenth century and the entire nineteenth century. Army officers were not united by a tradition focusing on professional matters. The United States and its new government were protected from professional adversaries, apart from some excursions and conflicts with the British navy, by two of the largest moats in the world: the Atlantic and Pacific Oceans. Also, the U.S. government could virtually ignore its army because it was never severely challenged by a social revolution as governments were in Europe. As a result, army officers, facing Indian tribes that were militarily underdeveloped from a European standpoint, were under no pressure to develop a high level of proficiency.

U.S. Army traditions expected officers to serve as models of courage and honor; they did not have to be particularly competent. An excess of either "cleverness" (intelligence) or zeal was bad form. The minuscule regular army officer corps expanded when it was necessary to conduct a war by appointing temporary officers. The primary qualification for a temporary commission, as well as for accelerated promotion in the regular army, was political influence—which often did not mean professional competence. There was almost no sociopolitical homogeneity in the officer corps, and little possibility of building common professional views. The army's police mission in the west and the country's incredible size influenced this, because officers were scattered in small posts throughout the country—and, after the Spanish-American War, in the Philippines.[14]

Officers in the peacetime army in this period spent much of their duty time in isolated locations engaged in recreation, sport, and social activities. Official duties occupied only two or three hours per day, and with notable exceptions, there was little emphasis on the study of leadership or other aspects of war making as in the German and French armies. One of the foremost U.S. Army manuals in 1864 devoted only eight pages to the organization of the army and the duties of officers in peace and war. This would be unremarkable were it not in stark contrast to more than two hundred pages describing and illustrating the 154 forms required by the subsistence, quartermaster, and adjutant general departments. When the army was not chasing bands of Indians or bandits, it turned to the time-honored tradition of "looking good at the cost of being good."[15]

The small regular army and its officer corps reacted to the War of 1812 and the Mexican War with improvisation and a reliance on the militia. The former conflict involved a British military whose primary focus was on fighting Napoleon and France in a continental war, while treating the American theater as a sideshow. The latter war pitted the U.S. Army against the colorful but poorly trained Mexican army and its incompetent leadership. This allowed the regular army to win all of the battles prior to the arrival of volunteer regiments.

The Mexican War was the first test for graduates of the new U.S. Military Academy. The engineer-focused curriculum at West Point, with its emphasis on the details of minor garrison activities, left out the study of the art of war. Many officers and prominent civilians felt that this deficient curriculum was validated by the performance of its new officers in the Mexican War. Even the shock of having to create a "modern army" for the American Civil War failed to wake the officer corps to the need for professionalism.

As a result of the "victories" in these two wars, lessons regarding poor performance were largely ignored, with the small regular army continuing to rely on both a politicized officer corps educated largely in engineering at West Point and a state militia system. The militia system resembled more of a social club than a ready reserve. It was hoped that time would allow both to expand rapidly to meet the demands of war.

That war was the Civil War, and the condition and size of the regular army prevented it from putting down the Southern rebellion early. It thus failed to prevent a long and bloody conflict. The army of the frontier and its officer corps were only prepared for police work. The officer corps had to move from concentrating on the small unit level (the army of the frontier fought bandits and Indians on the western plains, with an occasional excursion into Mexican territory) to learning the intricacies of "big" war, in a war that was similar to those fought in Europe during the nineteenth century.

The cost of the army's attitudes and traditions against professionalism lengthened the war and caused unnecessary casualties as officers learned their trade. The only lessons the army seemed to learn from "the last of the old, and the first of the new wars," however, were the wrong ones, as the regular army immediately returned to chasing Indians in the west and most of its veterans returned to civilian life.[16]

Writers after the Civil War (and even some historians up to the 1980s) "learned" lessons from the Civil War on the use of attrition warfare—Ulysses S. Grant was a butcher, while Robert E. Lee was a maneuverist.[17] Nothing could be further from the truth. Civilian officials and officers misinterpreted Grant's 1864 campaign against Lee in Virginia as one that seemed to focus on sheer attrition. They failed to look at the operational brilliance of Grant's plan for finishing the war.

In sheer numbers, Grant took substantial losses during his drive toward Richmond, yet Lee, who was on the defensive, lost a greater percentage of his army in killed, wounded, and captured. Grant achieved his goal. He tied down Lee and his army of northern Virginia, rightfully perceived as the Confederacy's military center of gravity. As a result of taking away Lee's offensive ability by constantly pounding him in Virginia, Grant freed up the remaining Union armies to conduct mobile campaigns.[18]

Despite the success of Grant's strategy, the focus afterward remained on the defeat of Lee and his army. Later writings focused on the attritionist approach and the material might which Grant had available to push Lee to capitulation at Appomattox. The attrition theme is reflected in the strategy employed in all U.S. wars thereafter. Long build-ups and train-ups produced thorough preparation to conduct overwhelming campaigns. Despite attempts by a few to move toward a standing professional army, the evolving strategy of attrition through intensive firepower, easily adopted by an amateur officer corps and its masses of conscripts, was coming in line with emerging business management techniques at the end of the nineteenth century.[19]

The Second Period: Upton and Root

The first reformer to attack the militia and frontier myths of improvisation was Maj. Gen. Emory Upton. He was a prominent advocate of military professionalism whose 1878 manuscript, *The Military Policy of the United States,* became "the bible of emerging American" military professionalism.[20] His ideas were no secret, nor were they confined to the narrow circle of professional soldiers. Upton was sent in 1875 to visit Europe and Asia and report on "the organization, tactics, discipline and maneuvers of the Armies of Italy, Germany, Austria, Russia, France and England." Upon his return Upton published his reports in his widely circulated book, *The Armies of Asia and Europe,* in 1878. Upton was impressed by the German military system and pleaded for the creation of an efficient, well-trained American regular army "free of the evils of favoritism," a force capable of facing the best European army.

Upton advocated an officer corps similar to the German officer corps, in which examinations would be used to determine entrance as well as promotion. Officers would be given professional education based on the model of the *Kriegsacademie* in Berlin. He advocated a general staff, staff-line officer rotation, and compulsory retirement based on age. He also wanted to create professional regiments employing a regimental depot unit-replacement system. While the European army example was one reason to change, the mechanization of warfare and the growing rivalries of great powers proved equally convincing reasons to build a more effective army.[21]

To accomplish Upton's goals, major cultural changes would have to take place, and they would have to be tolerated by the government, as well as by half of the officer corps that occupied the staff bureaus in the War Department. For the reforms to occur, the government and officer corps would have to plan for long-term commitments of men and resources. This ran counter to the popular confidence in improvisation and heroics, so much a part of the American militia tradition and myth.

Also, to build this professional army, officers would need to control access to and mobility within the officer corps, privileges that politicians were reluctant to concede. To the soldiers, the politicians' insistence upon accountability was a clever way to defend the home turf or the pork barrel. To politicians, it was the essence of democratic institutions to totally control the army and keep its power to a minimum by preventing its officers from becoming true professionals on the German model.

So the reformers failed. This denial of professionalism was not challenged again until the army entered the Spanish-American War. The emerging theories of management science provided the politicians with a comfortable substitute for solving the question of military professionalism.

The army and the War Department were exposed to the theories of management science and the organizational model of bureaucracy in 1899. As a result of the chaos within the War Department during the Spanish-American War, President McKinley appointed Elihu Root as Secretary of War. Root made much-needed changes to the War Department in 1899 through 1904, adapting tenets of management science and the bureaucratic organizational model, as well as pushing for reforms advocated by Upton, such as a general staff on the German model.[22]

Root introduced management science as used by the Pennsylvania Railroad into the army and the navy. In the 1890s the Pennsylvania Railroad was larger than the army, navy, and marine corps put together. The politicians and the public at large looked at the cultural prestige of these great businesses and believed that they had the answers to solve any problem, including military ones. The managerial revolution was embodied in the railroads and was the driving force behind Root's reorganization.[23]

The so-called management science was based on a philosophical assumption called "ethical egoism," which regards as true and proven the idea that individuals are motivated by self-interest—variously packaged as the positive incentives of money, pleasure, advancement, distinction, power, luxurious prestige goods, and amenities, or as the negative incentive of self-preservation. Management science was also based on another philosophical assumption: that only the individual person is real. Social entities are merely built up out of individuals.[24]

Root brought with him officers who rode the wave of the bureaucratic revolution sweeping the country at that time. Army reformers felt that in order to get their desired changes through Congress, they needed to ride the "progressive era." The new army and its officers based their efforts on the thesis that "military problems, like corporate and public problems, could be solved through effective organization and management." This effort was a reflection of the "era's general groping towards a satisfactory expression of the bureaucratic method of administration and control."[25]

Root's reforms eliminated serious defects that plagued the army, yet by understanding the longer-lasting effects on professionalism wrought by these reforms, we can understand why the army has implemented only minor reforms in the last fifty years. The larger and longer cost of transforming the army officer corps from a profession within an institution into a specialized workforce can be assessed by viewing this transition from an organizational prospective. Our army's personnel system currently provides an example of what Samuel P. Hays has called a "technical system"—a centralized bureaucratic mechanism for molding "highly specialized individuals" into a "coordinated workforce."[26]

The legacies of this culture had an immediate effect in World War I. It was management science, explicitly Taylorism, that led the army to change from a unit-based system for replacing casualties, as advocated by Emory Upton, to an individual replacement system. By the middle of the Korean War, based on the belief that this system was one of the reasons behind its victory in World War II, the army had enough computer power to treat every soldier as an item of inventory in order to implement an individual rotation policy. Root's reforms, while dramatic, contradicted what Upton had advocated when mixed with the emerging culture of management science. The reforms did not deliver a professional army based on a European model, but one based on American ideas of an army, which revolved around the advancement of the individual.[27]

Root's reforms paid short-term dividends; the United States was able to mobilize and deploy an army to fight in Europe in 1917. The new general staff advocated by Upton, and pushed by Root in the General Staff Act of 1903, made this possible.

However, at the end of World War I, American traditions of resistance toward a standing army and needed professionalism again took hold. All that remained of Root's ambitious reforms were a war plans division and smaller versions of the general staff system that had filtered down to battalions, which consisted of specialized sections involving personnel, intelligence, operations, and logistics. Stern selections and separate career paths within the staff were also abolished. The U.S. model was a watered-down version of the German model because of attempts to create fairness for individual officers and eliminate the appearance of elitism. Thus, the U.S. version of the general staff eliminated the very items that made the German model so successful: strenuous entrance requirements and cohesion.[28]

At the end of World War I, the army once again returned to its time-honored practice of appointing and promoting officers politically as it shrunk twentyfold to fourteen thousand officers and one hundred twenty thousand enlisted men. Although Root's reforms were effective in centralizing the staff bureaus at the War Department, the army suffered the interwar years with branch infighting that in effect stifled and reversed the progress begun by Root. Of all the modern armies of the time, the U.S. Army did little or no innovating in the interwar years to prepare for the next war. The wish of Upton—to transform the officer corps into one that mirrored the techniques used by the Germans—was washed away by the Allied victory in World War I.[29]

The Third Period: The Hand of George C. Marshall

The officer corps walked away from World War I with three practices that would be passed on. These were solidified in the interwar period and became almost impossible to break as traditions after the victory in World War II. First was an authoritarian style of leadership. The rapid expansion of the army, both in size and in responsibility for officers, meant that an officer's job was beyond the competence of most individuals. Adapting an authoritarian approach was secure and hid the flaws as rapidly promoted prewar regular officers had to direct the operations of thousands of amateurs led by amateurs.[30]

The next legacy was the army's adaptation of a doctrine of intense supporting firepower from the French. The doctrine was refined and was called fire-and-movement tactics. It relied on the simple process of one unit firing while another moved forward, supported by massed indirect fires. The tactics of fire-and-movement warfare were largely linear—parallel to the proven business practices of the day—and were centrally controlled.

Finally, shaped by a force structure that limited the army to eighty-nine divisions, the army institutionalized the practice of using individual replacements, which had been done during World War I. The army had gone into World War I planning to use unit replacements with one division in the United States supporting two divisions in France, but by the time units were committed to the fighting in 1918, attrition occurred so rapidly that there was not enough time to train new units to replace existing units. Instead of using the interwar period to study the lessons from World War I and improve or replace these legacies, the army officer corps sat stagnant under the strain of no money and a public and Congress that drifted into isolationism.

Entering World War II, Marshall was forced to create an army from scratch. His accomplishment of creating a victorious army from amateurs and equipping, training, and moving it overseas to fight and defeat the Axis powers left a lasting impression in his mind; he would not allow the next army to exist in a state of unpreparedness. He felt that the officer system that existed prior to World War II was to blame. Rightly so; the officer system had regressed to one that did not rely on evaluations or examinations to determine entrance into its ranks or potential for command. Short of committing a capital offense, poor officers could not be dismissed from the service. For example, Marshall had to relieve five hundred senior field-grade officers and general officers who were incapable of assuming field commands because they were too old, ultimately replacing them with younger officers.[31]

Immediately after World War II, Marshall and other senior army officers began to examine what was required to avoid repeating the mistakes that had occurred at the beginning of the army's expansion for World War II. Marshall was concerned about preparing the army for an immediate confrontation with the Soviet Union and its allies on the plains of central Europe. The army would not have three years, as it had at the beginning of World War II, to build up and train for war.

As a result of testimony by such prominent generals as Marshall and Eisenhower before Congress, as well as the mood of the country, which held the view that everything that came out of World War II was sanctified by the glow of victory and the moral purity of a crusade against evil, the Officer Personnel Act of 1947 was passed. It was the first piece of significant legislation affecting officers to come out of Congress since the passing of the Navy Personnel Act of 1916.[32] OPA would come to signify the faulty perceptions of senior leaders who considered the status of the United States superior to that of any future opponent. Thus, they believed that we could afford to be revolutionary in our pursuit of personnel laws and policies that favored the individual and bucked time-proven measures advocating cohesion.

OPA included three parts. First, it significantly increased the size of the officer corps in the middle and senior grades. Marshall felt that it was necessary for the army and the entire military to be able to expand fast to fight an all-out land war in Europe. Second, OPA adopted an "up-or-out" promotion system, in which an officer who was passed over for promotion would be forced out. In Marshall's eyes, this would prevent stagnation in the officer corps by maintaining a "youthful and vigorous" corps of officers.

Finally, to ensure that a steady stream of officers was maintained to keep "up-or-out" working, a twenty-year "all-or-nothing" retirement rule was implemented. Congress influenced this aspect of the measure to ensure that not only officers but all service members received proper compensation for their services. Congress also sought to ease their transitions into civilian careers. The passing of OPA appeared to demonstrate that Congress and the public recognized the importance of the individual and were determined not to see a repeat of the backlash of antimilitarism that had swept the country after World War I.[33]

OPA had several flaws, which, combined with the culture of management science that had been emerging since the turn of the century, would riddle the army with problems under the stress of combat. OPA institutionalized individual competition in "up-or-out" and set in stone the "all-or-nothing" twenty-year pension. This stood in contrast to the military cultures of successful armies, which emphasized powerful intrinsic rewards in a community of shared effort. The value pattern of the new officer corps required that all gratification come from the institutional rewards of money, prestige, and power. A culture based on system analysis of tangibles could not understand any rewards that came from solidarity; these were deemed irrational and suspect.

Another principle from management science built into OPA was the notion of the officer as a general manager whose competence did not have to be anything in particular, other than management itself. Marshall and other generals believed that the best way to prepare for war was to make every officer a generalist. Those who had risen rapidly at the outset of World War II had held a variety of positions in the prewar army.

Marshall and succeeding army chiefs of staff began directing personnel managers to formulate army policies that moved officers around frequently, so that they received a lot of experience in a multitude of positions, while always emphasizing the need to prepare for more responsibility at the highest levels of command. They also began to send instructions to promotion and selection boards to look for a wealth of experience at numerous positions and duties. When the next world war came and the army once again expanded to millions, its officers would have limited experience in a wide variety of jobs and would supposedly be able to lead the new formations.[34]

The division of labor so beloved of management-science advocates, as applied through the army's bureaucratic organization, declared the functional specificity of the general manager to be general management. This consisted of organization, communication, goal setting, division of labor, delegating, motivating by means of incentives and punishments, and recruiting. Merely technical competencies could be delegated. "Merely technical" seems to mean specific military competencies such as understanding the art of tactics—maneuvering combined arms units under fire—and making decisions.

There is much to study and practice at every level of the military that is specifically military in its content. These skills and competencies are perishable, like those of a surgeon. Yet based on the drive to create generalists and the results of the Doolittle Board, which stressed the need for more equality in the way the army conducted its personnel business, career equality became the newest tradition in the army.[35]

Career equality meant that every officer would get an equal chance, with the same amount of time at critical positions. Under the rigid management system that has evolved from 1947 to the present day, it is essential to give officers the "right" jobs to get them promoted. In fact, career equality, combined with a bloated officer corps, undercuts readiness. No officer spends enough time with troops for real mutual trust to develop based on performing strenuous missions or training events together. Well-founded trust is the best kind of vertical cohesion, but through the policies developed to support career equality and the up-or-out promotion system, the army prevents it from forming. Personnel managers and senior leaders seem to believe that placing enough emphasis on specific military competencies that relate to the art of war is unfair and impairs career equality for the bloated ranks of the officer corps.

The first failings of OPA and its influence on army personnel policies relating to the individual and the fairness concept occurred under the test of combat in Korea. At the Chosin Reservoir in the first week of December 1950, the army's 31st Regimental Combat Team of the 7th Infantry Division was destroyed. The specifics are more horrifying when one considers that only one in ten of the regimental combat team's thirty-three hundred soldiers were capable of continuing to fight. Furthermore, not one organized unit was able to function effectively after the 7th Infantry Division was evacuated from Wonsan. The regimental combat team, and most of the division for that matter, had to be rebuilt because all of its artillery, vehicles, and crew served weapons were left behind. Nearly half of the troops were captured, dead, or wounded.

On the west side of the reservoir, in the same terrain, with the same equipment, against the same Chinese troops in the same horrible weather, the marines successfully fought their way out of the Chinese envelopment. They brought out almost all of their artillery and vehicles and all of their wounded. Their losses were bad at 50 percent, but only two companies out of two regiments in the 1st Marine Division ceased to function as effective combat units. The division was rebuilt in a short time and acted as the Eighth Army operational reserve within weeks of its evacuation from Wonsan.[36]

The principal difference did not come from training, nor from institutional pride, nor from the Chinese massing on the army while ignoring the marines. They attempted to encircle both formations with equal-sized forces and the same intent. The difference lay with the different personnel policies of the army and the marine corps. The army assigned officers to battalion level and above on the basis of career equality. Most of them had not held previous commands and had served lengthy times on higher-level staffs or as aides-de-camp. Only one in four of the army battalion commanders had previous combat commands.

In contrast, the marines assigned senior combat commands to officers who had previously commanded in combat at the same or next-lower level. Three out of four of the marine commanders at the battalion level and higher had previous combat experience in command.[37] Combat in command in war and combat training in peacetime are not "general management." At Chosin, the marine officers had specific technical competencies that the army leaders did not. It was not that the army did not have leaders who had those competencies; it was that the army didn't assign them to command. Equality in policies was not the only practice that hampered the army throughout the Korean War.[38]

Despite the uproar from many veterans who had served in frontline infantry units in World War II, and who complained that the individual replacement system was worthless, it was again put into practice in Korea. By the time of the Korean War the army had institutionalized the practice of rotating individuals instead of units into combat based on the theory of mechanical metaphor. Individual soldiers were technically trained in specific tasks and were regarded by personnel managers as replaceable parts under the policies of equality.

There was nothing equal or fair about sending individuals to war with strangers. General Donn Starry, U.S. Army (Ret.), relates how in Korea "these new replacements would arrive in the evening with supper, and leave in the morning in body bags when breakfast arrived." This could be even worse when new officers arrived with only the seventeen weeks of training they had received prior to leaving the United States.

The problem in Korea, which tended to be overlooked after the war because stabilization allowed firepower and technology to hide the weaknesses of these policies, was that a small unit has to be stabilized and trained together for a long period. The mechanical metaphor learned at business schools is even more worthless than the individual replacement system, because everyone in a combat platoon needs to know everyone else's job. Soldiers need to know which other soldiers or leaders can do their jobs; they should be able to read each other's minds and give you the end result or solution before the leaders ask. By the end of the Korean War some senior leaders began to see the weaknesses in these policies of equality, and in the larger evolution of the management culture.

Chief of Staff General Matthew Ridgway's dispute with President Eisenhower was over more than his nuclear deterrence policy, called "New Look." He disagreed with the force behind the policy. He saw the downfalls of the culture of management science, and of where its new bureaucratically trained officers would lead the nation.

Ridgway, who had previously served as commander of the Eighth Army in Korea, was a gifted and brilliant leader who understood unit cohesion and leadership. That was why Ridgway stated shortly after resigning as chief of staff that one of his proudest legacies was that he had protected the mavericks. He saw that blind faith in nuclear delivery systems as our first defense and security priority would create adverse situations when the army was forced to fight conventional wars.

The joint chiefs of staff's focus became quantitative rather than qualitative, which favored the technically oriented air force and navy. This made the army the low man on priorities, although it would be forced to carry the brunt of the fighting in future conventional wars. Thus, the real danger in where the new culture was leading was that the army would be committed on the assumption that means (technology) would be the basis for defining ends. Tactics would be limited to techniques for exploiting means. This mindset was being fostered by two emerging focuses of the culture of management science: technology over strategy and management over tactics.[39]

As a result, the culture of management science and its love for technology, analytical comparisons, and quantitative measures got us into Vietnam. It kept us there while the emerging class of officer technocrats sought silver bullets to change our status and improve our role. It did not let us pull out honorably when our so-called doctrine proved erroneous.[40]

Many of our so-called experts do not have a clue as to why we lost Vietnam. The answer lies in three factors: a lack of professionalism, misdirected personnel policies, and the culture of management science. Generals Ridgway and Gavin recommended an enclave concept, which ironically would later serve as the basis for "Vietnamization." This proposal called for securing and defending key areas and only counteracting when U.S. forces could gain an advantage on U.S. terms and with minimum casualties. Had this approach been implemented, the results might have been different.[41]

Again, it was not that the army did not have officers who possessed tactical and leadership skills. It did, but its personnel policies emphasized constant rotation so that every officer would get a "fair" chance at command in combat to enhance his career progression. The pursuit of equality overrode the obvious need to maintain command and unit cohesion. Vietnam came to be seen by many as a passing phase through which to advance one's career.

From the introduction of combat units in 1965, and even before with advisors, rotations of individuals for twelve months became official policy, with no chance of building the necessary experience to use the right strategy and doctrine over a lengthy period of time. We entered Vietnam with a mechanical approach, employing a World War II–era doctrine that emphasized firepower, with manpower restricted by the ever-evolving personnel polices shaped by management science.[42]

In 1960 Secretary of Defense Robert McNamara caused management science to rule supreme by implementing system analysis into all decision-making processes affecting the military on and off the battlefield. McNamara not only forced bureaucratic traits on the officer corps; he institutionalized them. His solution to any problem was the use of system analysis and cost-effectiveness comparative analysis. He arrogantly commented to senior officers, "I am sure that no significant military problem will ever be wholly susceptible to purely quantitative analysis. But every piece of the total problem that can be quantitatively analyzed removes one more piece of uncertainty from our process of making a choice."[43]

The impacts of tools such as OPA, the emphasis by Maxwell Taylor on the "corporate" officer, and McNamara's institutionalization of system analysis began to transform the officer corps to such a point that even high-ranking civilian members of the government such as Secretary of State Henry Kissinger noticed that "a new breed of military officer emerged: men who learned the new jargon, who could present the system analysis arguments so much in vogue, more articulate than the older generation and more skillful in bureaucratic maneuvering."

Yet Dr. Kissinger also noticed the downfalls of the "new breed." He noted, "On some levels it eased civilian-military relationships; on a deeper level it deprived the policy process of the simpler, cruder, but perhaps more relevant assessments which in the final analysis are needed when issues are reduced to a test of arms."[44] This meant that the new culture had a hard time placing tangible measurements on the study, planning, and execution of war, and the necessary assets to conduct war effectively, such as the maintenance of unit cohesion.

Another example of the influence of management science on personnel policies was the implementation of the infusion program. Army combat personnel from the United States were initially introduced as units. Out of fear that entire units would rotate at the same time, units were stripped of part of their personnel upon arriving in Vietnam. New personnel with different departure dates were infused into each unit, so while the unit flag stayed, its personnel parts constantly changed, terribly disrupting unit cohesion.[45] Commanders and staff officers saw the destruction caused by these policies, but few spoke out. One of the reasons was the control that the technical and centralized officer-management system had over officers.

The officer personnel system's most distinguishing feature used to control its environment was a vastly inflated, negatively focused evaluation tool called the Officer Efficiency Report, or OER. The army has been using some type of written evaluation since the early 1800s. The written evaluation report has been the only tool used to evaluate the performance and potential of officers.

In 1881, upon the founding of the School of Infantry and Cavalry (the future Command and General Staff College) at Fort Leavenworth, reformists called "Uptonians" after Gen. Emory Upton attempted to implement formal and objective examinations using the Prussian military as a model. This move was severely resisted by most of the officer corps, who believed that the practice was undemocratic and unfair. In reality, they resisted it because the majority of officers, except for graduates of West Point, were largely uneducated, especially in the art of war. Examinations would expose the weaknesses of both the officer corps and the army as professionals to Congress and the public. This practice of resisting professionalism and intellect remained until after World War II, when once again the only tool comfortable for use for officer evaluations was a subjective one.[46]

The Officer Efficiency Report Series 67 was standardized in July 1947 in line with the reforms being pushed by Marshall, which culminated in OPA in 1947. The army has gone through ten versions of the OER since 1947. Because of its support of an up-or-out promotion system, the OER has always been prone to inflation by officers who want to project their subordinates as the best, or by raters or senior raters who do not have the moral courage to face their officers with average or below-average OERs, which might destroy their careers. The OER fits perfectly into the culture of management science, in which a generalist officer is measured by how well he pleases the boss. It is the boss or rater who makes or breaks the officer's career.[47]

The OER has been and is now used as the main tool on promotion and selection boards. During Vietnam every job had to receive a next-to-perfect OER for the officer to be promoted or selected to schools such as the Command and General Staff College or the war colleges. As the OER continued to gain strength, it could be used in one of two deleterious ways: first, to damage an officer's career or even end it. An officer with strong character who posed a threat to a commanding officer could be sabotaged. The second way was to advance a favorite of the brass rapidly up the ranks or into the right job. In both cases, writing an OER became an art for the career-minded officer, who learned how to employ the right words in the right places to make a point.[48]

The OER facade as a tool of careerism that did not create professionalism became apparent to many members of the officer corps. "There is now a total disbelief in the system and a concomitant question regarding the integrity of all of us who continue its use."

To the casual observer and many officers, no impact on the officer corps could be seen; everything looked good. The use of the OER, both then and now, reflects poorly on the ethical strength of the officer corps when officers cannot fairly assess performance and potential. All officers were caught up in the scandal. With a large officer corps operating under an inflated evaluation system, anyone who tried to use the system to fairly assess his officers would, in effect, destroy their careers.

The final damaging aspect of OPA in Vietnam was the size of the officer corps. From 1947 it had grown steadily, both in absolute size and as a percentage of the total force. In 1968 it reached an incredible fifteen percent of the total force. Effective armies in history such as the Legions of Rome, the Germans, and the Israelis have maintained an officer corps consisting of three to five percent of their total force. A large officer corps creates greater centralization and competition for critical positions under a rigorous management system. This causes the image and prestige of officers to suffer. During Vietnam, soldiers realized that the selection and promotion standards within the officer corps had deteriorated.[49]

One of the most severe criticisms on record of the cultural atmosphere caused by management-science-shaped officer policies came from the U.S. Army War College. Its *Study on Military Professionalism* found that the up-or-out promotion system and the emphasis on equality contributed significantly to much of the undesirable and unethical conduct of officers. This report found that misconduct, leading to a lack of trust in authority, was caused by "seniors who sacrificed integrity on the altar of personal success. . . . [Junior officers] were impatient with what they perceived as preoccupation with insignificant statistics."

Although Chief of Staff Gen. William Westmoreland had commissioned the study, he and other senior officers, conditioned by the culture of management science toward corporate loyalty, shelved the study for thirteen years when they saw the critical conclusions.[50]

The Fourth Period: A Noble Effort

Several officers who had served as junior and middle-grade officers in Vietnam were determined to reform the army's culture of management science into one that focused on war fighting. Four significant events occurred during the 1970s and 1980s that, together with an influx of material, enabled the army to perform effectively in Panama and the Gulf War.

The first three of the events were: The post-1973 doctrinal renaissance begun by Gen. William DePuy's advocacy of the doctrine of active defense, and furthered by Gen. Donn Starry as army doctrine evolving into the AirLand Battle concept; the army training revolution that produced realistic force-on-force training for army leaders, soldiers, and units, with lessons shaped by rank-blind, candid after-action reviews; and a force design that evolved on a parallel line with technologies and doctrine, including a continual development of air-assault doctrine begun in 1963. This development included the 1st Cavalry Division experiments in 1971 through 1974, the 9th Infantry Division (Motorized), High Technology Test Bed, and the 7th Infantry Division (Light), Army of Excellence force structure. These succeeded in preparing the army to conduct warfare with a Soviet-style heavy force.

The fourth significant event was an attempt to change the officer personnel system in light of the all-volunteer force, coupled with an attempt to switch from individual to unit replacements. These endeavors met with mixed results.[51]

The army has attempted to subtly adjust its officer personnel system since the *Study of Professionalism*. Three officer personnel management systems (OPMSs) have been implemented, in 1971, 1983, and 1997, to address officer management. The first two focused on providing "many roads to the top" by stressing that the best commanders would command and the best specialists would specialize. With minor adjustments only, the army never enforced the philosophy behind the first two OPMS studies, because the legacy of OPA and the army's "heroic" tradition continued to stress the importance of command.

Another reason the two systems failed was that the army was still affected by other factors outside the realm of OPMS: a bloated officer corps and the all-or-nothing twenty-year retirement policy. These factors continued to force officers up through the ranks at an incredible pace, not allowing them enough time to become proficient at command or specialization.[52] OPMS moved to eliminate any cracks in the personnel system's authority and control by centralizing more decisions at the Department of the Army in Washington, D.C.

What did occur as a result of OPMS 1971 was the centralization of selection and promotion boards in one location. On these boards, few individuals have enough time to measure an individual officer's worth in detail, especially in terms that measure strong character. Instead, the boards promote or select "strong files," providing questionable results when determining an individual officer's professional strengths and weaknesses. Despite the failures in officer management, strides were made with unit cohesion. At the end of the 1970s and the beginning of the 1980s, Chief of Staff of the Army Gen. Edward "Shy" Meyer began studying ways to implement a unit personnel system in the army. Two studies occurred almost simultaneously.

The first, begun in 1979 and conducted under the direction of the army inspector general, developed "the new unit manning system." The unit manning system was in effect a compromise in that officer career patterns, unlike in the regimental systems of other nations, would be unaffected by this system. The unit system would only involve enlisted ranks starting basic training, who would remain together for three years at the company and battalion level. Despite the perceived success of the unit manning system among junior officers in the 1980s, seniors conditioned by the management-science culture repudiated it as they refused to adopt an army structure that could be supported by a unit system.[53]

The other study was more dramatic in its recommendations. Under the guidance of the commander of training and doctrine command, Gen. Donn Starry, a true regimental system on the lines of the British system was designed to fit American society in 1980. Called the "application of the regimental system to the U.S. Army's combat arms," it addressed the details of training, recruitment, unit rotations, and personnel management. Some senior army leaders, the Department of the Army staff, and senior civilian personnel managers killed the plan in 1980 to 1981 because the organizational bureaucracy refused to change the policies that directed the massive centralized individual system.[54]

A spin-off of the unit manning system was the cohesion, operations, readiness, and training (COHORT) system of unit management. In the eyes of many officers and noncommissioned officers, it was a successful program. It failed because it was evolutionary, or a smaller part of a larger individual system. It also existed in only a few of the army's eighteen divisions, yet COHORT units received priority in personnel. It violated the tradition of equality because it created a "haves and have-nots" view among divisional and brigade commanders. Beyond the institutional failure, COHORT created cohesion and produced better units than those filled by individual replacements.[55]

The COHORT model succeeded in selected artillery and tank battalions and in the 7th Infantry Division because, even at the lowest ranks, a high degree of discipline prevailed. Every soldier knew from training, example, and peer pressure how to behave correctly in accordance with ethical and military standards. Positive motivation developed out of confidence, understanding, skills, and unanimity of purpose. A new and unfamiliar phenomenon emerged in cohesive units because of positive leadership: Soldiers who were self-motivated needed and wanted to be taught and guided, not driven.

Not only with COHORT, but in the entire army, positive changes were taking place, such as more emphasis on studying the art of war and military history in army schools, with the intent among some generals to break the mold of management science that was continually strengthened by new laws.[56]

Limitations were placed on the army by the Defense Officer Personnel Management Act (DOPMA) of 1980 and its rigid management policies. DOPMA standardized OPA 1947 across the services and continued to hold the army to a structure that would allow it to mobilize in case of a large land war against the Soviet Union. This meant that a larger-than-necessary officer corps bound by the up-or-out promotion system was maintained. Despite these restrictions, which were seen as the only way of doing business by much of the officer corps, policies were implemented at lower levels to circumvent the restrictive boundaries set by DOPMA, son of OPA.

General Meyer and Lt. Gen. Walter Ulmer, commander of III Corps, Fort Hood, moved to give officers more experience while creating a positive leadership environment. Command tours for battalion and brigade commanders were extended to as much as three years. Furthermore, General Ulmer moved to create a positive command climate in his corps that broke the tradition of top-down leadership doctrine. This style had evolved since World War I and had become the norm of the management-science culture because of the army's perceived success in World War II.

Top-down or authoritarian leadership requires blind, instant obedience from subordinates ruled by fear. Officers are to create Darwinian competition among subordinate commanders, dole out information to subordinates, lie to them freely, and make them lie to the senior when the truth would make the senior uncomfortable or make him look bad to his boss. In this style of leadership, the leader never takes responsibility for setting priorities, so when anything is left undone the senior can always find a subordinate to blame ("I told you that was top priority"—like everything).[57]

Some of these moves had lasting effects; the division commanders who went into Desert Shield and Desert Storm had a wealth of command experience at the battalion and brigade levels. Others did not last, as General Meyer and his immediate subordinates moved on to retirement. It seemed that the culture waited them out. Soon after General Meyer left, the new chief of staff, Gen. John Wickham, Jr., reversed his policies, which had created cohesion and experience, because of demands to maintain the tradition of equality that existed in personnel management.[58] Soon the glow of victory and moral purity of driving the evil Saddam Hussein out of Kuwait would ironically wash away any reforms in the personnel arena achieved in the 1980s, because the foundation they rested upon was not fixed, just covered up.

The Fifth Period: The Officer Corps of the Future

Even before the victorious troops returned from the Gulf War, two significant events occurred that would affect the post–Gulf War army. One was the drawdown of the army in light of the fall of the Soviet Union; the other was the development and fielding of the army's newest doctrine, based on emerging information technology. The drawdown effectively showed that the temporary fixes conducted in the 1970s and 1980s by OPMS 1971 and 1983 and by DOPMA were superficial. The larger culture shaped by the numerous traditions mentioned earlier—specifically OPA—remained. As a result, the dramatic strides attempted through the adoption of a new doctrine will be diminished as new technologies and their capabilities are placed over old organizations and cultural practices.

The 1990s drawdown was a catalyst that brought out the worst of the institutional culture. The words *careerism, self-promotion,* and *zero defects* continually appear in professional journals and papers. Several officers and civilian officials blame the current state of affairs on downsizing. An effort called OPMS XXI is already under way to correct the deficiencies of the culture caused by OPA, DOPMA, and the army's own rigid management policies. OPMS XXI causes the officer corps of the future to be specialized. After officers perform their initial duty with troops, and upon being promoted to major, they will be divided into four categories: the operations, information operations, institutional support, and operational support career fields.[67]

The benefits of OPMS XXI have yet to be seen, but the potential exists to put the officer corps on the right track. OPMS XXI's emphasis on specialization ensures that fewer officers will get an opportunity to command. This will be a small price to pay for the benefits of specialization. Arguments that more former commanders are needed for mobilization ignore the ability of staff officers and junior commanders to learn from good examples.

The larger benefit of OPMS XXI is the strengthening of critical staff specialties throughout the army. Excellent officers not selected for command can pursue successful careers through repeated assignments in one of the aforementioned fields. OPMS XXI's long-term goal is to eventually have well-qualified specialists selected as general officers, destroying the myth that command experience is essential to high-level advancement.

More importantly, the army would perform better without the influence of entrenched civilian bureaucrats, producing obvious benefits to the functioning of units in combat. OPMS XXI is a step in the right direction, yet more remains to be done outside its boundaries, such as addressing the problems caused by the up-or-out promotion system, the bloated officer corps, the all-or-nothing retirement system, and the lack of a unit personnel system.

In reality, OPMS XXI guarantees only that the competition will be fair. By moving many officers out of the old command track and into the other three fields, it can once again promise all starters who reach the grade of major an equal chance to win. In this way the army can continue to feed the up-or-out promotion system and fill numerous jobs mandated by laws. It can also ensure that few competitors will become prematurely discouraged in the race for status.

As mentioned previously, under OPMS XXI the symbol of status will swing somewhat away from the need to command, thus sustaining the generalist career pattern. This continues the trend of providing "many roads to the top" by increasing the chances for promotion and promising all majors attendance at the Command and General Staff College. OPMS XXI has streamlined fairness by remodeling the façade of the personnel system's customary mechanism for maintaining the tractability of the officer corps.

OPMS XXI maintains the competitive ethic caused by the up-or-out promotion system along with a bloated officer corps. OPMS XXI allows the organization to extract deference through competition. Like the two earlier OPMS systems, the new system uses competition more than ever as a lever to control the career soldier.

Under the culture of management science, from the day that officers receive their commissions, the army impresses upon them the importance of remaining competitive. Thus, officers must compete against each other to survive in the up-or-out system. The competitive ethic is used in an explicitly coercive manner. To become noncompetitive is to risk exclusion from the army officer profession altogether. Officers have felt and continue to feel compelled to give careful attention to the institution's performance cues. Certainly, the post–Gulf War drawdown has made the point clear to even the least attentive.

The army's officer system under OPMS XXI will continue to use competition, based on the theory that the best will rise to the top. In fact, competition corrupts. It creates an unhealthy strain that no officer can elude. The preference of adhering to the profession's ethical code yields to the grinding realization that the officer must also satisfy the institutional demand to remain competitive, if only out of self-preservation. It is ironic, given the strictness of the legislation governing our officer system and the culture, that the reforms under OPMS XXI are perhaps the best that could be applied to the officer corps.

The problem remains with broader issues manifested under the fear of mobilization and the undying belief in management science. Before any changes can really be termed reforms, the issues that generate careerism and undermine readiness must be discussed openly. Unfortunately, OPMS XXI's downfall, as with the previous two OPMS reforms, is that it leaves careerism unaffected because it emphasizes the competitive ethic which, despite specialization, will remain.

I hope the limitations of management science—the compulsion to maintain personnel policies around a system developed for mass mobilization, and the need to be fair, which in turn creates competition—will be recognized, allowing the army officer corps to move forward. OPMS XXI should be viewed as a bridge to more and better reforms in the near future. Eventually the army, like society, will create its own version of a new, flatter organization with inherent officer personnel policies revolving around the unit policies that must accompany them. As a result, the army will introduce professionalism into its officer corps.

If we are going to be bold with our new doctrine and its embrace of new technology, we need to be courageous enough to create an institutional culture that produces officers who can handle the tempo that the doctrine advocates for using future technology. This will be a different culture from the one we have now. We cannot continue to write glowing documents advocating an agile officer, yet subtly support peacetime practices that uphold bureaucratic qualities, rather than battlefield qualities, when officers are considered for promotion.[60]

To prepare the army for the twenty-first century and create the officer corps of the future, we must:

- Replace the organizational model bureaucracy with a flatter, more autonomous organization, including reducing the officer corps from 14.3 percent of the force to 3 to 5 percent of the force.
- Replace the individual personnel system with a unit personnel system. Revolve all personnel policies around a unit system and move to an army force structure supported by a unit replacement system.
- Eliminate the up-or-out promotion system and replace it with an up-or-stay promotion system.
- Replace the specific branches and place officers on a track or category system at the O-3 or O-4 level. Make officer management more flexible.
- Revise the officer evaluation system to use a narrative OER based on character, with periodic examinations for promo-

tions as well as attendance at the Command and General Staff College.

• Revise the educational system so that mid-level education is conducted earlier in an officer's career, as well as moving to an educational system that emphasizes the art of war, including the study of military history.

• Do away with the all-or-nothing retirement system.

The purpose of all these reforms is to change incentives. They seek to reward strength of character, especially as manifested by a willingness to make decisions and take action, and penalize those who get by—by doing nothing controversial. It does no good to call for promoting the risk takers when the incentives all work the other way. Once strength of character is rewarded, then loyalty to the nation, the army, and the unit can be established over loyalty to the self. The personnel system's advocacy of the individualistic focus, "Be all you can be," as well as the belief that people must be moved frequently, promoted, and given make-work, must be done away with.[61]

The first ingredient in the reforms to prepare the officer corps and the army for combat in the twenty-first century is to discard a force structure manned by a top- and middle-heavy officer corps. Surprisingly, we still employ a table of organization and equipment similar to the one used in World War II. The army's primitive structure, despite the age of e-mail, faxes, telecommunications, and quicker intelligence-gathering and assessment systems, still consists of Industrial Age hierarchies. This means many layers of supervisors, colonels, and generals, all practicing perfection in a bureaucracy brought on board by Elihu Root in 1903.

The army has the worst officer-to-enlisted ratio ever: one to six. At the same time, the number of senior officers, especially at the middle and general officer levels, has become bloated, with one field-grade officer for each junior officer and one general for every eleven hundred soldiers.

This is not simply a matter of inefficiency or the army's preoccupation with mobilization. When there is a surplus, officers must frequently be assigned to make-work jobs that are not relevant to war fighting and in which military skills atrophy. Personnel turnover and competition increase as officers fight for moves from make-work to critical branch-qualifying jobs such as company command for captains, battalion operations and executive officer jobs for majors, and battalion command for lieutenant colonels. Further, an officer surplus leads to centralization as officers at senior levels create work for themselves by pulling decisions up to their own level.[62]

A gradual 50 percent reduction of the officer corps at the major level and above, plus a reduction of the entire officer corps to 3 to 5 percent of the force (minus doctors, lawyers, and dentists) is necessary. Remaining officers will gain more experience and will have more time to learn the art of war. Reducing the officer corps will extend each officer's time as a platoon leader, company commander, or battalion commander or in a primary staff position. The challenge for the army—for the entire military, since everyone falls under DOPMA—is prioritizing which positions are important and which are unimportant: those unrelated to combat or the structure necessary to support combat units.

Congress needs to revise DOPMA, tailoring the law specifically to the needs of each service. For example, the air force is more technically and individually oriented, whereas the army should revolve its policies around a mandated unit personnel system. A unit personnel system would increase collective training and maintain the band of excellence longer, ease personnel turnover, lower personnel costs, create a larger pool of readily available units for deployment, and diminish the need to pour massive amounts of money into "surge" training in anticipation of the start of a conflict.[63]

Future warfare of the type envisaged by think tanks and doctrine writers will rarely be of the Desert Shield/Desert Storm model, in which the army received the personnel cohesion it needed by default because its opponent allowed it six months to build up and train.

Future operations will consist of rapid deployment and entry operations (preemptive offensive operations) in which success will depend on the units at the forefront of the operation. Precision fires will sweep future battlefields when an opponent dares to fight the U.S. Army in the open. Many operations will occur in urban or suburban environments where the stress of combat will be at its height, requiring unit cohesion.

We have to switch our dependence on physical mass to a reliance on agility and tempo in these types of environments. "Attrition doctrine requires mere numbers and massive firepower, while maneuver requires quality in the very best units, able to use selective firepower." A maneuver-style doctrine supported by a maneuver-style culture allows a unit system that is a battalion package configured under brigade combat teams. The second part of a unit system is a regimental-type replacement system enabling battle-tried units to be pulled off the line and reconstituted in unit packets from a regimental depot. This requires what many analysts in the upper echelons of the Department of Defense and those advising Congress would view as extra or uncommitted battalions and companies.[64]

Unlike COHORT, in which the officer personnel system was divorced from the unit because of concerns about officer career opportunities, all personnel—officers and enlisted—are assigned regimentally and seconded from their regiments. Regiments become administrative or horizontal headquarters in various locations throughout the country, with specified units such as those in the logistical branches covering broader areas and overlapping those of combat regiments.

Battalions will rotate through three phases in a three- or four-year cycle. The first and third phases come under the regiment. In the first phase the battalion gathers and trains for combat at the individual and team levels. In the final phase it draws down and its members form a cadre to conduct many missions, including post support, advising reserve units that also constitute battalions within the regiment, and a host of duties that are normally filled by military manpower. A regimental colonel oversees these phases.

During the second phase the battalions fall under a vertical or command headquarters of a brigade. The force structure, designed to interlace with a unit system, would have two-thirds of the thirty-two brigades of armor and infantry, but the remaining twenty-four brigades would be far more deployable, with a "ready-now" status.[65]

The final aspect of this system is the management of its personnel. Army units today train, administer, and fight their component battalions. A unit replacement or rotational system works differently. A regimental depot administers and trains its battalions in the first phase and administers them in the third phase. Depending on the corps and the number of brigades the regiment supports, it can supervise any number of battalions. For example, an infantry depot located on the East Coast may support a light, mechanized, and armor brigade, located respectively at Forts Drum, Benning, and Stewart. Needing a total of five infantry battalions in phase two, the regiment would have to administer a total of ten battalions in all three phases. The management of regiments also means that the way officers are managed and developed must change.

The new officer-management law should also eliminate up-or-out promotions and replace them with an up-or-stay system. The new system would allow officers the time to develop the ability to grasp changes in situations rapidly and exercise initiative through independent planning.[66] An officer currently spends his or her career on a treadmill, developing anxiety about getting promoted.[67]

The new promotion system will be more decentralized.[68] Those who know an officer can best promote or select that officer. This means that regimental and division boards will be able to view fewer officers for longer periods of time. With commanders remaining at their positions longer, they will be able to better assess on a first-hand basis which officers deserve to be promoted or selected for higher education. Brigade and division commanders should be empowered to appoint boards to promote officers up through the rank of lieutenant colonel.

With the field narrowed by a smaller officer corps, centralized boards could then decide who gets promoted to the rank of colonel and higher, and could select officers to command brigades and larger formations. All boards at all levels will use three tools: the OER (written solely in regard to the officer's character), an examination taken yearly, and the personal conduct of the officer in front of the board, to determine promotions and selections. The bottom line in using such stringent tools is that leadership and professionalism are critically important—too important to rest on the sixty-second consensus opinions of uninterested officers serving the political agenda of the army.[69]

The type of officer needed for combat in the future must possess many qualities that may cause uneasiness among superiors developed and raised in the culture of management science. A leader with strong character and imagination will always focus a unit on training for war. He will spend time on studying the art of war and not waste time in the diversions called for by the up-or-out system. Currently, the officers that Force XXI and the Army After Next writers are calling for are getting out or are getting relegated to the backwaters of failed careers.

A study on personalities (using the Myers-Briggs Type Indicator) and their relationship to rank in the air force was conducted in 1991.[70] It found that Air Force Academy cadets had a wide variety of personality types. When an analysis of the personalities of army O-5s and air force O-5s was conducted, it showed similar personality groupings with no statistically significant differences. When the O-5s were compared to the cadets, there were statistical differences (using the Chi-Square statistic Chi Square = 59.57 at the p = .05 level). When a group of 161 army generals was compared to the army and air force O-5s, there was again no statistical difference.

When the group of O-7s was compared to air force cadets, there was a significant statistical difference (Chi-Square=73.04 at the p=.05 level). Some 56 percent of the O-7s comprised two personality types: introvert sensing thinking judgment (ISTJ) and extrovert sensing thinking judgment (ESTJ).

In analyzing the two predominant personality types, ISTJ and ESTJ, it was found that these types have a preference for stability and the avoidance of organizational conflict. In other words, they tend to be "corporate men" or bureaucrats with a "don't rock the boat" attitude.

Psychologist Otto Kroger has been holding seminars on the Myers-Briggs Type Indicator at the National Defense University since 1979. Kroger states that if his students traded their uniforms for business suits, it would be impossible to distinguish them from the corporate executives he also tests. Somewhere between the grades of O-3 and O-5, it is postulated that there is a significant shift toward these preferences. Officers are either weeded out with the up-or-out system, or they get out because they do not want to conform to the management-science cultural mindset of "playing the game."[71]

In an up-or-stay promotion system, an officer will still enter the officer corps from one of three commissioning sources, but accessions will be more selective than ever before with a smaller officer corps. This will allow the army to return to advertising for potential officers using the ideas of service to the country and duty to the people as the primary reasons for officers to serve.[72]

First all potential officers will serve a minimum of two years with a national guard or reserve unit as enlisted soldiers (similar to the simultaneous membership program employed in conjunction with ROTC programs now), gaining experience with the reserves. Next the commissioning sources will select and strenuously prepare their candidates to become officers. Meeting missions and filling quotas should not be the concerns of the commissioning sources; they should only be concerned with having candidates who meet standards. Quality, not quantity, is what the sources should strive for and obtain.

Prior to becoming commissioned, officers will be required to pass a comprehensive entrance exam. They will then serve an initial four-year tour with a regiment. Branches will be eliminated and replaced by combined arms, logistics, and specialists. An initial tour in a specific area will not determine the officer's path for the rest of his or her career. An officer may move from one area to another throughout a career or remain in one area as long as he or she performs admirably. This makes room for the late bloomer, something that does not occur now.[73]

At the end of this first tour (which aligns with the four-year, three-phase life of a battalion), accession into the professional corps will occur based on how well officers have scored on their second entrance examinations and performed in their regiments, with a decentralized selection board examining these tools. The board will also determine the specialty of each officer in one of three tracks—tactical, operational, or technical—while serving in one of three areas: combined arms, logistics, or specialist.

Under this system the army would be able to spend substantial time on the development, assessment, and evaluation of its officers, instead of the sixty-second look-over officers currently get on promotion and selection boards searching for the one discriminator in their files.[74] Through the use of a multitude of evaluation tools and a smaller officer corps, the army will become more objective in its personnel decisions, benefiting the nation, the army, and the officers. The following paragraphs briefly touch upon the reorganization of the officer-management branches and officer specialties. The army will have to recode several military occupational specialties to align them with the new broader fields.

The tactical track ensures that an officer will remain at the company, battalion, or regimental/brigade level for the rest of his or her career. After selection to the tactical track, the officer will attend a tactical course focusing on small unit leadership, decision making, and tactics. The officer may rotate from positions within one of the tactical levels to instructor positions and back. This track includes all units from both combined arms and logistical units involved at the tactical level. Officers may remain in this track, with the option of being promoted to the level of colonel and the possibility of commanding a brigade.

Those officers who score in the top 15 to 20 percent on their entrance examinations and perform outstandingly in front of the board will be admitted to the operational track. Additional requirements for the operational level will include an understanding of the art of war, demonstrated on the officers' entrance exams, and proficiency in a foreign language.

The operational track will consist of officers who become the operational experts of the army. They will rotate between command and staff assignments at divisional or higher levels and back to the army or joint staff. These officers will attend a combined version of the Command and General Staff College and the School of Advanced Military Science, a two-year version of graduate school in the art and science of war. These officers will become the institutional cradle for proficiency at the operational and strategic levels.[75]

The technical track will relate to specific abilities associated with a more technologically advanced army and the management of the tables of distribution and allowances. This field involves far more than the medical and law professions; it includes positions that require graduate-level civilian education or technical training such as an acquisition corps, academic instructors, operations research system analysts, comptrollers, computer programmers, communications specialists, and facilities managers.

Officers in this category could remain captains with prorated pay, but would have to continually demonstrate their proficiency with periodic examinations combined with reviews of their evaluation reports. Officers could opt for promotion as the technical experts at division or higher levels, while the appropriate higher-level ranks would correspond with higher headquarters and responsibilities.[76]

The education system, as touched upon earlier, will change dramatically as well. A true education is much more than the learning of skills or the acquisition of facts. Rather, it means acquiring a broad understanding of the art of war, including its ideas, principles, and history. This education must also give officers a thorough grounding in the warrior/leader culture, with a heavy emphasis on decision making.

The conduct of maneuver warfare, needed to permit the noted reductions in force structure and manpower, demands a shift from mere mental training to truly educating our officers. Instead of giving all branches, regardless of their relationship to the battlefield, "equality" in attending Command and General Staff College, leaders with a particular mindset will be chosen for a culture that rewards audacity, tempo, and creative decision making.[77] As a people, Americans possess the requisite skills to be successful in maneuver warfare, but our military professionals require education that will encourage boldness and mental agility.

Current military training has caused concern at all levels of government. Numerous journals have noted the absence of the study of war at our various war colleges. Alumni have watched in disbelief as the focus of the service academies migrates away from preparing young officers for combat and obligated national service. Graduated cadets now voice impatience to "get out to Wall Street."

Instead of being the repositories for innovative thought, most intermediate service schools remain Cartesian in their training methods. Training is mired in memorization and adherence to formulas, advancing immutable formats, principles, and processes that, if properly learned and applied, will supposedly bring victory. Schools emphasizing such rules, reinforced with the necessary formatted, quantitative decision aids and tables, serve only to stifle creativity in leadership.[78]

Making military education relevant to future warfare, with its myriad changes and challenges, will not be easy. Already, the missions of military operations other than war and their equally difficult adjunct, peacekeeping, demand officers who understand the political and strategic implications of their actions (particularly in light of the impact of real-time media). With rules of engagement that impose limitations on their operational and tactical capabilities, the officers of the next century will face unique challenges.

Because the officer corps will be relatively small and there will be fewer officers in the operational track, Command and General Staff College should come after officers are selected for the specialty. The war college should also come sooner, perhaps at the tenth to twelfth year of officer service, with selected officers from both the tactical and operational fields attending. There the curriculum would be dramatically refocused. All officers would be encouraged to get an education from new universities such as the American Military University that provide unique educational opportunities from "cradle to grave" in military art and sciences.[79]

How should the curricula at the schools that remain be refocused to show how to fight in the high-tempo, nonlinear environment of projected future warfare? Our officers, commissioned and noncommissioned alike, must be educated in the classical sense. Their education must be grounded in the art of war, but also in aggressively challenging their instructors, questioning a status quo that in fact should no longer exist. The professional must understand why principles evolved and when they are best used or amended. This demands training that provides not set-piece scenarios, but the chaos inherent in the nature of war.[80]

Classroom education is still necessary, but it must be focused on the case study, demanding critical analysis of historic examples. Leaders must move beyond rote memorization of techniques to experimentation with unorthodox solutions. Using interactive tactical decision tools already available in the civilian sector, they should formulate, discuss, and debate imaginative solutions. As they progress through the curriculum, it should introduce the often-missing combat intangible of simulation: a living opponent, possessing its own will, with an incentive to win.

Force-on-force war gaming provides the best available training for leaders and decision makers. "Free-play" exercises should be taken to their natural conclusion, allowing for clear winners and losers. This provides leaders with invaluable learning and the context-based experience necessary for the development of cognitive and intuitive skills. In addition, it is a vehicle to identify those who fully understand the intricacies of command and possess the intuition and innovativeness for success.[81]

These must be more than exercises pitting school-trained officers against similarly trained officers. There must be an enemy who is asymmetrical in experience as well as armament and weaponry. Here our ability to integrate "reach-back" technology and unorthodox opponents can provide a distinct advantage. A young former gang member from Los Angeles can teach our most senior officers more about fourth-generation warfare in an urban environment than most might want to admit. Although not skilled in the military art, such opponents offer the conventional soldier a means to assess the challenges of those surviving through instinct. Certainly, the Russians could have used this before Grozny.

Augmenting aggressors by employing and training with local guard and reserves, and/or military or academic foreign-area experts familiar with a given area and culture can also enhance the learning of twenty-first-century students. In the case of the reserves, this is a win-win situation benefiting both training and preparedness.

The advantages of this type of competition-based education are found in history. We are all aware of the successes and innovations of the *Militarische Gesellschaft* of the Prussian army in the early 1800s and its successor, the Prussian/German general staff.[82] Less well known, likely because of a lack of national institutionalization, is Gen. Al Gray's reformation of marine corps education in the late 1980s.[83]

Both initiatives recognized that training dominated by principles and formulas was outmoded. Both instituted the development of officers with a higher degree of intelligence, possessed of a favorable attitude toward change and innovation, with a propensity to assess and take risks as needed. Both challenged their students to approach problems realistically, rewarding decisions and judgments that demonstrated their ability to incorporate innovation, tactical logic, situational awareness, and boldness—essentially out-OODA looping (observe-orient-decide-act-looping) their competitors. Their mastery was determined not by methodical application of predetermined school solutions, but by their ability to win. This is the type of education that will best prepare our leaders for the battles ahead.

Selection for attendance at these reformed war-fighting schools (as well as for promotions) must also be reconsidered. Advanced readings assigned to specific tracks must be accomplished well before attendance at formal schools. An officer at the appropriate level must clearly demonstrate a capacity for decision making beyond his or her current grade. Whether by mentor or board evaluation (as in the defense of a thesis) or by examination, officers should be carefully screened prior to selection for attendance.

The program of instruction should be arduous and demanding, in contrast to the "year with the family tour" or "time to make contacts" mentality now advanced throughout the army. It is appalling to see a nonresident program use no readings and the resident course used as a career advancer. It is acknowledged as an unwritten policy that for those who want to serve with troops at the major level, it is mandatory to attend resident Command and General Staff College. In what other profession would a major school reduce the course load in response to complaints from students? In what other profession are the implications of ignorance more grave?

Finally, to reform our school system the army has to change the officer personnel priority for assignments to the faculty at army schools. As the last drawdown demonstrated, the first officers at the middle grades to be cut were instructors at the service schools.[84] In most Western armies, the top officers are chosen to be instructors at their service schools. This also occurred in the U.S. Army in the 1920s and 1930s with the Command and General Staff College and the War College.[85]

Officers and academicians selected for faculties must be among the most well schooled in their military subject areas. Other than command, no assignment should be more sought after than instructing. We must institutionalize this mindset among the officer corps and inculcate our juniors with the desire to become instructors as they help shape our officer corps. This is not currently the case; although change is coming, it needs to be expedited. The final reform, that of changing the retirement system, would create more flexibility in allowing officers to move back and forth between instructor positions and troop assignments.[86]

The final element in forming a strong foundation for the building of the officer corps is to change the retirement system that evolved out of OPA 1947. The current system, with its focus on all-or-nothing at twenty years, undercuts moral courage in those with twelve to twenty years of service. Moral courage must be present daily in order to practice it under the strain of combat. Instead of the twenty-year all-or-nothing concept, we should adopt a retirement system that allows officers to retire at ten years, with benefits beginning at age fifty-five.

The vested in ten, benefits at fifty-five system would allow officers to focus entirely on war-fighting skills. They could retire any time after ten years as long as they remained competent in their fields. Retirement pay would be increased for each year an officer remained after ten years.

Another issue that must be resolved is at what point officers should be forced to retire. I suggest captains at twenty-five years of service, majors at thirty, and all higher ranks at thirty-five or forty years.

There are several additional reasons for changing the army's retirement system. The first is cost. Retirement allotments paid to retired officers in 1995 were $5.1 billion. The second reason is that with almost one-fourth of officers retiring in their late thirties to early forties, the army loses a lot of experienced talent. This occurs in an age when people are living longer and healthier lives. This will have an impact on units in the future army, which can be led only by seasoned officers who have experienced several missions. Officers today naturally use their last years to prepare for second careers. Instead, officers should be constantly concentrating on and studying war as it continues to evolve.[87]

Effectiveness for the army is not an option; it is an imperative. The officer corps of the future, of the new culture, must execute the type of missions imagined for the future. This is sine qua non to the effectiveness of the army. Many officers and civilian leaders believe that technology makes the difference, but as John Boyd said, it is the people who do this, especially when there is effective leadership. The personnel system is the linchpin that will directly affect combat effectiveness, doctrine, and a host of other critical issues pertaining to the army of the future. The culture must adjust its course before the army can execute the high tempo and rapidly changing warfare of the future.

Conclusion: The Keystone of National Security

These reforms will readjust the army's management-science culture from a negative one to one that is professionally focused and built upon trust. The fundamental reason for instituting serious reform is that our national security construct, from our national security strategy down to the smallest military organization and how we manage our personnel, is not keeping pace with rapid changes under way in the world today. The army's officer and enlisted personnel system is an outdated follow-on to the system designed for the Cold War. Most officers are uncomfortable with our system, knowing that it is insufficient—that something is lacking. They feel this way because they understand that our current culture is founded on the organizational model that was used almost one hundred years ago to reform the old War Department.

A lot that is bad today is the result of good intentions that have produced unintended consequences. One must acknowledge that reformists of the maneuver warfare culture value competing goals. The people who have upheld the culture of management science for the last one hundred years and those who put these systems in place were trying to do the right thing. Their only fault is that they have since ignored the problems created by their implementations.

The army bureaucracy has become a weighted organization with its own logic, tradition, and inertia. The implementation of new doctrinal and unit organizational reforms is apt to take a long time. The army bureaucracy has a thick-hide resistance to taking risks and making changes. The army needs to follow the lead of General

Ridgway, who said, "My greatest contribution as chief of staff was to nourish the mavericks."[88] This will lead to creativity, vision, and innovation. Army officers must understand that it is desirable to have a love quarrel with the institution that they serve while still remaining loyal. The army must adapt an organizational model and personnel system to nourish the mavericks and nurture the innovators.

True professional soldiers, who are not popular in peacetime, must be kept around because the art of war is best learned through the course of several campaigns. It is time the army paid attention to our officer corps and its need to become more professional. It will defend us in our old age, and more importantly, it will defend our progeny. No utopian, brave, new, politically correct, gender-neutral, nonlethal, high-tech-clean-war generation is stepping forward to replace the hard chargers now deserting the army, and none will.[89]

In the future, war may be short and intense and require important decision making at many different levels of command. Much depends on proper planning and preparation to ensure that leaders and their units can perform in the best way possible during the initial days of combat. The army will not have three years to prepare for war, nor six months nor even one month to organize. The army needs to be ready beyond what technology can provide us with today. The army needs to go beyond technology. It requires a complex change led by extraordinary civilian and military leaders possessing vision. Our leaders should provide the beginnings of a peaceful revolution more dramatic than those conducted by Elihu Root and George Marshall.

The author would like to thank Col. Carl Bernard, U.S. Army (Ret.); Col. Dan Bolger, U.S. Army (Ret.); Dr. Steve Canby; Lt. Col. Robert Chase, U.S. Marine Corps; Ms. Barbara Graves; Mr. Bruce Gudmundsson; Col. David H. Hackworth, U.S. Army; Lt. Col. Jan Horvath, U.S. Army; Maj. Timothy Jackson, U.S. Marine Corps; Dr. Faris Kirkland, U.S. Army (Ret.); Lt. Col. Robert Leonhard, U.S. Army (Ret.); Mr. William Lind; Brig. Gen. Mike Lynch, U.S. Army (Ret.); Lt. Col. Paul Maubert, U.S. Marine Corps; Gen. Edward Meyer, U.S. Army (Ret.); Dr. Williamson Murray; Maj. Carl Rehberg, U.S. Air Force; Dr. Jonathan Shay; Mr. Franklin Spinney; Gen. Donn Starry, U.S. Army (Ret.); Mr. John Tillson; Lt. Gen. Richard Trefry, U.S. Army (Ret.); Lt. Gen. Walter Ulmer, U.S. Army (Ret.); Dr. Charles White; Col. Mike Wyly, U.S. Marine Corps (Ret.); and Maj. Chris Yunker, U.S. Marine Corps, for their insights and input.

Notes

1. John Boyd, "A Discourse on Winning and Losing," unpublished briefing, Washington, D.C., August 1987, 5–7.

2. Franklin C. Spinney, "Pork Barrels and Budgeteers: What Went Wrong with the Quadrennial Defense Reviews?" *Strategic Review* (Fall 1997): 29–39.

3. Robert A. Doughty, *The Seeds of Disaster* (Hamden, Conn.: Archon, 1985): 3–7.

4. Joint Chiefs of Staff, *Joint Vision 2010* (Washington, D.C.: Chairman of the Joint Chiefs of Staff, January 1997): 11–16.

5. Samuel P. Hays, introduction to *Building the Organizational Society,* ed. Jerry Israel (New York: The Free Press, 1971): 3.

6. Ibid., 3.

7. Franklin C. Spinney, "Evolutionary Epistemology: A Personal Interpretation of John Boyd's Destruction and Creation," unpublished briefing, Washington, D.C., September 1997. The Pentagon uses the term *revolution* in the wrong meaning and context. Revolutions, such as the German development of "Blitzkrieg" took twenty years, occurred in evolutionary increments. The bureaucratic culture uses "evolutionary change" as a method to ignore the need for necessary change, when in fact it is nothing but a strengthening of the current status quo. A revolution of cultural change is how we think, organize, and fight, but it will take a series of evolutionary changes over the next few years, spanning a generation of officers, for the proposals outlined in this essay to take place.

8. Donald E. Vandergriff, "Without the Proper Culture: Why Our Army Cannot Practice Maneuver Warfare," *Armor* (January–February 1998): 20–24.

9. For a thorough analysis of the German military culture see Bruce Gudmundsson, "Maneuver Warfare: The German Tradition," in *Maneuver Warfare: An Anthology,* ed. Richard D. Hooker, Jr. (Novato, Calif.: Presidio Press, 1993): 277–78.

10. Franklin C. Spinney, "Aviation from the Sea (AFTS): Innovation & Evolving Requirements via Operational Prototyping & Experimentation," unpublished brief, Washington, D.C., 17 November 1997, 5.

11. David H. Hackworth, "God's Work in Hell: Somalia, 1992–1993," in *Hazardous Duty* (New York: William Morrow, 1996), 119–32. Many of the problems seen in Vietnam appeared in Somalia, such as dual chains of command, competitiveness among senior officers for a share of the fighting (for career enhancement), as well as services competing for a share of the mission, and an organization trained in doctrine to fight a second generation war, i.e., support units of the 10th Mountain Division asking the Marines to pull their security because their own soldiers were technicians.

12. Chester I. Bernard, *The Functions of the Executive* (Cambridge, Mass.: Harvard University Press, 1938), 132–40. In regard to reform, there are five types of reform: administrative, organizational, sociopolitical, doctrinal, and technological. Reforms may overlap.

13. Walter Millis, ed., *American Military Thought* (Indianapolis, Ind.: Bobbs-Merrill, 1966), 12–14. George Washington had proposed a federal Continental Militia, a small regular army, and a military academy as the system best suited for defense. Again, in 1790, Secretary of War Henry Knox proposed a universal professional militia controlled by the Federal government. Both moves died in Congress.

14. Edward M. Coffman, *The Old Army: A Portrait of the American Army in Peacetime 1784–1898* (New York: Oxford University Press, 1986), 61–64 and 194–98. John R. Elting, *American Army Life* (New York: Scribner's, 1982), 55 and 84. A period of social reform preceded the Root reforms during the period between the Civil War and the Spanish-American War. See also Jack D. Foner, *The United States Soldier Between Two Wars: Army Life and Reforms, 1865–1898* (New York: Humanities Press, 1970). Foner discerns two distinct periods of reform, the first in the early 1880s and the second in the late 1880s and early 1890s. Spurred by the civil service reform movement of the early 1880s and later by what became the progressive movement, the army instituted numerous social reforms, all aimed at making service life more attractive for the enlisted soldier.

15. Discussions with Dr. Faris Kirkland, 12 April and 8 May 1998. Faris Kirkland, "The Gap Between Leadership Policy and Practice: A Historical Perspective," *Parameters* (September 1990): 54–55. Also see Coffman, 23–40, 101–03, and 176–80; and Elting, 38–45 and 76–78.

The army reformers under Upton failed to reform West Point on the German model. In 1881, Gen. John Schofield resigned as Superintendent citing political meddling when he tried to change the curriculum from an engineer focus to a military art focus. Gradually some technical courses were replaced with more broad, liberal, and military art aspects as in the German system. Several officers including William T. Sherman did see the failure of the army's organization and policies during the Civil War. A small group of officers called "Uptopians," after General Emory Upton attempted some reforms for three decades after the Civil War, met largely with failure.

16. Russell F. Weigley, "American Strategy from Its Beginnings Through the First World War," in *Makers of Modern Strategy from Machiavelli to the Nuclear Age,* ed. Peter Paret (Princeton, N.J.: Princeton University Press, 1986), 439–41.

17. James F. Dunnigan, *How to Make War* (New York: William Morrow, 1993), 584–85. Dunnigan presents a succinct comparison between maneuver and attrition warfare: "Through most of its wars, the United States successfully used the attrition approach. It is easier to be proficient at this type of warfare. You need to master only the simplest military skills and possess enormous quantities of arms and munitions."

18. Bruce Catton, *Grant Takes Command* (New York: Little, Brown, 1969), 389–90. Catton is explicit in his analysis of Grant's brilliant yet simple strategy, and he breaks the traditional perception of Grant's overall strategy as general in chief. Grant wanted to destroy the enemy army, but he preferred to do it through maneuver instead of attrition.

19. Weigley, 439–41.

20. Jack C. Lane, *Armed Progressive* (San Rafael, Calif.: Presidio Press, 1978), 150.

21. Emory Upton, *The Armies of Asia and Europe* (Washington, D.C.: Government Printing Office, 1878), 219. Upton considered the U.S. Army experience misguided and disastrous. He considered the overall performance of the U.S. Army in all previous wars unprofessional and wasteful of lives. He attributed these results to ineffective policy regarding an amateur officer corps, reliance on a militia system, and faulty organization.

22. John Dickinson, *The Building of an Army* (New York: The Century Co., 1922), 245–70. At the time of Dickinson's writing, the officer corps was not professional. Examinations and efficiency reports were used, but nothing was done when officers failed them or received bad reports; promotions, commissions, and appointments were more often based upon favoritism and political pull than merit. The most common argument in favor of the up-or-out promotion system is, "Look what happened during the Civil War and World War II, when we had hundreds of officers too old to perform in the field, and they had to be replaced by younger and more vigorous officers." This argument ignores the fact that, unlike today, no mental and physical evaluations existed then.

23. Paul Y. Hammond, *Organizing for Defense: The American Military Establishment in the Twentieth Century* (Princeton, N.J.: Princeton University Press, 1961), 10. Hammond asserts that President McKinley brought in Root "to clean up the mess" left by the Spanish-American War. Also see Graham A. Cosmas, *An Army for Empire: The U.S. Army in the Spanish-American War* (Columbia, Mo.: University of Missouri Press, 1971), 311. Cosmas claims that "McKinley strove to organize the army on the principles elaborated by Emory Upton."

24. Bernard, 148.

25. Russell F. Weigley, "Elihu Root Reforms and the Progressive Era," in *Command and Commanders in Modern Warfare,* ed. William Geffen (Washington, D.C.: Office of Air Force History, 1971), 24. Jack C. Lane, "The Military Profession's Search for Identity," *Marine Corps Gazette* (June 1973): 40.

26. Hays, 3 and 10.

27. Bernard, 133.

28. For the best explanation regarding the "Americanization" of the general staff, see John M. Palmer, *America in Arms: The Experience of the United States with Military Organization* (New Haven, Conn.: Yale University Press, 1941), 125. "In the correct sense, a General Staff officer is distinctly a specialist in the highest of all military specialties and not a generalists as most of us assumed him to be when Congress passed the General Staff Act of 1903. To us [the officer corps], the new General Staff appeared to be a sort of a busybody staff created to butt into the business of every other staff activ-

ity. . . . Secretary Root did not want his new General Staff to be a super administrative agency to do what was already being done."

Also see Robert L. Goldich, "Evolution of Congressional Attitudes toward a General Staff in the Twentieth Century," *Defense Organization* (Washington, D.C.: Senate Armed Services Committee, 1980), 244–74.

Also see William H. Carter, "Army Reformers," *North American Review* (October 1918): 548–55. This is a critical evaluation of those who had hindered effective army reform, such as the bureau chiefs of cavalry, artillery, and infantry and the National Guard Association.

29. Allan R. Millett, *The General: Robert L. Bullard and Officership in the U.S. Army 1881—1925* (Westport, Conn.: Greenwood, 1975), 208–10. Millett talks about Lt. Col. Robert L. Bullard's perceptions of the influence of the emerging culture of management science: "Bullard thought that modern society had made leadership especially difficult because it produced 'a common lack of manly honor and self-respect' among soldiers by its impersonality and its materialistic value system." Millett goes on, quoting Bullard: "The straining life of highly organized society has undoubtedly made men more nervous, more hysterical and less able to face danger, suffering and death. . . . The frequent necessity of defense of self and rights, have made them more than ever loth [sic] to risk their lives in war and battle."

Also see Russell F. Weigley, *History of the U.S. Army* (Bloomington, Ind.: Indiana University Press, 1984), 598–600.

30. Millett, 309–45. Millett talks extensively about how Gen. John Pershing, commander of the AEF in France in World War I, adopted a command climate of fear to impress on the French and British the professionalism of U.S. officers. This tradition, later called "zero defects," was emphasized at the Infantry School and the Command and General Staff College at Fort Leavenworth in the 1920s and 1930s.

Marshall believed in the centralized control of subordinates. See Daniel P. Bolger, "Zero Defects: Command Climate in the First U.S. Army, 1944–45," *Military Review* (May 1991): 66–67. Marshall wrote, "Control presupposes that the leader knows the location of all elements of his command at all times and can communicate with any element at any time." Marshall emphasized that his students, his instructors, and later his subordinates understood that knowing the rules and procedures overcame friction. In Marshall's tenure at the Infantry School and as chief of staff of the army, "the requirement [of control] was absolute."

This command and leadership philosophy relates to the fact that Marshall did not have a professional army to speak of at the beginning of World War II, so at least initially, he had to resort to this style of leadership in training. It persisted to the end of World War II and was carried on after the war.

See also Robert L. Bateman, "Shifting Gears: Tanks, Radios and the Changing Tempo of Warfare between the World Wars" (M.A. thesis, Ohio State University, 1998), 113.

31. U.S. Senate Committee on Armed Services, *Officer Personnel Act of 1947,* 80th Cong., 1st sess., 1947. From the testimonies of Generals Eisenhower and Marshall.

32. *Congressional Quarterly Almanac* (Washington, D.C.: Congressional Quarterly, 1916), 321–22. The introduction of up-or-out came with the Navy Personnel Act of 1916. It floundered in the interwar years because the navy did not possess a large officer corps to support up-or-out. "The new rapid-promotion system for men of special ability would make the military career more attractive to brilliant men, and the bill would also increase military efficiency by making it possible to get rid of unqualified officers."

33. U.S. War Department, Bureau of Public Relations, *Report of the Secretary of War's Board on Officer-Enlisted Man Relationships* (Washington, D.C.: U.S. War Department, May 1946), 2–3.

34. William L. Hauser, *Restoring Military Professionalism* (Washington, D.C.: The Heritage Foundation, 1985), 1–3. This article specifically discusses the effects of OPA 1947 .

35. Kenneth Kay, "How the Air Force Learns from Business," *Air Force Magazine* (August 1956): 144–50 and 155. Twenty-five Army officers attended Harvard, Stanford, Columbia, and Wharton Business Schools for postgraduate studies in business and personnel management. After their education, officers were assigned to service schools and command headquarters to teach and formulate management and personnel policies.

36. Kirkland, "Soldiers and Marines at Chosin Reservoir: Criteria for Assignment to Combat Command," *Armed Forces and Society*, Vol. 22, No. 2, (Baltimore, Md.: Holy Locks Press, 1996), 258.

37. Ibid.

38. Of the six division commanders who initially went into Korea, four were relieved by December. Of those four, none had previously commanded a division.

39. Discussions with Brig. Gen. Mike Lynch, U.S. Army (Ret.), 29 May 1998. "Despite today's rhetoric, a replay of Vietnam with today's wonder weapons would produce the same result. We'd just kill more people and destroy more enemy means. And we wouldn't understand that the North Vietnamese won with the appropriate measures."

40. The so-called "search and destroy" concept, developed by then Maj. Gen. William DePuy, assistant to Gen. William Westmoreland, violated the basic tenet of protecting terrain and preserving combat resources. It was based on the faulty perceptions of leaders who, based on World War II, considered our status to be superior. It was planned by subordinates schooled in the French way of war. They erroneously assumed we could control events. It was carried out by a legion of dedicated grunts who trustingly presumed that its architects were professionally qualified.

41. Cinncinatinus, *Self-Destruction, The Disintegration and Decay of the U.S. Army During the Vietnam Era* (New York: W. W. Norton, 1981), 132–40.

42. William D. Henderson, *Cohesion: The Human Element in Combat* (Washington, D.C.: National Defense University Press, 1985). This book compares the personnel policies that affected cohesion, leadership, and training in Israel, Vietnam, the United States, and the Soviet Union. The U.S. Army does not fare well in this book.

43. Henry L. Trewhitt, *McNamara* (New York: Harper & Row, 1971), 4–12 and 34–56. McNamara had been brought up on the quantitative measurements approach since his days at the Harvard Graduate School of Business Administration. His military experience in World War II was limited to the sterile environment where he worked as a captain for the army air corps in accounting problems. He emerged as part of the growing management-science culture.

44. U.S. Army, Deputy Chief of Staff for Personnel, *Study of the Twelve Month Vietnam Tour* (Washington, D.C.: Government Printing Office, 29 June 1970), 3–10. Also see U.S. Army, *U.S. Army Replacement System: DCSPER Staff Study* (Washington, D.C.: Government Printing Office, 10 March 1959).

45. H. P. Ball, *Of Responsible Command* (Carlisle Barracks, Pa.: U.S. Army War College, 1983), 180–82. Also see W. V. Pratt, *The U.S. Navy War College—A Staff Study* (Newport, R.I.: U.S. Naval War College, 1954). This book provides a thorough history of the U.S. military's resistance to the use of examinations. In 1903 at the Naval War College, a proposal was laid out that examinations be used to determine standings in the class; this was resisted on the ground that its use was "undemocratic."

46. Sam C. Sarkesian, *The Professional Army Officer in a Changing Society* (Chicago: Nelson-Hall, 1975), 67.

47. Larry H. Ingraham, "The OER Cudgel: Radical Surgery Needed," *Army* (March 1986): 8–16.

48. J. T. Miller, "Integrity and Reality in Writing up OERs," *Army* (April 1977) 16–18. This article was also reproduced in a Command and General Staff College ethics pamphlet, pamphlet L1-AS-2–5.

49. Paul L. Savage and Richard Gabriel, "Turning Away from Managerialism: The Environment of Military Leadership," *Military Review* (July 1980): 57.

50. U.S. Army War College, *Study on Military Professionalism* (Carlisle, Pa.: U.S. Army War College, 1970), 12 and abstract.

51. Center for Army Lessons Learned, *How to Change an Army* (Fort Leavenworth, Kan.: U.S. Army Command and General Staff College, 1997), slides 1 and 2.

52. Andrew J. Bacevich, "Progressivism, Professionalism, and Reform," Parameters,(Carlisle, PA, U.S. Army War College) Vol.9, No.1, March 1975, 6–7. For a thorough assessment of OPMS 1971, see William Hauser, "The Peacetime Army: Retrospect and Prospect," in *The U.S. Army in Peacetime,* ed. Robin Higham and Carol Brandt (Manhattan, Kan.: Military Affairs/Aerospace Publishing, 1975), 217. Also see David McCormick, *The Downsized Warrior: America's Army in Transition* (New York: New York University Press, 1998).

53. Discussions with Lt. Gen. Richard Trefry, U.S. Army (Ret.), 4 and 11 May 1998. General Trefry sheds a realistic light on the inability of the U.S. Army to adopt a unit personnel system. The demands of a bloated officer corps at the middle and upper ranks force the army to maintain a force structure filled with numerous headquarters manned by thousands of officers and soldiers, which does not allow the army to create enough units to rotate with one another based on the manpower cap set by Congress. Trefry says this is because "there are not enough faces to fill the spaces." He also states that the army officer corps does not have the discipline to maintain a unit system because as soon as a cohesive unit arrives to replace losses, it is instantly broken up because of "the priorities of the commander."

54. Discussions with Gen. Donn Starry, U.S. Army (Ret.), 7 November 1997. Also see P. W. Faith and D. I. Ross, *Application of the Regimental System to the U.S. Army's Combat Arms* (Fort Monroe, Va.: Training and Doctrine Command, April 1980).

55. Informal surveys conducted by the author among former platoon leaders, sergeants, and company commanders of COHORT units.

56. *Army Research Institute* newsletter, vol. 9, June 1992. The effect of "climate" on trust, cohesion, and unit effectiveness has been validated in many studies. The army has considerable experience with a variety of surveys beginning with the *Study of Professionalism*. It is the use of data, not the gathering of it, that has been the primary flaw in the army's survey efforts.

57. Walter F. Ulmer, Jr., "Military Leadership into the 21st Century: Another 'Bridge Too Far?'" *Parameters* (Spring 1998): 4–25.

58. Discussions with Gen. Edward Meyer, U.S. Army (Ret.), 29 January 1998.

59. Author worked periodically with the OPMS XXI group from September 1996 through March 1997. The members that composed the OPMS XXI task force were some of the best and the brightest the army had to offer.

60. Donald E. Chipman, "The Military Courtier and the Illusion of Competence," *Air University Review* (March 1983): 15–24.

61. Ibid. Doughty, 7–12, 33–41, 56–57, 113–17. Bacevich, 61.

62. Edward N. Luttwak, *The Pentagon and the Art of War* (New York: Simon and Schuster, 1985), 188. In 1995 the army had 70,203 commissioned officers for 422,073 enlisted personnel. Even after the latest cuts, the ratio will remain the same. Also see James Bennett, "So Many Officers, So Little to Do," *Washington Monthly* (February 1990): 23. Also see Nick Koltz, "Where Have All the Warriors Gone," *Washingtonian* (July 1984): 25.

63. John C. Tillson, Merle L. Roberson, and Stanley A. Horowitz, *Alternative Approaches to Organizing, Training and Assessing Army and Marine Corps Units* (Alexandria, Va.: Institute for Defense Analysis, November 1992), 23. A band of excellence resembles a roller coaster of training ups and downs, with the band representing the average of the surges of training that occur with the constant inflow and outflow of personnel.

64. Discussions with Dr. Steven Canby and Mr. John Tillson. Both of these individuals are experts on unit cohesion systems, and they have developed a system of unit development and replacement for use by the U.S. Army and Marine Corps.

65. This system comes from a mixture of the systems employed by the Germans, Israelis, and British, and proposals put forth by Dr. Canby and Mr. Tillson. A separate essay could be written about the new system. This is used as a foundation on which to place the officer corps' focus.

66. U.S. Army, *TRADOC Pamphlet 525–5: Force XXI Operations* (Fort Monroe, Va.: Training and Doctrine Command, August 1994), 3–4 and 3–5.

67. Koltz, 27–30.

68. OPMS 1971 did away with the decentralization of promoting officers and selecting them for command by division commanders. During the Vietnam War, it was perceived that rampant favoritism occurred in this process. General officers were concerned about the lack of trust in their ability to pick future commanders. See Memorandum from Office of the Chief of Staff for Personnel to Col. Jimmie H. Leach, U.S. Army (Ret.), dated 7 December 1977, regarding concerns about the centralized promotion and selection system. See also a letter dated 23 December 1977 from Brig. Gen. J. McKinley Gibson, U.S. Army (Ret.), to Gen. Bruce C. Clarke, regarding

the feeling among general officers about the new centralized promotion and selection system.

69. Donovan R. Bigelow, "Equal but Separate: Can the Army's Affirmative Action Program Withstand Judicial Scrutiny After Croson?" *Military Law Review* (Winter 1991): 12–13. This article, written after extensive research by Captain Bigelow, talks of the influence projected over centralized boards by the army in the pursuit of "goals" for promoting women and minorities.

70. "Truth" Rehberg, "An Exploratory Study of Psychological Type with Respect to Rank in the USAF" (master's thesis, University of South Dakota, March 1991). Discussions with Major Rehberg.

71. Ibid., 86–91. Chipman, 33–34. Defense Manpower Commission, *Defense Manpower: The Keystone of National Security, Report to the President and the Congress* (Washington, D.C.: U.S. Congress, March 1976), 261. "One of the most controversial subjects deals with the 'up or out' promotion system in the personnel management area . . . [which] has created morale problems . . . has caused personnel turbulence and general hardship [and is] failure oriented." This was also one of the reasons Senator Sam Nunn of Georgia, head of the Senate Armed Forces Committee, resisted DOPMA for four years, stating that it is "expensive to force officers up through the ranks and a waste of experience to get rid of others."

72. Dr. Charlie Moskos of Northwestern University, considered the leading military sociologist in the nation, has conducted extensive research and written several books about the impact of the military using economic incentives and turning the military profession into a job instead of a profession.

73. Ralph Peters, "Twelve Steps to Army Reform," *Army Times*, 8 June 1998. "Revise the personnel system to attract and retain talent instead of driving it away [and] terminate the 'up or out' [policy]." This article is concise and provides a road map for army reform.

74. Bigelow, 15, describes in detail the workings of the army's centralized boards.

75. Sam C. Sarkesian and William Taylor, "The Case for Civilian Graduate Education for Professional Officers," *Armed Forces and Society* 1, No. 2 (New York: Scribner's, 1975), 251–61. "The effective command of complex military units and organizations remain as

much an art as a science. Development of the capacity for exercising command effectively is advanced by studies ranging from history to understanding the human condition to ethics and psychology of leadership, before the processes of decision, the capabilities of weapons, the elements of alliance relationships, the thought patterns, culture and doctrine of possible opponents, and the whole gamut of professional military considerations are even broached."

76. D. Nowowiejski, "Leader Development and Why It Remains Important," *Military Review* 4 (1995): 70–75.

77. P. J. Dermer, "CGSC—Learning Institution or Inhibitor?" (term paper, U.S. Army Command and General Staff College, 1996), 3–4. This paper describes the shortcomings of U.S. Army education from the view of the students.

78. Informal author survey of former students of army schools, journalists, and military historians.

79. Discussions with Dr. Charles White and Mr. Jim Etter, president and founder of American Military University. Dr. Martin van Creveld, *The Training of Officers* (New York: Free Press, 1990), 145–56. van Creveld recommends that the army move up education and refocus. Also see his *Fighting Power,* in which he compares U.S. and German training methods.

80. Dermer, 9–12. Dermer and other former students of Command & General Staff College, as well as developers at TRADOC, talk about the army using the same scenarios to teach processes as well as validating new tactical and operational concepts. One familiar scenario is the Fulda Gap scenario in central Germany, using a Soviet-style enemy.

81. Dr. Christopher Bassford, *The Spit Shine Syndrome: Organizational Irrationality in the American Field Army* (Westport, Conn.: Greenwood Press, 1988), 84. Dr. Bassford provides a solid recommendation for how to instill cohesion and create effective team force-on-force evaluations.

82. Charles E. White, *The Enlightened Soldier:* Scharnhorst *and the* Militaerische Gesellschaft *in Berlin* (New York: Praeger, 1989), 34–40, 105–06, and 123.

83. Discussions with Mr. Bruce Gudmundsson, Mr. William Lind, and Col. Mike Wyly, U.S. Marine Corps (Ret.)

84. McCormick, 120–56. McCormick talks about the selections for early retirement boards, used to help accomplish the army's drawdown.

85. These ideas about education are based on discussions with Lt. Col. Robert Chase, U.S. Marine Corps, and Dr. Charles White. Subjects of discussion included Marshall's legacy; several of his instructors at the Infantry School in Fort Benning later became general officers in World War II, and J. Lawton Collins was assigned to the faculty of the War College in the late 1930s.

86. In the mid-1980s the army implemented a personnel policy called Project Warrior. It took top officers in company command and sent them to be observer controllers, then rotated them to be small-group tactical instructors at the branch schools. Today the pendulum has swung back the other way, with the army placing its fast trackers in the Pentagon or at Personnel Command to serve in the bureaucracy.

87. Donald E. Vandergriff, "Creating the Officer Corps to Execute Force XXI Blitzkrieg," *Armor* (March-April 1997): 29.

88. William E. Rosenback and Robert L. Taylor, *Contemporary Issues in Leadership* (Boulder, Colo.: Westview Press, 1984), 87.

Discussions with Brig. Gen. Mike Lynch, 24 May 1998. "Ridgway's mavericks all got in trouble when his successors, such as General Maxwell Taylor, did not think like he did and emphasized the corporate man over the warrior."

89. Discussions with Lt. Col. Paul Maubert, U.S. Marine Corps, 12 May 1998.

Ed Offley

There will be more than one front in future wars. Because of the explosion of communications technology, from the apparent omnipresence of the Cable News Network to the volumes of material available almost instantaneously via the Internet, the military needs to address the future of the military-media relationship. There is now a second battlefield, and the objective at stake is the support of the military by the American people. Since this is the case, this anthology could not be complete without addressing that battlefield through the eyes of one of those who occupy that ground: a member of the media.

Ed Offley has been a military reporter for the *Seattle Post-Intelligencer* since 1987. In this role he is responsible for covering military commands, units, operations, and training exercises in Washington state and the Pacific Northwest region. He focuses on the work of about eighty thousand Department of Defense military and civilian employees at eleven major military installations in the state. With more than fifteen years "on the beat," he has, like many military affairs reporters, developed a deep affinity with the subjects of his reporting. Yet in those years it has not always been easy for a reporter to break through the barriers erected by both the military and the media in the aftermath of the Vietnam War. Offley has succeeded because, unlike many of his peers, he has "seen the elephant," serving as a sailor in the U.S. Navy in Vietnam.

Among his other qualifications, he is current chairman of the Military Reporters Organizing Committee, which is working to form a national association of military journalists. During Operation Desert Storm, Offley covered the outbreak of the war and served in a media combat pool. He has covered military operations and exercises in eighteen foreign countries, including the former Soviet Union, Somalia, Panama, and South Korea. He has been qualified by both the air force and the navy to fly in combat planes, and has flown in more than twenty types of military aircraft. He has also covered a Trident missile submarine on submerged nuclear patrol, an air force resupply mission to the South Pole, and special operations units.

With these credentials from both sides of the debate, Offley is one of the best qualified of all authors to comment on the past and the potential future of the media-military relationship in the digital era. This is a strategic-level question that addresses the very heart of the digital revolution: How will the military relate to the people it protects in the future?

The Military-Media Relationship in the Digital Age

The explosion in digital computer technology is transforming American society and revolutionizing the art and conduct of war. It can be stated as a given that the relationship between the military and the media is being profoundly altered by advances in digital computers and related gains in other communications hardware.

In the decade now ending, U.S. and international reporters have covered U.S. military operations in Panama, the Persian Gulf, Somalia, Haiti, the Balkans, and Africa, as well as crisis response measures from the east coast of Africa to the Taiwan Straits. In each of the operations, ranging from small-force civilian evacuation missions to the U.S.-led air and ground war in Operation Desert Storm, print reporters and broadcast journalists have seized upon the gains in technology to improve the quality of military coverage and the speed of transmission from the field.

News coverage of recent nonmilitary events in Washington, D.C.—particularly the Office of Independent Counsel's investigation of President Clinton, the referral to Congress of the investigative files, and the decision of the House of Representatives in September 1998 to release the bulk of the investigative files, including the president's videotaped grand jury appearance—further confirms the power of advanced computer technology to deliver immense amounts of news material to the public practically instantaneously.

The power of this new technology is having—and will continue to have—a profound effect on the coverage of military operations. It has already sparked countermoves by the Pentagon to exploit the new technology for its institutional interests while attempting to preserve operational security, as we will analyze in this chapter.

Still, the technology revolution is not taking place in a vacuum. A number of other developments within the military arena and the journalism profession will intersect with the computer revolution to shape the landscape of future military-media relations.

On the military side, the maturing of joint military doctrine and interservice cooperation under the guidance of the 1986 Goldwater-Nichols Act continues to erode the historical cultural differences in military-media relations among the four uniformed services and even their subcomponents. A decade of shrinking Pentagon budgets has impelled even the most conservative and hesitant military subcultures to use the press as a venue to advance their public images, programs, and budget requests.[1] By and large, a new generation of military commanders and senior public affairs officers has discarded the generation-old antipathy toward the press and taken to heart the PAO "lessons learned" from the 1991 Persian Gulf War: The news media is not the enemy, but rather the battleground on which the struggle for public support, congressional funding, and political decision making will be fought.[2]

The American journalism profession has also experienced a wave of change during the past decade that directly affects its approach and effectiveness in covering the military. Masked by the explosion of "new media" such as cable television and online publications, both newspapers and broadcast outlets have for the past decade experienced severe economic pressures that have resulted in fewer full-time international news bureaus, a reliance on third-nation journalists for initial on-site coverage in a crisis, a decimation of the number of full-time military reporting specialists, and a continued decline in budgets for in-depth coverage and travel. Moreover, the national security and defense beats have declined in prestige within the journalism profession since the end of the Cold War, even while the pace of military operations and the number of international crises involving U.S. military forces have continued unabated.

Some media analysts are convinced that the very nature of news will be transformed by the spread of computers and global communications. The merger of the Internet, television, digital audio and video signals, and text will make it possible for wars (and other intense human dramas) to be provided to the American public not as stories to be read or viewed, but as multimedia events that can range from text to computer graphic simulations.

Both the military and the media are separately and together grappling with the long-term implications of digital computer power.

In peacetime, computers promise to help narrow a gap between the military and civil society that has widened as an inadvertent consequence of the end of the draft in 1973 and the shrinking of the military community to a smaller number of base clusters scattered throughout the country.

Within the military, computer-driven information, whether news or private e-mail, has become a powerful tool to help military service members retain a connection to their families and home communities even when they are deployed half a globe away.

But it is in the coverage of future conflicts that the computer revolution will have the most dramatic impact.

Few military operations in the digital age will elude intense, detailed coverage by the news media at practically a real-time pace. Both the military and the news media will be forced to grapple with the operational security and privacy implications of the digital computer revolution.

An examination of current trends in computer technology, particularly the explosion of online journalism, suggests the following issues for the military and the media in the cyberspace revolution:

- Coverage of peacetime military subjects will improve somewhat as a result of the Pentagon's commitment to using its Web sites to promulgate timely information ranging from briefing transcripts to unclassified publications. A similar profusion of other federal and nongovernmental Web sites, such as the sites of the General Accounting Office, Congress' Thomas system, and scores of policy think tanks and research institutes, will also expand the scope of rapid information gathering on military and national security subjects. News media organizations versed in computer-assisted reporting will expand the current level of reporting on issues, employing Department of Defense computer databases for information on important issues.

• However, the gains in media access to national security information will be offset somewhat by a continued decline in the number of full-time military reporting professionals, a trend that has accelerated in the aftermath of Operation Desert Storm.[3]

• As Internet and e-mail capability spreads throughout the news media to include smaller, community-oriented publications and broadcast outlets, the Pentagon will be able to expand its grassroots public affairs presence using computerized "home town" news releases, feature profile news releases, and even use digital imagery.

• Journalists will have more powerful tools to conduct wartime coverage independent of the military, including direct uplinks from portable laptop computers to commercial communications satellites that avoid any dependency on military communications networks. This is particularly true in crisis areas where U.S. journalists already have an established presence before the armed forces arrive.

• Large media organizations will be able to obtain, analyze, and publish satellite imagery of crisis areas or battlefields independent of the Pentagon and official spokesmen.

• Broadcast media using smaller, more refined technology will place more pressure on the military to allow it to record actual combat footage. (An example would be installing cockpit-mounted television "finger" cameras such as those currently used by the air force on its Thunderbirds flight demonstration team.) The expansion of digital computer technology, such as the Intervehicle Information System showing real-time positions of tanks and infantry vehicles, will create additional forms of digital battlefield depictions that the news media will want—and demand—to use.

• Both the military and the media will have to cooperate and effectively work together under a news cycle that is even more intense than the twenty-four-hours-per-day, seven-days-per-week pattern that began on cable television and now exists on the Internet. Both institutions will have to learn how to manage the enormous strain of demands to "get it right," while avoiding the release of information that could threaten the success of an operation and the lives of U.S. service people.

• In the absence of a particular television image, news organizations will have an arsenal of computer-driven graphics at their fingertips, including animated simulations as well as static visual depictions, to serve as gap fillers during coverage of critical military operations or events.

• The administration and the Pentagon will find themselves competing with outside experts and analysts in the diplomatic and public relations aspects of a conflict. Even the enemy, whether a hostile state or a subnational ethnic group, will be able to wage a public relations campaign in cyberspace as the battlefield struggle proceeds. The Pentagon will learn to use cyberspace as it previously used live television to send its message "around" the news media directly to the American people and global bystanders.

• The Pentagon will have to expand an information and technical campaign unveiled in September 1998 throughout the armed services to balance the policy of open information against the equally pressing needs for operational security and privacy protection.

As journalists and generals alike prepare for the next conflict, it is imperative that they come to grips with the powerful two-edged sword that is digital computer technology. If there is one consensus among computer users and communications experts alike, it is that the unintended consequences of the digital computer revolution on military-media relations will be immense, even as the specifics elude concrete prediction.

Earlier Revolutions

It is a supreme irony, to those studying the evolution of military-media relations, that one of the most deeply imbedded icons in print journalism (and by transference, broadcast reporting as well) owes its existence to shoddy reporting on the military. Seventeen years after the invention of the telegraph in 1844, reporters on both sides flocked to cover the American Civil War and found the military's use of telegraphic communications a revolutionary new means to send their dispatches in for publication in a matter of hours—not days or weeks. As media analyst Johanna Neuman recounts:

"There was a magic to the times, an intoxication about the 'telegraphic' newspaper. 'We marvel that it has become possible to convey, print and circulate upon the streets facts concerning a pending battle hundreds of miles away,' said one of the Civil War military telegraph operators. . . . (But) none of this, however, made the reporting terribly accurate. Journalism from Civil War battles is, with few exceptions, a disappointing chapter in the profession's history."

Initially, Neuman writes, publishers topped these electronic dispatches with the line, "By Telegraph," which signaled to the readers their immediacy.

However, it was a disgusted Union Gen. Joseph Hooker who forever changed the face of print journalism. Fed up with inaccurate reporting within his camp, Hooker in 1863 ordered reporters to affix their names atop their stories—as a matter of public accountability and to promote accuracy.

Thus was born the newspaper byline.[4]

The impact of new communications technology on society transcends the narrower debate over military-media relations, but historical responses to other media technology advances offer hints about how the digital computer revolution may affect not only media coverage of future military operations, but the relationship between the public and policymakers as well.

What is clear is that no new technology has appeared without sparking resistance and condemnation. Yet there is evidence that such innovations not only advance the specific new technologies, but reinvigorate other, older forms of media as well.

As early as 1453, when Johannes Gutenberg invented moveable type, which would lead to the hand-powered printing press, the reaction among political and cultural leaders—who presided over intellectual, religious, and government institutions long habituated to hand-written manuscripts available only to a limited number of educated readers—was immediate and negative. "It was ferociously adjudged that [Gutenberg] was in league with the devil," one early historian said.[5]

Never mind that with Gutenberg's press came an explosion of publishing, writing, and reading that historians link to several major historical events, particularly Martin Luther's assault on the Roman Catholic Church's monopoly on liturgy. "Barely a few years after the [Gutenberg] Bible had been printed, printing presses were set up all over Europe," writes historian Alberto Manguel. He notes, "It may be useful to bear in mind that printing did not, in spite of the obvious 'end of the world' predictions, eradicate the taste for hand-written text. . . . It is interesting to note how often a technological development such as Gutenberg's, promotes rather than eliminates that which it is supposed to supercede, making us aware of old-fashioned virtues we might otherwise have overlooked or dismissed as of negligible importance. In our day, computer technology and proliferation of books on CD-ROM have not affected—as far as statistics show—the production and sale of books in their codex form."[6]

Each new advance in media technology has sparked the same cry of apocalypse and doom: A Rhode Island newspaper damned the invention of the telephone in 1876 as an element of the "powers of darkness." One of the inventors of the radio, Lee De Forest, was savagely criticized by the prosecutor in a 1913 fraud trial (regarding the sale of stock in his America Wireless Company) for the "absurd and deliberately misleading" assertion that it would be possible to transmit voice and music over radio waves in the future. The *Times of London* reported in 1926 that there was no future in a technology that "only sends shadows," an instant rebuke to the concept of television.[7]

By the end of World War I, the telegraphic revolution was truly global with the steady growth of undersea marine telephone cable networks. The electronic media of that era, as Neuman writes, led many leaders such as President Woodrow Wilson to lament, "All the impulses of mankind are thrown out upon the air and reach to the ends of the earth; quietly upon steamships, silently under the cover of the Postal Service, with the tongue of the wireless and the tongue of the telegraph, all the suggestions of disorder are spread through the world."[8] But the new media did something else, Neuman writes: "What [telegraph and wireless technology] actually did was speed the input of public opinion" into government decision making.

So did radio and television, and now cyberspace.

Fighting the Last War—E-Mail in the Gulf

The Iraqi invasion of Kuwait on 2 August 1990 set the stage for a U.S.-led coalition air and ground war five months later, which is noted by military historians as unveiling a new generation of weapons and tactics that some say signaled the transformation of combat.

The air force unleashed the radar-evading F-117A stealth fighter and a previously classified air-launched cruise missile against Iraqi targets; navy submarines and surface ships for the first time fired Tomahawk cruise missiles; the army dominated the ground offensive with a host of weapons ranging from the Multiple Launch Rocket System to the AH-64 Apache helicopter gunship and the computer-aided 120mm main gun of the M1A1 Abrams tank.

Less visible but equally effective were the complex computer-driven command-and-control system, the phalanx of air- and space-based satellite sensors, and other high-technology systems that gave the coalition total information dominance on the battlefield.

The news media, too, brought a computer-driven arsenal to the Arabian desert. A postwar survey of Desert Storm news coverage found ten examples of high-technology innovation brought to bear for the first time to cover war, including:[9]

1. Electronic mail and computer-to-computer communications
2. Digital transmission of still photographs
3. Fax transmissions
4. Portable satellite telephones
5. Remotely sensed satellite imagery
6. Frame capture of video images to print

7. Portable laptop computers
8. International data transmission networks
9. Flyaway satellite uplinks
10. Computer graphics (both video and print)

The most visible innovation in the Gulf conflict was, of course, the ability of CNN and other television operations to provide real-time coverage of the conflict (although the events being covered live were a small fraction of the overall campaign).

Whereas in Vietnam, filmed stories of battle often took at least twenty-four hours to be processed and transmitted from the war zone to New York for airing, CNN's breaking news coverage of the air battle over Baghdad—initially limited to a telephone description of Iraqi antiaircraft gunners firing blindly into the night skies—marked a major advancement in news technology's ability to bring events as they occurred into living rooms around the world.

Despite the steep costs in license fees for satellite transponders (about $75,000 a month in Saudi Arabia), the major television networks did not hesitate to maximize their use of the technology. "The key change is the ability to go live any time, every time, to see any Scud (missile) attack," NBC News production director David Schmerler told the Gannett study.

Each of those technologies were put to intensive use by various newspaper, radio, and television organizations with personnel deployed in Saudi Arabia and other nations in the region.

An inevitable result of the satellite television breakthrough was that it was not just viewed by ordinary citizens.

"As CNN's Bernard Shaw, Peter Arnett and John Holliman described the sights and sounds of aerial attacks outside their hotel window in Baghdad," media analyst Johanna Neuman would later write, "viewers could watch war. Thatcher watched in Britain. Yeltsin watched in Moscow. Bush watched in Washington. Shamir watched in Jerusalem. Even Libya's Qaddafi watched in his tent in Tripoli. . . . There is simply no precedence for this experience."[10]

The other computer-driven technologies also played an important role in the collection and production of news.

"This was an e-mail war," said Charles Borst, then director of the Knight-Ridder photo service, when interviewed for the Gannett study. Despite the uneven quality of service by the Saudi telephone system and the constraints posed by time and distance throughout the region, Borst said that the electronic system performed well both in allowing internal communication within his organization's U.S. and foreign sites and in transmitting stories and photographs once they had cleared the Joint Information Bureau in Dhahran.

Although the advanced technologies described here did help reporters, photojournalists, and television producers, the hardware and software by themselves did not overcome several significant obstacles—political and physical—that existed in the Desert Storm area of operations.

Eight years before Operation Desert Shield began in August 1990, the British fought a brief war against Argentina over the Falkland Islands. That ten-week conflict saw the most severe imposition of press restrictions in post–World War II history in the West. U.S. military officials watched the British tightly control the number of reporters allowed to accompany their task force. Dispatches were severely censored and often delayed (they had to be sent over military communications channels).

The following year the Pentagon imposed a ban on journalists during the initial stages of the Grenada intervention, going so far as to detain reporters who had managed to get to the island on their own. Even after a military-media commission devised the concept of a pool of experienced military reporters to accompany deploying forces, the 1989 invasion of Panama resulted in a similar, albeit de facto exclusion when the Pentagon press pool was sidetracked in Panama and not allowed to cover the scene until after the fighting had ended.[11]

Several major studies of military-media relations during the Gulf War have examined in depth the roots of hostility between the Vietnam-era military and news media, and its resulting impact on the Central Command decision to limit both the number of journalists on the battlefield and their access to combat units and personnel while under close PAO escort. Rather than imposing formal censorship, the command used its monopoly on in-theater transportation, a policy of limited access to units, and the dependency of reporters upon the military communications system to control coverage.[12]

These physical limitations and policy constraints neutralized much of the new technology that journalists brought to the war zone, and in fact hindered much coverage of the campaign that the military itself later conceded would have been positive.

The Revolution in Public Affairs

In the aftermath of Operation Desert Storm, computer technology continued to expand in power throughout the U.S. journalism profession even as a postwar recession struck both the print and broadcast sectors with severe consequences. (At least eight daily newspapers that sent correspondents to the Gulf War would shut down during the recession or shortly thereafter.)

At the same time, key leaders in the military began reassessing the Cold War–era public affairs policies that in large part had shaped the stringent controls on the press during the Gulf War.

The convergence of these three trends—the rapid reduction in military coverage by U.S. newspapers and television broadcast organizations, a radical turnaround in Pentagon PAO policy, and new gains in communications technology—produced a revolution in the military-media relationship that did not become evident for some time.

For example, the U.S. Pacific Command in the summer of 1992 conducted a major multiservice training exercise in the southern California region that ran from July 1–24, with a week set aside for reporters to observe a wide variety of simulated combat events involving a marine expeditionary unit, a navy carrier battle group, army and air force units, and Special Operations Command (SOCCOM) elements.

Among the concepts being tested were a new set of Pentagon press guidelines adopted after the Gulf War that formally ended the restrictive policies that had hampered coverage.[13]

For an entire week, the task force commander and his battle staff provided military transportation across the area of operations and conducted detailed staff briefings on both the exercise scenario events and the forces participating in the exercise—including the previously walled-off Joint Special Operations Task Force headquarters established as a commando supporting element for the twenty-thousand-man war game.

Moreover, navy units participating invited reporters to field-test a new ship-mounted international marine satellite ground station that provided direct laptop computer connectivity between reporters and their newspapers hundreds of miles away. In addition, navy combat camera photographers were in the field with a new generation of digital still cameras and offered to test-transmit imagery directly from the field to newspaper publishing sites.[14]

Five months later, the Tandem Thrust participants made world headlines in Somalia as the 15th Marine Expeditionary Unit went ashore in Mogadishu supported by the USS *Kitty Hawk* carrier battle group and the USS *Tripoli* amphibious ready group offshore. Their practice with the new press guidelines and journalists' high-technology equipment during Exercise Tandem Thrust were immediately put to the test.

The Somalia intervention occurred at a time when more and more newspaper and broadcast operations were introducing new generations of computing equipment, including more powerful laptop models that could, with computer modems, provide faster transmission of articles and photographs from the field to home offices. Somalia also heralded a decade of "operations other than war," in which the rules for reporters were different, even if there were still antagonists nearby with loaded weapons.

Somalia became a laboratory not for computers per se, but for the continued gains in portable satellite uplink capabilities that provided the broadcast media with the means to transmit the beginning of a major military operation beyond the control of military PAO officers or any hint of censorship. (Media technologies such as satellite television broadcasting and remote satellite sensing are included in the scope of this chapter because their development is inherently linked to advances in computer processing power.)

When the 15th Marine Expeditionary Unit landed at Mogadishu in December 1992, it was met not by friendly Somalis or hostile ethnic factions, but by a large group of television and print journalists who descended on the arriving troops with camera lights glaring. Half a world away, Secretary of Defense Dick Cheney was furious.

"My immediate reaction was one of anger," said Cheney, who previously had refused to allow the Pentagon press pool into Panama in time for the takedown of the Panamanian Defense Force, and who had imposed a total news blackout (lifted twenty-four hours afterward) on coverage of the Desert Storm ground offensive despite formal negotiations over pool access and coverage prior to the war.

The public contretemps about coverage of the Somalia landing—one poor commando was filmed by CNN as he cleared his rifle and squinted into the camera lights, only to be morphed by digital graphics into the cable network's formal logo for subsequent news reports—quickly passed as the force solidified its positions without major incident. As it turned out, the incident was an honest miscommunication between the in-country press and the U.S. military public affairs officers, who had specifically told them the time and location of the landing and invited them to cover it, only for both sides to forget the impact of bright television lights on the soldiers' night vision.[15]

Somalia also would trigger an intense debate ten months after the December 1992 intervention when the U.S. forces withdrew over the same beach to their warships offshore. The question was: Had televised and print images of a slain U.S. soldier being dragged through the streets of Mogadishu precipitated the U.S. pullout?

The issue of the specific coverage of the fierce firefight between army rangers and Delta commandos on one side, and hundreds of Somali fighters on the other, does not directly hinge on the gains in news-gathering technology being discussed here. But the debate over the "CNN effect," about whether such intensive, continuous coverage actually can hijack the nation's foreign policy, is a valid debate topic—still unresolved—stemming from the news media communications revolution.

"In assessing the influence of television on international diplomacy in the last years of the 20th century, Bosnia and Somalia are most often cited as proof that satellite television, its lens trained on human suffering, was driving diplomacy," analyst Johanna Neuman writes. "In Somalia, the conventional wisdom holds that pictures got the United States in, and pictures forced the United States out."[16]

But a deeper look not only at Somalia but at other ethnic disasters such as the Sudan or Bosnia in the early 1990s show a less-than-consistent pattern, Neuman and other analysts note. Although media coverage played some role, other factors, including domestic politics, NATO internal disagreements, and "words of caution" from experts who warned of the dangers of precipitous military involvement, led away from intervention in Bosnia, Rwanda, and the Sudan at key points in the early 1990s.

A quieter, less noticed development marked the Somalia experience. Reporters and television journalists throughout the United States were invited into a pool for military coverage of units deploying after the initial landing. In one case, two newspaper reporters, a television reporter, and a television cameraman from four regional outlets in western Washington deployed aboard a Military Airlift Command C-141B from McChord Air Force Base and flew to Mogadishu with only two fueling stops en route. Under the post–Desert Storm press guidelines, air force officials secured them aircraft space and acted as true liaisons instead of interfering with their coverage from the time of embarkation, during a hectic ten days of coverage in Somalia and nearby Kenya, and on the return flight home. Nor was there any interference with article transmission (a moot point since the pools relied on commercial communications links in Kenya).[17]

Another positive sign of change in the military-media relationship emerged in January 1993, when the Bush administration ordered a massive bombing campaign against Iraqi military targets in southern Iraq using the carrier USS *Kitty Hawk* and land-based fighters from Saudi Arabia.

When the Saudi government for political reasons refused to permit U.S. journalists to enter the kingdom to cover the event, the Pentagon and the navy allowed a group of twenty journalists to fly to the carrier in the Persian Gulf. The access came in stark contrast to the conflict that had ended the year before, when several carrier group commanders had flatly refused to allow any journalists aboard their ships for the duration of the war. The press contingent was permitted aboard the carrier, given access to commanders and aviators, and provided communications links. In return, the journalists agreed to a news embargo prior to the air raids to preserve operational security.[18]

By the time of the U.S. intervention in Haiti in September 1994 and the introduction of a U.S.-led peacekeeping contingent in Bosnia the following year, the Pentagon and the news media had emerged from the standoff of the Persian Gulf War to achieve a set of guidelines that balanced operational security requirements against the media's need for access and timely transmission of dispatches.

When Task Force Eagle deployed from Hungary into Bosnia, the Pentagon launched what one subsequent report would term "a bold and innovative plan in military-media relations."[19] Journalists were "embedded" in the German-based army units earmarked for deployment as NATO's implementation force. They traveled with the units and remained with them in Bosnia for two or three weeks after their arrival.

This constituted a full reversal from the earlier pool arrangements in the Gulf, which had allowed only brief and transitory visits with deployed units. Now the journalists were considered part of the military unit itself, a concept that had not been seen since World War II. A total of thirty-three journalists, including twenty-four Americans, took part in the plan.

"The rationale for embedded media was to foster familiarity on the part of the journalists with the unit and its soldiers," one participant later wrote. "The assumption was that as the reporters grew to know the unit and its soldiers, there would be a more positive attitude on the part of the reporters toward the military's mission."[20] Except for one incident in which a brigade commander was quoted alleging that Croats were racist, which sparked several days of intense press scrutiny, the deployment was deemed a success by all parties.

It was within this context that the sudden explosion of the Internet and the widespread availability of powerful computers added an entirely new dimension to the relationship between the generals and the journalists.

The change manifested itself in more than one area, as the following examples will show.

Case Studies: High-Technology Military Reporting

Computer-Assisted Reporting and the Military

It was an investigative reporting project that simply could not have been achieved before the computer era.

When reporters Russell Carollo and Jeff Nesmith set out to do a major investigation of military medical malpractice in 1996, they faced a labyrinth of seemingly inaccessible information. Not only did each of the armed services maintain a separate set of files and records on its military medical personnel, but a number of laws enacted by Congress from the 1940s through 1990 permitted the Pentagon to withhold information that civilian hospitals and medical firms were mandated to disclose. Further exacerbating the reporting challenge were apparent gaps in reporting by many military hospitals and commands.

But the two reporters for the *Dayton* [Ohio] *Daily News* had a powerful ally: off-the-shelf computer software programs that enabled them to download and cross-correlate several dozen military medical databases containing the information they sought—even though the data was unevenly spread throughout millions of bits of other information. (They relied on the federal Freedom of Information Act to litigate the release of several databases that the military unsuccessfully attempted to withhold from them.)

The software allowed Carollo and Nesmith to compile and analyze more than 100,000 separate records from more than a dozen separate military databases. The development of powerful Internet search engines that allow users to track individuals by their addresses and telephone numbers also played a role in the reporters' success in locating both victims of medical malpractice and the doctors accused of poor performance, which otherwise could have been an impossibly difficult task to achieve.

Carollo and Nesmith then took that computer-driven data and crisscrossed the nation conducting interviews with scores of people. The result was a powerful package of articles titled "Military Medicine: Flawed and Sometimes Deadly," which appeared in the Dayton newspaper during 5–11 October 1997.

The series revealed that existing laws and Pentagon policies had inadvertently turned the military medical system into a magnet for problem doctors; the existing system allowed at least seventy-seven physicians without state medical licenses to practice medicine with "special licenses" that bypassed the fact that most of them had repeatedly failed state licensing exams. The reporters discovered that more than seventy-five military medical facilities had failed to report incidents of malpractice to a federal database created by Congress to protect the public from problem doctors—while those very facilities had been the targets of claims alleging more than one thousand malpractice incidents.

The statistics unearthed and deciphered by the two newspaper reporters provided them with the skeleton for a package of articles that described in heart-rending detail the tragedies that had befallen hundreds of military service people and their family members.

As a result of their reporting, both the Pentagon and Congress moved to instigate reforms to ensure quality of care and accountability among military physicians and medical commands. The package won the 1997 Pulitzer Prize for national reporting.

Investigative reporter Andrew Schneider, who has won major national recognition, including two Pulitzer Prizes, for investigative reporting projects, said at an early conference on computer-assisted journalism, "We reconfirmed the fact that computers will not transform bad reporters into good ones." But, he added, "The potential of computer-assisted journalism is limited only by the imagination of the reporters who use it."[21]

Projects such as the 1996 *Dayton Daily News* investigation of military medicine reflect a growing maturity and sophistication among mainstream media in their ability to use the computing power available today to shine a bright spotlight on military topics that were once practically immune from scrutiny. The trend will continue.

DefenseLink and "Data Mining" for Defense News

The army's Delta Force and the Naval Special Warfare Development Group—two of the "black" components of the U.S. Special Operations Command—do not talk to the press. But thanks to the Pentagon's open information policy and the power of contemporary digital computers to search the Internet for available information, an in-depth news story on their specific role in countering the proliferation of weapons of mass destruction was possible to assemble and publish.

On 29 August 1998, the *Tampa Tribune* published a front-page article titled "MacDill brass targets terrorists," written by the author of this chapter for the *Seattle Post-Intelligencer* and sent out over the *New York Times* News Service for other newspapers to use.[22]

The article revealed:

- Units of the multiservice U.S. Special Operations Command (headquartered at MacDill Air Force Base in Tampa) have been training for "extremis" missions to seize nuclear, chemical, or biological weapons in the hands of terrorists or rogue nations.
- Because the 1991 aerial campaign in Operation Desert Storm had demonstrated the extreme vulnerability of all targets located aboveground, nations such as North Korea and Libya in recent years have been building nuclear and chemical facilities deep under hardened rock with the intent of evading aerial destruction.
- Experts say some of these sites, particularly the North Korean nuclear complex at Yongbyon, may be impervious to even tactical nuclear weapons because of their depth under hard rock formations.
- U.S. commandos, charged with the "render safe" and seizure of loose nukes (and presumably the simpler destruction of targeted chemical or biological sites), have actually practiced for combat under the earth at the U.S. National Test Site in Nevada, where for decades the United States set off its own test nuclear devices.

None of the information in the article was classified.

The significance of this article was that its factual foundation was available on the Pentagon's DefenseLink Web site for anyone who wanted to read it. Each year, the secretary of defense files a formal "threat and response" report to Congress itemizing the state of preparedness for countering nuclear, biological, and chemical proliferation. Another unclassified report available through PAO channels is the annual report to Congress by the Pentagon's Counterproliferation Review Committee. Both documents provide a broad overview of U.S. counterproliferation strategy and goals, as well as detailed status reports on various technology initiatives and budget requests.

A central element of the program, one report states, is "supporting, training and equipping SOF teams to detect, neutralize and 'render safe' . . . weapons and devices in permissive and nonpermissive environments both in the United States and overseas."[23]

Having assembled this unambiguous profile of the SOCCOM response to the threat of proliferation, the author had no difficulty securing on-the-record interviews with knowledgeable sources to amplify and explain the issue, including former joint chiefs chairman Gen. John Shalikashvili and retired Gen. Wayne Downing, who headed up the U.S. Special Operations Command during 1993 to 1997.

Satellite Imagery and the Media

It was a remarkable story that was lost in the overall drumbeat of press articles presaging the outbreak of war in the Persian Gulf.

On 6 January 1991, reporter Jean Heller of the *St. Petersburg Times* wrote an article challenging the Bush administration's earlier contention that Iraqi army units directly threatened Saudi Arabia shortly after the 2 August 1990 invasion of Kuwait.

The newspaper's source? Satellite photographs of southern Kuwait shot by an orbiting Soviet photo-reconnaissance satellite that were analyzed for the newspaper by two experts not affiliated with the U.S. government.[24]

"The photos are not conclusive proof that the administration overestimated Iraq's buildup along the Saudi border, a buildup that was cited as a justification for the deployment of U.S. troops," the article said. "But two American satellite imaging experts who examined the photos could find no evidence of a massive Iraqi presence in Kuwait in September (1990)." The Soviet satellite photographed Kuwait on 13 September, which was forty-two days after the invasion.

The newspaper sought a Department of Defense explanation of the discrepancy between Department of Defense statements and the apparent lack of Iraqi troops in the overhead photographs, but a Pentagon spokesman declined to respond, Heller wrote.

The venture into independent satellite reconnaissance came subsequent to an attempt by ABC News to obtain the same evidence. The newspaper reported that ABC News had decided not to air its photographs because they did not include "the strategically important area of southern Kuwait" where Iraq was thought to have laagered its army units. The newspaper alleged that the photographs it had purchased from the Soviet commercial space operation constituted the missing images.

The Pentagon had reported on 18 September 1990 that there were 360,000 Iraqi troops and 2,800 tanks in or near Kuwait. At the time of the *St. Petersburg Times* article, the Bush administration estimated that there were 500,000 soldiers in the occupied emirate.

In hindsight it is not possible to definitively resolve the contradiction suggested by the newspaper's foray into satellite imagery analysis. One account of Operation Desert Shield noted that after the initial strike into Kuwait, which included Iraqi units advancing toward the Saudi border, Iraq after less than a week pulled the Republican Guard out of Kuwait into southern Iraq and left only a handful of conventional units within a short distance of the border.[25] The newspaper's implied accusation of Bush administration deception was neither proved nor disproved.

At the time of the newspaper's scoop, the United States had been operating a wide range of photographic, radar, and electronic intelligence satellites aimed at the Soviet Union and its allies. Because of the nature of technical intelligence gathering, the complexities of the systems involved, and—most particularly—the need to prevent the adversary from knowing the extent of U.S. satellite accuracy and photographic precision, the program had been classified special compartmented information, a security classification more restrictive than top secret, author William Burrows wrote.[26]

Thus, one thing is clear: The newspaper's decision to obtain and use its own satellite imaging source constituted a major turning point in the ongoing high-technology revolution of news coverage.

Journalists were now willing to challenge the U.S. government on its single most valuable intelligence capability, its eyes in space.

(Unconfirmed reports have it that the Iraqis in 1990 were trying to obtain the same area imagery from the French SPOT photo satellite, but the United States persuaded the French consortium to refuse selling it to Baghdad.)

The commercialization of space imagery comes as another inevitable consequence of the end of the Cold War. Although it remains a relatively unexplored frontier to journalists nearly a decade after Operation Desert Storm, space satellite photography is yet another medium that the computer revolution will soon make easy to exploit by the news media.

"The rapid advancement of both communications and computational power is going to forever change the way we fight wars and disseminate information," Jeffrey Harris told a recent military-media conference. Harris, a former assistant secretary of the Air Force for Space, currently is president of Space Imaging Corporation (SIC), one of eleven civilian firms that have cropped up in this decade that are marketing space imagery as a business and media tool.[27]

For reporters covering military affairs, commercial satellites whose imagery resolutions are as small as one meter—the minimum now allowed by the U.S. government—offer photographic coverage from space that rivals the capabilities of U.S. intelligence agencies just a few decades ago. "The media will be a regular customer for data products and information products (from commercial satellites)—floods, earthquakes, fires, tidal waves, refugee camps," Harris told a 1997 Cantigny conference of military officials and defense journalists convened by the Robert R. McCormick Tribune Foundation.

Another implication is that journalism outlets will inevitably consider obtaining for independent analysis satellite imagery of crisis areas that could be as large as the Korean demilitarized zone or as small as a Kosovo village being pillaged by Serbian security forces.

Harris and other experts agree that connecting this imagery with existing computer power offers a new dimension for how television and print journalists can illustrate a breaking military story and independently assess what their government is saying about the enemy.

The impact of journalistic insertion into what has always been a strategic intelligence function—thanks to satellites and related computer processing power—sparks strong debate between the military and the media.

"The next time there's a crisis on the Korean peninsula, the media will have imagery that's almost as good as that available to the military," one military officer theorized at the 1997 Cantigny military-media conference.[28] "What is likely to happen is that a debate will erupt in Washington in which the president says, 'The situation is X, and therefore, I'm going to do Y,' and the media is going to go to Jeff Harris and buy imagery, either real-time or archived imagery of U.S. troop deployments in South Korea and of troop deployments in North Korea, and they're going to say, 'Ah, the situation's not what the president says. It's Z.' And they're going to find some retired general who's going to say, 'That's right. I have grave concern. . . .' And it's going to make decision making enormously more difficult."

Like Woodrow Wilson, who lamented of telegraphy, "All the impulses of mankind are thrown out upon the air and reach to the ends of the earth," the military man was decrying the advance of the news media—and its customers, the public—into a domain that for decades had been the impenetrable sanctuary of the SCI-cleared experts.

Monica Lewinsky and the Internet War

When the Clinton administration ordered a cruise missile attack on suspected terrorist sites in Afghanistan and Sudan on 21 August 1998, the Pentagon imposed an information blackout on the identity and location of the military units involved.

But it took only five minutes on unclassified Pentagon Internet sites for the author and other journalists to learn the specific names of the navy warships that had fired the Tomahawks.[29]

In the fall of 1998, the Pentagon had a sudden spasm of self-doubt about its four-year love affair with the World Wide Web. Confronted with an escalating struggle against nonstate-sponsored terrorism and the continuing threat of proliferating weapons of mass destruction, Department of Defense leaders suddenly wondered if the new technology that enabled them to publish information about defense programs might pose a genuine security risk by doing just that.

Under a Department of Defense information policy spelled out by Secretary of Defense William Cohen sixteen months earlier, in April 1997, the Pentagon is required "to make available timely and accurate information so that the public, Congress and the news media may assess and understand the facts about national security and defense strategy." Cohen's policy statement added that the Pentagon requires that "information be withheld only when disclosure would adversely affect national security or threaten the men and women of the armed forces."

But Cohen and his military subordinates quickly learned in the aftermath of the missile strikes and a separate inquiry into Pentagon Web site content that striking such a balance between openness and operational security is going to be difficult to achieve. The very nature of digital computer power, when harnessed to the Internet and a host of powerful search engines available online, makes it impossible to prevent even an amateur user from amassing critical information from isolated bits and pieces scattered at various sites—none of which by themselves constitute particularly sensitive data.

Military leaders used a term with sinister tones to describe the problem: "data mining."

Journalists call it journalism.

A case in point is the Afghan and Sudanese incident in the fall of 1998. Information continuously provided by the navy on various Web sites (and available from the service's information office in the Pentagon) revealed that there were only two groupings of naval warships in the region immediately prior to the incident: the USS *Abraham Lincoln* carrier battle group and several surface warships assigned to the Navy Middle East Task Force.

The *Abraham Lincoln,* like most major navy ships and shore commands, has created an informative, information-packed Web site in recent years aimed at informing crew family members and the public about the carrier, its embarked carrier air wing, the other escort and logistics ships assigned to the battle group, and even the biographies of senior commanders.

To further help family members keep track of their loved ones, the carrier's Web site contained one link that provided a day-by-day location map from the time the ship left on deployment from its base in Everett, Washington, until the present time. (For security, the ship suspended precise latitude-longitude markings whenever it entered the Persian Gulf, stating only that the ship was operating in the waterway.)

A check of the *Lincoln*'s locator map the day of the missile strikes turned up a tantalizing and revealing clue: The daily entries for the carrier and its battle group had abruptly ended several days before. (The dog in Sherlock Holmes' account had abruptly stopped barking.)

It then only required several minutes of examining the unclassified descriptions of the *Abraham Lincoln* escorts and the current Middle East Task Force ships through an unclassified reference manual[30] on naval ships to glean the list of those armed with Tomahawk cruise missiles.

At the same time that the United States engaged in its retaliatory strikes against the terrorists who had set off bombs at two U.S. embassies in east Africa, a pair of military officers presented a briefing to senior Pentagon officials on Web security issues.[31]

The two members of the joint staff demonstrated how they had successfully compiled information on selected military commanders using commercially available Internet search engines that amassed separate pieces of information that—when seen in the aggregate—"could translate into a vulnerability." Taking one general officer as a text case, the two staffers were "able to extract his complete address, unlisted phone number, and using a map search engine, build a map and directions to his house," according to an AFPS report.

In response to the experiment, Deputy Secretary of Defense John Hamre on 25 September 1998 directed a comprehensive review of information placed on publicly available Department of Defense Internet sites.

"The World Wide Web provides the Department of Defense with a powerful tool to convey information quickly and efficiently on a broad range of topics," stated a Department of Defense press release posted on the DefenseLink Web site on 25 September. "The global reach of the Web makes information, whether a press release or a statistical chart, easily available to everyone from individual service members to the international community."

Still, Hamre ordered all military Web site administrators to remove certain categories of information from Web sites accessible to the public, including:

- Plans or lessons learned that would reveal sensitive military operations
- Information on sensitive movements of military assets or the location of units, installations, or personnel where uncertainty regarding location is an element of the security of a military plan or program
- Personnel data such as social security account numbers, complete dates of birth, home addresses, and telephone numbers other than public telephone numbers of duty offices. In addition, names, locations, and other identifying information about family members of Department of Defense employees and military personnel should be removed

Hamre's order also created a task force to review overall Internet information policies and establish a security awareness program for defense organizations.

Military journalists who have adopted the Internet as their new operating arena say that the Pentagon cannot succeed in halting the impact of the Web on how journalists (and ordinary citizens for that matter) use its power to rapidly collect, collate, and synthesize information.

"There is a fundamental lack of understanding about the Web (at the Pentagon)," says Neff Hudson, general manager for Military City Online, the multifaceted Internet site for the *Army, Navy,* and

Air Force Times newspapers. "Once you let information out, it's out: you can't put that genie back in the bottle."[32]

A privately owned newspaper group that has covered the military for its members for fifty years in 1998, the Army Times Publishing Co., is looking at the new technologies of the Internet and digital computers as an expanding opportunity to both present conventional news accounts of defense issues and explore innovations such as digital video and audio segments, issue-related computer bulletin boards, and chat rooms for those interested in military topics, Hudson says.

The Pentagon's dilemma is best summarized in a feature story that Military City Online put together during Gen. John Shalikashvili's tenure as chairman of the joint chiefs of staff. Using digital video animation techniques, MCO (as it's known on the Web) created a "virtual tour" of the chairman's private residence at Quarters 6 at Fort Myer, Virginia.

"When [Gen. Hugh] Shelton came in as chairman, he asked us to take it down as a security risk," Hudson said. "So we took it down."

The lesson from this, Hudson continued, is that "there tends to be a thought that all of this information is new out there. It's not. The difference is the speed with which we can get it."

The most dramatic confirmation of the Internet's power and speed did not come through a military Web site and did not concern the military or reporters who cover military topics. But the extraordinary demonstration of Internet capacity that occurred with the release of the Office of Independent Counsel report on President Clinton and former White House intern Monica Lewinsky on 21 September 1998 offers a clear indication of the dynamics that the Department of Defense must contend with in the next major military crisis or war.

In releasing the 453-page report directly onto the Internet, Independent Counsel Kenneth Starr inadvertently gave the new media technology its most severe test since the Internet exploded into popular use five years earlier.

By all accounts, the computer network easily handled a historic "spike" of computer users switching to one of several sites to download or simply read the report. "The decision [to utilize the Internet] prompted a digital rush hour of historic dimensions. Various Web sites and Internet service providers reported increases over normal usage with log-ons about 10 percent above normal," wrote computer columnists Brit Hume and T. R. Reid on 26 September. "And the system survived."

An article in the *New York Times* called the Starr Report release, and the subsequent live broadcasting of the president's grand jury appearance via broadcast television, cable, and direct Internet outlets, a "defining moment" in the history of the Internet.[33]

It's also a bellwether for what the military can expect as user sites continue to proliferate and new software programs that offer sophisticated delivery of computer graphic animation and video and audio signals improve.

Simply put, military crises and battles—and the underlying policy debates governing the deployment of forces to overseas hot spots—are now totally in the public domain. This is because the Internet in just five years has attained the data capacity, bandwidth, and sophistication to provide all levels of information in a user-attainable, comprehensible, and compelling array of forms.

Some experts say a new role for military journalists will be to simply sort out the truly important issues and facts from a torrent of raw data that could overwhelm the individual Internet subscriber and his or her favorite search engine. With more than 1,500 Web sites currently dedicated to military topics, military analyst Bill Arkin warns that the sheer mass of information is now posing the biggest challenge to Internet users seeking military and defense data.

"It is no longer economical or even technically possible for the commercial search engines and mega-portals to index everything that is online, nor to do so in a timely and reliable manner," Arkin warns. "For a segment of the Internet such as the .mil domain, the result is that more material goes largely unindexed and is more difficult to find."[34]

Hudson, the MCO general manager, said the Internet itself is helping to redefine the root definition of a news story. In the future, he said, Internet users who are tracking military forces in a foreign conflict will switch on not just to a textual account or a video clip or a digital photograph, but to an integrated package of all of these, with additional elements added.

A review of existing online capabilities can complete Hudson's comment: In the next war, the citizen-subscriber to the Internet will also connect to a computer simulation of a bombing mission or Tomahawk strike, then switch to a live satellite image of the battle zone. Further subject familiarity will come by accessing a three-dimensional topographical map of the target area. Other links will integrate the latest wire-service news with various homepages of research think tanks that have published policy papers or op-ed essays on the conflict.

Then, having taken in all of that data, the subscriber-citizen will be able to e-mail his or her comments on the operation to the White House and join a chat room of citizens discussing the foreign operation.

The Internet will directly involve U.S. journalists—and citizens—as never before in the activities and operations of its armed forces, in peace and war.

The threat and the promise are the same.

Sidebar—Then and Now

What a difference a decade makes.

In May 1990, freelance reporter and California State University journalism professor Gib Johnson profiled the high-technology equipment reporters were using to cover the news in crises and in remote foreign locations.[35]

He noted the experience of CBS producer David Hawthorne, who survived the crash of an airliner on takeoff into the East River, then climbed back into the fuselage to retrieve his "cumbersome" cellular phone, which at that time consisted of a telephone carried in a satchel encumbered with a heavy battery unit weighing several pounds. Still, the phone allowed him to dictate a breaking story of the crash.

A review by Johnson of high-technology journalism from that year underscores the steady evolution of communications capability used by the press (as well as documenting the significant increase in capability from both existing and new technologies). In 1990 there were laptop computers, the Johnson article recounts. But the state-of-the-art model was the Tandy 200 laptop, which had a total internal memory of 25,000 bytes (about one-fortieth of the current 3.5-inch disk) and no floppy drive. Still, it was state of the art and could send stories over a clear phone line.

Other standard gear in 1990 included battery-operated tape recorders, fax machines, nine-band shortwave radios (for getting news in the bush), and compact television sets.

Fast-forward to late 1998.

Correspondent Nicholas D. Kristof of the *New York Times* empties his rucksack to demonstrate to his newspaper readers the fundamental equipment required of the high-technology reporter.[36]

"The centerpiece [of my gear] is my Thrane & Thrane satellite phone, which I can set up in about 30 seconds in the middle of the jungle clearing," Kristof writes. The unit, which retails for about $3,000, allows "voice and data transmission from any place on the planet outside the Polar zones."

Kristof notes that just two years earlier, off-the-shelf satellite phones were the size of suitcases. Now the standard model is the size of a small laptop computer, complete with a directional antenna to lock in on the satellite. The device permits voice phone calls, e-mail transmissions, and full computer connectivity with the Internet (which did not exist in a recognizable form ten years ago) or home paper, he writes. Instead of lugging a heavy backup battery, the unit has a solar panel which recharges the built-in power pack.

Some items are timeless, however: Kristof carries a small insecticide coil that will drive away the mosquitoes, if not the computer bugs.

Reading List

The following books and articles further explore the issues of military secrecy, computer technology, and journalism events relevant to the military-media relationship.

Books

Arkin, William. *The U.S. Military Online: A Directory for Internet Access to the Department of Defense.* 2d ed. Brassey's, 1998.

Dunnigan, James F. *Digital Soldiers.* St. Martin's, 1996.

Fialka, John J. *Hotel Warriors: Covering the Gulf War.* Woodrow Wilson Center Press, 1991.

Neuman, Johanna. *Lights, Camera, War.* St. Martin's, 1996.

Richelson, Jeffrey T. *The U.S. Intelligence Community.* Ballinger, 1985.

Sharkey, Jacqueline. *Under Fire: U.S. Military Restrictions on the Media from Grenada to the Persian Gulf War.* The Center for Public Integrity, 1991.

Woodward, Bob. *The Commanders.* Pocket Star Books, 1991.

Reports and Documents

Aukofer, Frank, and William P. Lawrence, Vice Adm., U.S. Navy (Ret.). *America's Team: The Odd Couple—A Report on the Relationship Between the Media and the Military.* Freedom Forum First Amendment Center, September 1995.

Committee on Governmental Affairs, U.S. Senate. *Pentagon Rules on Media Access to the Persian Gulf War.* Washington, D.C.: Government Printing Office, 20 February 1991.

Dennis, Everett et. al., eds. *The Media at War: The Press and the Persian Gulf Conflict.* Gannett Foundation (later Freedom Forum), June 1991.

Ethiel, Nancy, series ed. *The Military and the Media: Facing the Future.* Cantigny Conference Series, Robert R. McCormick Tribune Foundation, 1998.

Moskos, Charles C., with Thomas R. Ricks. *Reporting War When There Is No War.* Cantigny Conference Series, Robert R. McCormick Tribune Foundation, 1996.

Notes

1. The U.S. Special Operations Command, Navy Submarine Service, and Naval Reactors Branch (NAVSEA-08) of the Naval Sea Systems Command are three military components that have shown significant openness in recent years, contrasted with previous policies of minimal interaction with the news media.

2. Rear Admiral Brent Baker, chief of navy information during the 1991 Persian Gulf War, is credited with the first use of the term "battlefield" to describe the news media. During a 5 April 1991 military-media conference at the U.S. Marine Corps Command and Staff College, Baker said, "The sad fact is that if we remain silent on the media battlefield, we have just surrendered." (*The Public Affairs Communicator,* May/June 1991).

3. Ed Offley, "Reinforcing the Future, a Strategy for Strengthening the Military Beat" (research paper sponsored by the Robert R. McCormick Tribune Foundation, 1995). Surveys of major U.S. newspapers and other print outlets showed a reduction of full-time defense reporters from about 120 in 1989 to less than sixty in 1995. Roughly half of each group covered the Pentagon and other defense agencies in Washington, D.C., and the rest worked for regional publications with a significant military or defense industrial presence in their primary circulation areas.

4. Johanna Neuman, *Lights, Camera, War* (St. Martin's, 1996), 33.

5. Henry Lemoine, *Typographic Antiquities: Origin and History of the Art of Printing, Foreign and Domestic* (S. Fisher, 1797).

6. Alfredo Manguel, *A History of Reading* (Viking Press, 1996).

7. Neuman, various chapters.

8. Neuman, 98.

9. Everett Dennis et. al., eds., *The Media at War: The Press and the Persian Gulf Conflict* (Gannett Foundation [later Freedom Forum], June 1991).

10. Neuman, 212.

11. Jacqueline Sharkey, *Under Fire: U.S. Military Restrictions on the Media from Grenada to the Persian Gulf War* (The Center for Public Integrity, 1991).

12. See John J. Fialka, *Hotel Warriors: Covering the Gulf War* (Woodrow Wilson Center Press, 1991). Also see Sharkey. Also see

Frank Aukofer and William P. Lawrence, Vice Adm., U.S. Navy (Ret.), *America's Team: The Odd Couple—A Report on the Relationship between the Media and the Military* (Freedom Forum First Amendment Center, September 1995). Also see Committee on Governmental Affairs, U.S. Senate, *Pentagon Rules on Media Access to the Persian Gulf War* (Washington, D.C.: Government Printing Office, 20 February 1991). Also see Dennis.

13. Reporters attending the Tandem Thrust exercise were handed a memorandum that clearly stated the new ground rules. Highlights of the "Department of Defense principles for news media coverage of Department of Defense battlefield operations" include: (1) Open and independent coverage will be the principal means of coverage of U.S. military operations. (2) Media pools are not to serve as the standard means of covering U.S. military operations. Pools may sometimes provide the only feasible means of early access to a military operation. Pools should be as large as possible and disbanded at the earliest opportunity—within twenty-four to thirty-six hours when possible. The arrival of early-access pools will not cancel the principle of independent coverage for journalists already in the area. (3) Journalists will be provided access to all major military units. Special operations restrictions may limit access in some cases. (4) Military public affairs officers should act as liaisons but should not interfere with the reporting process. (5) Under conditions of open coverage, field commanders should be instructed to permit journalists to ride on military vehicles and aircraft wherever feasible. (6) Consistent with its capabilities, the military will supply PAOs with facilities to enable timely, secure, compatible transmission of pool material. The military will not ban communications systems operated by news organizations, but electromagnetic operational security in battlefield situations may require limited restrictions.

14. Memorandum from the author to Charles J. Lewis, 5 August 1992, "Field test of new military-media coverage guidelines" to the Washington Bureau Chiefs liaison committee with the Department of Defense.

15. Debra Gersh, "It's Hollywood! No Somalia!" *Editor & Publisher* (19 December 1992) 5.

16. Neuman, 228.

17. Author's notes from Somalia coverage, December 1992.

18. "Reporters on *Kitty Hawk* Operated on Agreed Guidelines," Associated Press, 13 January 1993.

19. Charles Moskos and Thomas Ricks, *Reporting War When There Is No War* (Robert R. McCormick Tribune Foundation report, 1996), 24.

20. Moskos and Ricks, 25.

21. Andrew Schneider, "Computer-Assisted Journalism and What It's Doing to Our Profession" (presented at the Conference on Advanced Investigative Methods, (Indianapolis, IN: Indiana University School of Journalism, 16 March 1990).

22. Also see Ed Offley, "Raids show Pentagon strategy to head off terrorist attacks," *Seattle Post-Intelligencer,* 21 August 1998. This earlier "overview" article on counterproliferation had been written and was being edited on the day the Clinton administration launched a volley of cruise missiles against Afghanistan and Sudan. Although the raids showed the timeliness and relevance of counterproliferation, the author was the beneficiary of good luck in the specific timing of publication.

23. Report to the Congress by the Department of Defense Counterproliferation Review Committee (unclassified), 1 May 1998.

24. Jean Heller, "Photos don't show buildup," *St. Petersburg Times,* 4 January 1991.

25. Bob Woodward, *The Commanders* (New York: Pocket Star Books, 1991), 250.

26. William Burrows, *Deep Black: The Startling Truth behind America's Top-Secret Spy Satellites* (Berkeley, Calif.: Berkeley Press, 1988).

27. *The Military and the Media: Facing the Future,* a report by the Robert R. McCormick Tribune Foundation (Chicago: 1997).

28. By pre-agreement, all Cantigny Conference participants speak and debate "on background." In journalistic conventions, "on background" means that no individual names are cited, but that the speakers' comments may be generally attributed in context.

29. Ed Offley, "Puget Sound–based sailors played a role in missile attacks," *The Seattle Post-Intelligencer,* 22 August 1998.

30. Norman Polmar, *The Ships and Aircraft of the U.S. Fleet* (Annapolis, MD: Naval Institute Press1996).

31. Paul Stone, "Internet Presents Web of Security Issues," American Forces Press Service via DefenseLink, 25 September 1998.

32. Neff Hudson, interview with author, 1 October 1998.

33. Lisa Napoli, "The Post-Lewinsky Winner Is the Web," *New York Times,* 28 September 1998.

34. Bill Arkin, e-mail to author, 18 September 1998. "Domains" are classifications of computers based on the area of the Internet from which they operate or the purpose for which they are used. Common domains are .com and .edu, used by commercial sites and education sites, respectively. The domain .mil is unique to the U.S. military.

35. Gib Johnson, "The Compleat Reporter—With a few essentials the journalist is wired to the world," *Washington Journalism Review* (May 1990), 16–19.

36. Nicholas Kristof, "Have Adapter, Will Travel—a Foreign Correspondent Reflects on the Technotricks of Life on, and off, the Road," *New York Times,* 24 September 1998.

Robert L. Bateman III

Conclusion: Looking Back—The Napoleonic Revolution

One of the guiding principles of the department of history of the U.S. Military Academy at West Point is the idea that although we may not be able to derive hard and fast lessons from history, we can obtain wisdom by studying history. This was, for several of the authors, an implied goal if not an explicitly stated one, as it should be. History, well researched and analyzed, is a solid foundation for those seeking to extrapolate into the future as we have done here. Yet for all that was presented here, we have yet to fully explore the breadth of the issue of the impact of digitization on the future of war, let alone the depth of any one element.

As suggested by General Sullivan in his introduction, I am hopeful that this book will serve as a springboard for additional debate and dialogue about issues relating to the impact of digital technology. Many of the authors are members of the traditional maneuver arms of the U.S. Army, infantry and armor. The obvious missing links are the advocates of precision fires, the leaders in the artillery and aviation communities, as well as the logisticians—the people who make war possible across strategic and operational distances. Also missing are opinions from the sister services: the navy, air force, and marine corps. They too are wrestling with many of the same issues, so we must educate ourselves on their developments, which may be following parallel lines. Yet even this may produce a field of vision too narrow to capture the essence of what the "digital revolution" really means.

For many leaders and thinkers in all branches and arms of the military, the essence of the digital revolution comes down to an analysis of what the potential effects of technology may be on weapon systems, command-and-control systems, and organizational structures. All of these are undoubtedly important, at least in the short term, but perhaps we should look back into history once more to develop an appreciation for a broader possible interpretation of what this revolution may hold in store.

In the preface I explained the common definition of a "revolution in military affairs" to be used in this book: a fundamental change in the nature of war occurring in a relatively short period of time, stemming from changes in organization; military doctrine; economic, social, or political factors; or technology. In this book we have addressed organization, doctrine, and technology. Perhaps because of the common denominator of our profession, we have not addressed the other potential variable: the economic, social, and political factors. To open that topic within a context with which military leaders may be familiar requires looking back more than two hundred years, to the era of the French Revolution and the subsequent empire of Napoleon.

In the introduction General Sullivan mentioned that he was being credited for the digitization of the U.S. Army; in the same breath he denied that it was actually his doing. What he does accept is that he formalized the investigation into the effects of a phenomenon already well under way when he became chief of staff. Were Napoleon less a megalomaniac, he too might well have admitted that the "Napoleonic revolution" was not of his making; he was merely the jockey who rode that horse when it showed up at the gate.

It is not overstating the case to say that from roughly 1796 through his final defeat at Waterloo in 1815, Napoleon's system of warfare reigned supreme. That is, all belligerents, if they were to maintain any hope for success, either had to adopt some aspects of the Napoleonic system or develop tools of their own to counteract it. In either case, even after the apogee of the French empire passed, all belligerents were in a reactive mode in relation to the empire of Napoleon.

Until relatively recent times, the Napoleonic revolution in military affairs was credited to Napoleon himself. Technology was not considered a significant factor, and Napoleon was credited with the institution of organizational changes within the structure of the French armed forces. Current interpretations, however, suggest otherwise. Napoleon was merely the right man at the right time, and for all his genius, arguably he was merely the jockey riding the best horse in town. What, then, was the basis for the phenomenal French success during this era? To answer that, and to pull a little wisdom from history, requires some understanding of the Napoleonic system.

The components of the system have been studied and dissected for more than two hundred years. Perhaps the major factor that contributed to Napoleon's success was his relative velocity in comparison to his opponents at all levels of warfare. Speed was the name of the Napoleonic game; it was achieved through several interrelated changes.

At the strategic and operational levels of warfare, Napoleon achieved speed because, unlike armies of the preceding era of limited warfare, he could move his large armies along widely dispersed parallel routes. Thus his entire army could cross a border at three or more locations simultaneously rather than sequentially. A cavalry corps spread out across the entire front of his moving army collected information and denied the same to the enemy as the whole mass moved forward. This system, perfected in the operational-level formation of the *battalion carré* ("battalion square," although the primary units in its makeup are corps and the formation actually resembles a diamond), subdivided Napoleon's army into corps units, each capable of independent defensive operations against an enemy force for up to twenty-four hours. Not coincidentally, each element of the formation could reinforce the others within twenty-four hours, thus massing the entire army in one location.

Yet these developments were not the intellectual property of Napoleon; he was merely the commander given the chance to implement them. Military theorists preceding Napoleon had advocated such formations and concepts, but the armies of the ancien régime were not able to implement the ideas of the theorists at the time. Operating in multiple columns as a matter of course requires two other developments: a competent officer corps and the ability to break free of the restrictions of eighteenth-century logistics. Napoleon solved both of these problems.

The individuals in the French officer corps of the Napoleonic era were promoted based on merit. Numerous historians have pointed to the early siege of Toulon in 1793, when Napoleon was a mere artillery captain. During the course of that siege he came in contact with several other French leaders, men who within little more than a decade would be generals or marshals of France. These were men such as Jean Junot (a sergeant), André Massena (an ex-smuggler and former company sergeant), Auguste Marmont (an artillery sergeant, later a major at Toulon), Claude Victor (an infantry sergeant who led an assault at Toulon), and Louis Suchet (a common soldier).

Men earned their positions primarily through the demonstration of their abilities. While other armies of the day permitted the purchase of nearly all ranks, with the attendant inconsistencies of quality, the French had a system that found the best and elevated them. Without this system the operation of independent columns operating under general guidance (as opposed to restrictive directions) would likely have fallen apart under the pressure of enemy contact. This raises the obvious question: If merit-based promotion was so advantageous, why were the other nations of Europe unable or unwilling to use it?

Similarly, the French achieved speed through their reversal of the traditional methods of logistic support. Foraging while on the move required fewer resources and was faster than support from the rear. The armies of the age of limited war, which preceded Napoleon's, relied on an extensive system of supply bases, creating a logistics tail stretching from the operations area back to the strategic center of the nation. Napoleon instead relied primarily on foraging.

This was another reason that he dispersed his forces. It took considerable territory to support a corps or army on the move. Had he moved along a single route, the surrounding territory would have been stripped clean by the lead corps. This would have left no alternative for the following corps but to rely on logistics pushed from the rear. By using multiple avenues, he spread the logistic burden across a broader front. But this also was not an original idea of Napoleon's, merely one that he was in a unique position to implement.

Given that these ideas—foraging, the use of multiple routes to achieve speed and flexibility, promotion by merit, and so forth—were not new when Napoleon put them into effect, why hadn't other armies initiated them first? Why did the world have to wait for Napoleon?

I believe the other nations were not prepared socially; they were incapable of effecting the same changes within their societies as the French. Remember that the definition of a revolution in military affairs that we have used throughout this work encompasses changes in technology, organization, doctrine, and/or social, political, and economic factors. It was in fact the social changes brought to the front by the French Revolution that were responsible for the Napoleonic revolution.

For example, the use of independent corps formations, which many think was one of the key elements in Napoleon's success, depended on the existence of competent officers provided by a system of merit-based promotion. In eighteenth-century Europe, merit-based promotion was an idea that was only possible in a nation that embraced the idea of equality. At that time this attitude was found in only one European nation: revolutionary France.

Along a similar line, the great advantage in speed that the French enjoyed was because of their using a logistics system based on foraging. This also depended on social changes, in this case the effects of nationalism. Soldiers of revolutionary France were motivated to fight for the new idea of the French nation, something in which they participated, not for some distant king. These men generally were less prone to desert, the great bane of the royal armies of the era. This was important, especially if large numbers of soldiers were allowed to disperse across the countryside with little "loyal" (read officer) supervision in search of provisions. The true change that enabled the French shift in logistics and increased their relative speed, therefore, was not a change in technology or even a change in the military organization; it was a social concept that was born with the French Revolution.

Finally, there is the issue of manpower. It has been suggested that the genius of Napoleon was that not only was he capable of great operational intuition, but he could use this to bring great force to bear at a single point. This would not have been possible were the French nation not able to provide for large ground forces. The French mobilized their nation for defense, and later aggression, on a scale that other nations could not match initially. The French tapped into the great reserves of national manpower not only through the genius of the system of the *leveé en masse* implemented by Lazar Carnot, but also through the potential of their entire economy.

Although other nations of the day arguably had the potential to implement the measures needed for mobilization on the scale that the French achieved, they were incapable of doing so for social reasons. With the "nationalization" of many former aristocratic holdings and the centralization of power that the French empire achieved, the French could man and equip a larger force than any other nation. Again, these were changes that were only possible because of the social and political revolutions that the French had gone through.

Where then is the "wisdom through history" that we might derive from this short jaunt through the Napoleonic era?

Perhaps we need look no further than General Sullivan's words in the introduction. When asked about the decision to digitize, he replied, "It was easy to make because it had already been made and frankly, I could have been quiet on the issue and it would have happened in the course of time." Something similar could be said about Napoleon, and perhaps for many of the same reasons. Neither military leader created the conditions for which he is now credited, nor were the conditions, at their root, military ones. Napoleon capitalized on social changes coming from the French Revolution; General Sullivan formalized investigation into the implications of technological changes going on in his era. Both leaders rode the horses that were there when they arrived; neither provided the horse himself.

Alternatively, perhaps the wisdom we seek might be found by considering the idea that the true revolution we are now experiencing is not a technological one, but a social one. Might the real importance of the digital revolution be found not in the artifacts of technology but in the changing nature of the society that uses it?

Arguably many of the nations we now consider potential future rivals will never be able to implement the benefits of digital command and control if the members of their societies encounter technology only late in life. Concepts such as digitally shared databases and networked real-time cooperation are not intuitive. As today's generation of senior leaders will readily acknowledge, technology is not always easy to grasp for those who come to it late in life.

We all know, even in our society, a few technology holdouts—people just not able or willing to use to their fullest potential the machines to which they have access. What might be the effects of this retardation of technical familiarity on a nation unwilling to open itself to the potentially socially disruptive influences of the Internet? In some nations that we may face in the future, most people live their lives without access to anything like the information technology or digital machinery with which our children are familiar from a very young age. American children, the leaders of the twenty-first-century military, start becoming adept at the manipulation of high technology from the first time they play on a Nintendo 64. Should this, therefore, be the real focus of our investigations into the course and direction that our future military forces should take?

These are all questions that must be wrestled with, for it is only through discourse that we will arrive at the best possible answer. I look forward to participating in that process, and I hope that many of you who have read this book will too.